Praise for Aha!

"If you are a learner and believe you can create the life you want, **Aha!** is an essential tool in your toolbox. It has the conceptual model and practical how-tos for different learning styles."—Charlotte Roberts, coauthor of *Fifth Discipline Fieldbook*

"If **Aha!** doesn't kickstart your creativity, nothing will! A compendium of sure-fire methods to help you see the world in a whole new way!" —DeWitt Jones, corporate creativity consultant and *National Geographic* freelance photographer

"Leading authorities in business know that you're nowhere today unless you can tap into a steady stream of ideas that you can take to the bank. Read Jordan Ayan's book to keep those creative, bankable ideas flowing."—W. E. Williams, president and CEO, The Executive Committee, an international organizationof CEOs

"Jordan Ayan—the Wizard of Aha!s—has presented us with a treasure trove of techniques to stimulate our creative juices. A lot of fun!"— Roger von Oech, author of *A Whack on the Side of the Head* and creator of the Creative Whack Pack

"**Aha!** is an extremely well-written, entertaining, action-ready guide for anyone who wants to live a more successful life. All success is rooted in great ideas. **Aha!** shows you how to create ideas that will take you from where you are to where you want to be."—Michael LeBoeuf, author of *How to Win Customers and Keep Them for Life* and *The Perfect Business*

"It's simply a very superb new book by a very cool writer that will never let you run out of ways to be creative, ever. I think there's enough ideas and information on any one page to be worth the cost of the book. So you get all the other pages free!"—Marsh Fisher, cofounder of Century 21 Real Estate and chairman of IdeaFisher Systems, Inc.

"**Aha!** makes the magic of creativity accessible to even the 'creatively challenged.' It's chock full of practical strategies, resources, and ideas for putting zing and sizzle into your work and your life. Buy it and you too will say Aha!"—Thomas Armstrong, author of *7 Kinds of Smart* and *Awakening Your Child's Natural Genius*

"If you've ever wondered if you're creative, stop! Read Jordan Ayan's **Aha!** and you will not only recognize your creative potential, but also understand how to release it. **Aha!** is a life-changing book."—Joyce Wycoff, executive director of the Innovation Network and author of *Mindmapping* and *Transformation Thinking*

"What a great book! **Aha!** takes a topic that you may think defies logic and presents it in a logical manner that anyone can follow. Jordan Ayan is the creativity coach who can lead you to winning ideas."—Susan RoAne, professional speaker and author of *How to Work a Room*

"Jordan Ayan's **Aha!** is a gift to all who seek a more creative path. This extraordinary map to powerful ideas is fun to read and easy to use."—Chip R. Bell, author of *Customers as Partners* and *Managers as Mentors*

"Everyone is creative, innovative, and original. What we each have to find individually, before we find it collectively, is our own unique way to make a difference; a life-long contribution to yourself, your family, your country, and the world. I totally believe **Aha!** will free your greatness."—Mark Victor Hansen, coauthor of the best-selling series *Chicken Soup for the Soul*

"In today's fast-changing environment, this book is a tremendously valuable tool for helping you to tap into your creativity to turn challenges into opportunites."—Paul and Sarah Edwards, authors of *Working from Home, Finding Your Perfect Work*, and coauthors of *Teaming Up*

Aha!

10 Ways to Free Your Creative Spirit and Find Your Great Ideas

JORDAN AYAN

RICK BENZEL, EDITOR
THREE RIVERS PRESS
NEW YORK

To Jan, Ashley, and Christopher, the creative inspiration in my life

Miss Spider's Tea Party™ cover © GTM Callaway & Kirk Company LLC
reproduced by permission of the author.
PEANUTS reprinted by permission of United Features Syndicate, Inc.

Published by Three Rivers Press, a division of Crown Publishers, Inc.,
201 East 50th Street, New York, New York 10022. Member of the Crown Publishing Group.

Random House, Inc. New York, Toronto, London, Sydney, Auckland
www.randomhouse.com

THREE RIVERS PRESS and colophon are trademarks of Crown Publishers, Inc.

C.O.R.E.® is a registered trademark of Create-It! Inc.

Printed in the United States of America

Design by Elizabeth Van Itallie

Library of Congress Cataloging-in-Publication Data
Ayan, Jordan E.
Aha! : 10 ways to free your creative spirit and
find your great ideas / by Jordan E. Ayan.
Includes index.
1. Creative thinking. 2. Creative ability. 3. Creation (Literary, artistic, etc.). I. Title.
BF408.A94   1997   153.3'5—dc21   96-49431

ISBN 0-517-88400-3

10 9 8 7

acknowledgments

So many people have shared their ideas, inspiration, and support in helping me get the words on paper.

My family has been key to birthing this project. My wife and soulmate Jan's loving support, faith, wise counsel, and many hours spent reading and rereading the manuscript have kept me going. Her ideas have strengthened each chapter, and her inspiration provided the great title. My children, Ashley and Christopher, who sacrificed many weekends and evenings with Dad, have provided great ideas, stories, suggestions, and love that fueled me through the process.

Others have made essential contributions, especially:

Rick Benzel, my tireless editorial collaborator, who worked with me to shape my original ideas and drafts into a finely polished manuscript;

Jeff Herman, my agent, who saw potential in a rough proposal and had the creative persistence to find a publisher who shared our view of the project;

Pam Krauss, my editor, Margot Schupf, Jane Treuhaft, Andrea Peabbles, Barbara Marks, Elizabeth Van Itallie (whose wonderful design has brought the words on each page to life), and all the people at Crown who helped shape the manuscript and develop a wonderful book;

Deanna Berg, my friend and collaborator in creative seminars and workshops, who has provided great guidance and insight into the field of creativity.

Finally, I want to extend my gratitude to many others who have shared research, stories, ideas, and assistance: Carol Adrienn, Dr. Mihaly Csikszentmihalyi, Betty Edwards, Joyce Florey, Patricia Fripp, Dr. Joel Goodman, Dale Irvin, Dewitt Jones, Michael LeBoeuf, Dr. Joseph Lee, Mary LoVerde, John Pearson, Dr. G. Clotaire Rapaille, Susan RoAne, Anne Durrum Robinson, Dr. Martin Rossman, Paul Rousseau, Mike Ryder, Dr. Robert Schwander, Dai Tie-Sheng, Jeff Slutsky, Stephen Snyder, Juanelle Teague, Robert L. A. Troost, Anna Wise, and Joyce Wycoff.

contents

preface

Most of us wish we were more creative. We may dream of someday inventing an amazing new product or technology, directing a movie, writing a popular song, or painting a masterpiece. We may envision ourselves as great political leaders solving social problems, renowned business leaders brilliantly running a successful company, or respected humanitarians bringing new ideas and peace to the world. Or we may hope to be exciting and wonderful parents who can bring joy and excitement to our children day after day through our creative efforts.

The good news is that increasing your creativity is truly possible. Whatever your educational background or current creative experience, you can achieve far beyond what you had previously imagined or dreamed. You can direct an Academy Award–winning film, write a best-selling book, discover a drug, or pioneer a new theory. You can channel your creativity into improving an existing process at your workplace, developing an artistic hobby for yourself, or becoming a creative force in your community. If you fear your creativity has been stifled or lost, be assured that you can revitalize it and take it to new heights.

I wrote this book because I am a firm believer in *living* a creative life. For all of us, being creative is much more enjoyable and inspiring than living a life of monotonous routine. A creative life increases understanding and appreciation of new ideas, of other people, and of the world in general. Creativity unlocks the mind and makes the spirit soar. In a word, creativity is what makes you feel *alive*.

As we approach the year 2000, I, along with many other experts, predict that creativity will become one of the most important personal and business strategies for survival and success. The world is becoming more complex each day, and our societal problems are becoming increasingly difficult to solve. The world faces a multitude of issues begging for creative solutions. Our schools are in need of a major overhaul, there is crime in nearly every community, and many areas like health care, family relationships, and world peace are full of problems that remain unresolved. In the business world, too, the need for creative thinking is becoming ever more crucial as companies find that their traditional methods of operation are failing. With increased global competition and more sophisticated consumers who no longer want me-too products and services, large and small companies everywhere are scrambling to invent new ways to manufacture, manage, and market themselves. Many businesses suffer from a dearth of originality—and they need the creativity of every individual in their organizations to compete and thrive.

How I Came to Appreciate the Power of Creativity

A few years ago, I started a consulting firm focusing on innovation, technology, and creativity. I entered this field following a successful and exciting career as an executive with Donnelley Marketing in Chicago, until recently a division of the Dun & Bradstreet Corporation. Donnelley is a database marketing company, and one of the largest consumer direct-mail firms in the world. While at Donnelley, I developed a new service, called FastData, which creatively transformed the company's database into an on-line information resource of great value to other companies. To the amazement of many senior managers with whom I worked, the service I created with the help of my colleagues grew enormously and in just a few years was sold and licensed for nearly $50 million.

When FastData was sold, I was offered another job with Donnelley, but I decided not to accept the new job because I had become fascinated by the power of creativity. I came to see that it is the most powerful force a business can have. Moreover, when I examined my past, I realized that the best times in my life had been when I was doing creative work or was around creative people. From that point on I focused on turning my passion for creativity into a business.

I began to read widely in the literature on creativity and the mind, devouring the works of authors such as Howard Gardner, Mihaly Csikszentmihalyi, Edward deBono, Roger von Oech, Tony Buzan, Joyce Wycoff, Betty Edwards, and many others. I began attending a variety of professional meetings for people involved in creative work, such as the Creative Problem Solving Institute (CPSI) at the State University of New York at Buffalo, and the Innovation Network in Santa Barbara, California. I had the chance to meet and talk with many creative people, and I became ever more inspired to work in this field.

Gradually the consulting business grew, and today our clients include companies, associations, and government agencies. We conduct work for their executives and employees on being more creative and incorporating innovation into their organizations. Our clients include Kimberly-Clark, Freddie Mac, Allied-Signal, and Lucent Technologies as well as many banks, computer firms, and a variety of aerospace and engineering firms.

But creativity has application far beyond government and industry. This book is the result of years of research and consulting work, and a lifetime of experience. It synthesizes the many ideas and strategies I have developed and field-tested with great success in hundreds of workshops and seminars all over the world. Thousands of people—from senior-level executives to teams of workers on the shop floor—have used these concepts, techniques, and suggestions to benefit themselves and their organizations.

This book has many applications. First and foremost, you can use it to learn how to live more creatively in all aspects of your life. A creative life brings enjoyment and enrichment to you and everyone you meet. You can also use this book to learn how to solve specific problems in your business, community, or the world at large. As you read, you will find many suggestions for how to burst through blocks or generate ideas immediately. Finally, if you are a writer, painter, musician, singer, dancer, potter, or craftsperson of any kind, you can read this book to learn how to find the inspiration for your next project or how to get unstuck.

I sincerely hope the strategies that follow will help you gain new confidence about your creative capacities and help you use them to solve a problem or invent something that changes the world, improves your own life, or enhances the joy and happiness of your family and friends.

Part 1

under-
standing
your
creative
C.O.R.E.

Reclaiming Your Creative Power

Do you find yourself drawn to newspaper articles about people who invent new products and wonder why you can't do it, too? Do you admire such vanguards of popular culture as Steven Spielberg, John Grisham, Jerry Seinfeld, David Letterman, k. d. lang—even Madonna—and wish you could tap into the same vein of creativity (and success) that they have? Do you think about coming up with an idea to start a new business or help your employer's company prosper and grow? Or would you like to improve your painting, writing, acting, or musical abilities?

If the answer to any of these questions is yes, congratulations! You are ready to tap into your creativity and learn how you can expand it, refine it, and make it a more integral part of your life.

More and more people today recognize that being creative plays a crucial role in their personal happiness and their professional accomplishment. Creative people are the ones who get ahead in their jobs, start new businesses, invent products, build buildings and design homes, produce films and plays, compose music, paint pictures, and make things of beauty. Creative people often are those leading exciting and stimulating social lives, meeting other people, and going to interesting places, so that they are constantly learning and doing. Creativity is also an important aspect of a healthy family environment; creative parents know how to help their children grow into adults who love life and choose to get the most out of it. Creative people become our top business and community leaders, people who understand how to solve problems or inspire others to improve their lot in life.

Unfortunately there is a prevailing belief that creativity is an inborn trait that cannot be cultivated—either that you are creative or you're not. Few people understand that they can *learn* to be more creative. They don't know which techniques to use to generate new ideas or how to develop their natural artistic talents. They don't have any training or background in creativity.

Their parents didn't teach them about it, and their schools and universities didn't offer courses on the subject.

People often feel very frustrated by creative blocks—those times when they are stuck and cannot get the new idea they need or solve a pressing problem. This causes them to lose self-confidence and momentum in their work. Even when they come up with a great idea, they worry about other people ridiculing or criticizing them instead of moving forward with the idea and making it happen.

MINI WORKSHOP

HOW CREATIVE DO YOU FEEL?

Throughout the book, you will find projects like this one that will help you make the information you find in the chapters more relevant to your own life and creative efforts. I invite you to do as many of the activities as you want.

How do you feel about the level of creativity in your life right now? This project will help you assess your feeling. Close your eyes and think back to your childhood. Try to recapture a moment when you recall being highly creative.

If you are like most people, you can probably conjure up many instances of tremendous creativity. A large, empty cardboard box that became a house; the elegant ballet you choreographed and performed to the score of your favorite children's album; a snow fort you constructed that was transformed into a massive medieval castle in your imagination. You can probably still feel the sensation of finger paint dripping over your fingers, ready to be smeared across a glossy white sheet of paper, or recall the pleasurable sensation of molding Play-Doh into a worm or pancake as smooth and lustrous as any of Rodin's or Michelangelo's creations.

Now hold these images of youthful creativity in your mind for a moment. Do you still feel the same urge to create? Are you as excited about life as you were as a child? Are you as curious? As willing to experiment and play? As adventurous and fun loving?

In all likelihood, you are not. Sadly, most of us just don't feel as creative as we did when we were younger. As adults, we constrain our imaginations and limit our abilities to experiment and explore. We no longer experience the joyful curiosity of our youth. We no longer climb jungle gyms, and we hate playing with mud!

But take heart. You can change your beliefs and feelings by reconnecting with your creative spirit and learning some techniques to boost your creativity. This book will show you how.

Losing Our Natural Creativity

The irony about creativity is that we were born with many creative skills. As babies, we were naturally curious and eager to explore the world around us. We enjoyed color, light, movement, and sound. We wanted to taste, grasp, and manipulate whatever came into our view. We were quite satisfied to spend our days playing and experimenting with objects, toys, and the elements of nature (rain, sand, mud, and so on). As infants and toddlers, we were natural builders, artists, craftspeople, poets, and musicians.

Most of us begin limiting our creative pursuits and abilities sometime during our early years. It usually starts when we enter elementary school, where our creativity is slowly reined in by traditional education. We sit in rows or groups with twenty to thirty other students and are expected to adhere to strict rules and procedures—many of which limit creative thinking. We often learn by rote rather than through exploration, questions, and experimentation. As we go through elementary school, junior high, high school, and beyond, we wind up exercising our natural creativity less and less, and it slowly atrophies.

Think back, for example, to the first day you went off to kindergarten or nursery school. In all likelihood you received a box of crayons, maybe even the giant sixty-four-color box of Crayolas (the one with a sharpener on the back) filled with a kaleidoscope of color including Periwinkle, Melon, Gold, and Carnation Pink. What has happened to the color and creativity a mere twelve years later? We graduate from high school with the equivalent of an eighty-nine-cent, disposable ballpoint pen in our pockets. The endless possibilities represented by those sixty-four colors have been

reduced to a single standardized outlook, and, unfortunately, with them goes some of our imagination, wonder, and awe. In my mind, this is a powerful metaphor for what happens to our creativity as we move from childhood into our adult lives.

I saw another example of how the educational system can draw off some of our natural creativity when my son, Christopher, was in kindergarten. My wife and I went to a parent-teacher conference and were informed that our budding refrigerator artist would be receiving a grade of Unsatisfactory in art. We were shocked. How could any child—let alone our child —receive a poor grade in art at such a young age? His teacher informed us that he had refused to color within the lines, which was a state requirement for demonstrating grade-level motor skills. It became clear that the teacher spent so much time focusing on getting the kids to color inside the lines that their creative impulses were ignored. Or, worse yet, criticized. When the teacher explained to him the need to rein in his creativity on classwork and fulfill her requirements, our son started bringing home very somber pictures done in dark colors. When he did art at home, the drawings he made were beautiful and color filled. At home, we stressed the fact that there were no rules when he was playing in the art cabinet.

But our educational system is not the only limit on our creativity. We often experience criticism and negative feedback, rather than support and encouragement, in response to our creative efforts. When a teacher, friend, parent, or sibling wittingly or unconsciously comments disparagingly about a clay sculpture we've made, a watercolor we've painted, a dance we've invented, or a poem we've written, the insult hurts deeply. We decide that it is safer to withdraw and not express our creativity again rather than risk ridicule or embarrassment.

As we move from school to work, relationships, and perhaps a family, another factor that blocks us from fully utilizing our creativity is *stress*. We experience many pressures in our day-to-day lives that sap our energy. It is difficult to be creative when you have to run from meeting to meeting, arrange activities for your kids, and tend to a home simultaneously. Lack of leisure time and overcommitment are major deterrents to building the calm, reflective environment needed for certain kinds of creative work, such as painting, writing, or even inventing. You can be sure that many of the most famous artists, poets, and musicians in history would never have achieved their impressive body of work if they had faced the same level of stress as modern adults do.

Finally, many people do not develop their full creative potential because they are never shown how to take advantage of their natural creative skills or how to expand their repertoire of techniques. Few schools offer specific courses in creativity, and many of those who have mastered creativity in their fields are not available for mentoring or taking on apprentices. As a result, most people end up using far less of their creative powers than they could, and never learn to work through their creative blocks.

MINI WORKSHOP

CREATIVITY TESTING
PART I

Take the following informal test of creativity. Read the directions and then begin: In one minute, think of all the possible uses for an empty tin can. Write your answers on a separate piece of paper. Try to come up with as many uses as you can. Ready? Go.

PART II

You have just taken an adapted version of a creativity test based on the Torrance Test of Creative Thinking, developed by Dr. J. P. Torrance. Since creativity usually results from your ability to make many connections, this test illustrates how divergent your thinking is.

The full Torrance test measures four key creative abilities that are linked to divergent thinkers. In the tin can example, trained scorers would look at your responses and award points based on how they fell into the following four categories:

- Fluency — the ability to generate a large volume of ideas. In other words, how many ideas did you come up with in total?
- Flexibility — the ability to generate ideas in a number of categories. How many different types of uses did you devise for a tin can? The most common is a container, but it can also be used as a toy, a communications device, and so on.

- Originality — the ability to generate unique and unusual ideas. Any answer associated with typical uses of tin cans would receive zero points. More unexpected applications, such as "a hat for dolls," would receive two points.
- Elaboration — the ability to add details or to expand on the item itself. Ideas that require something to be added or a change in form are awarded points for elaboration. For example, if your idea required that the can be melted, ground up, painted, or even combined with another can, you would be awarded more points.

So, how did you do on the tin can test? Were your ideas fluent, flexible, original, and elaborative? If you have children, give them the test and see what they come up with.

I often use this test in my seminars with adults and have also tried it in classes of children. Children generally score higher than adults. For example, compare your answers with some of these interesting ones generated by one group of second-graders:

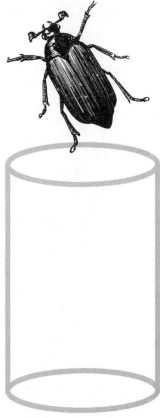

a bug keeper
an ant home
a bank
playing kick the can
a washing machine for small people
a hat for your doll
a Barbie doll pool
a telephone
a musical instrument
stilts
melt it down and "morph" it into
    Power Rangers

It is not that adults lack the ability to dream up new solutions, it is just that we use far less of our creative powers than we could and never learn to work through our blocks. Throughout life, we are often taught, as one of my favorite commercials pointed out, to "stay between the lines; the lines are your friends." In reality, however, if you really want your creativity to flow, you sometimes need to think like a child!

Research bears out the loss of creativity from childhood to adulthood. One study looked at the ability to generate original ideas. The resulting scores comparing "original" and "standard" answers stacked up as follows:

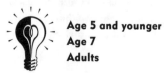

Age 5 and younger	**90 percent originality**
Age 7	**20 percent originality**
Adults	**2 percent originality**

The loss of originality is astonishing. No wonder that, by the time we reach our forties, fifties, or sixties, many of us end up feeling disappointed or defeated whenever we try to do something creative.

Rekindling Your Creative Power

If we all repress our natural creativity, or fail to use it to its maximum potential in our early years, the logical question is, What can we do as adults to awaken it, reinvigorate it, and expand it in the pursuit of our personal and professional goals?

That is precisely what this book is about. In the following chapters, you will find strategies for living a more creative life in general and learning how to harness your creativity whenever you need it to solve problems or generate ideas. The foundation of this book is learning to use ten key strategies that help you creatively address artistic or life challenges of any kind—be they related to your work, your craft, your family, or your community. The strategies are as follows:

1. **Connect with People**
2. **Design an Enriching Environment**
3. **Get out of Your Box Through Travel**
4. **Be Sparked by Play and Humor**
5. **Expand Your Mind Through Reading**
6. **Take up the Arts**
7. **Plug into Technology**
8. **PowerThink Your Challenges**
9. **Release Your Alterconscious**
10. **Connect with Your Creative Soul**

The concept of *Aha!* and the ten strategies are based on my personal experience and research into the field indicating that many means and methods are required to find the spark that inspires great ideas. Whether you want to paint a watercolor, write a novel, solve a business problem, invent a new product, or negotiate a conflict, these strategies can help you by providing more ways to discover your own Aha's.

These strategies can be employed in many ways. First and foremost, they stimulate your thinking. They open you to new possibilities and vistas, and they expand your horizons so you can make connections—the essential ingredients in the creative process.

Second, the strategies help you bulldoze through the mountainous blocks that can arrest your thinking and frustrate your efforts to move an idea or project forward. Some do this by helping you focus when your mind is racing too fast for quality creative work. Others help you relax and reinvigorate, allowing partially formed thoughts and ideas to simmer in the background until they are "cooked."

Finally these strategies will show you how to take advantage of one of the most potent yet largely unrecognized aspects of creativity, what some call luck or good fortune. There are many opportunities in the world begging for someone to discover and implement them. Opportunities probably cross your path daily, but unless you see them and recognize them as opportunities, they go to waste.

Of course, some of these strategies are also creative fields in and of themselves. Many writers commonly employ the Reading strategy to learn about other authors or to get ideas for their next novel or screenplay. Artists use the Arts strategy in the sense that they spend much of their time studying the great masters of their field so they can become better painters, sculptors, or musicians. And inventors and computer experts use the Technology strategy as their point of reference when they seek to invent new gizmos and gadgets that take technology one step further.

The thrust of this book is holistic: Use all ten strategies as broadly as possible for your inspiration in *any* creative endeavor. Don't restrict yourself to the strategies that relate to your field. If you are a sculptor or a dancer, you may benefit most from employing new **technology,** or working with other **people** to develop new ideas for your next artistic project. If you are a songwriter or a novelist, **PowerThinking** or **reading** may be the best way to get inspiration. And if you are a businessperson or inventor, experimentation with **travel** or your **alterconscious** could most effectively help you identify solutions to your vexing problems. In fact, viewing challenges through the lens of an unrelated discipline often sheds the most light. As Abraham Maslow said, "When all you have is a hammer, everything starts to look like a nail."

There are times, of course, when one strategy is more appropriate than another. For example, you may not have time to use the Travel strategy if you need to solve a problem or develop a new concept within the next twenty-four hours. Or you may find that some strategies appeal to you more than others.

Nevertheless, the overall goal of this book is to teach you to use all ten strategies frequently as part of a *fully creative lifestyle*. By incorporating the ten strategies into your daily routine, you will find yourself developing a natural talent for creative thinking that gives you a wide range of tools from which to draw inspiration, fertilize the growth of new ideas, and develop solutions to many of your challenges.

THINKING ABOUT YOUR CREATIVE LIFE

1. Reflect for a moment on the idea of living a creative lifestyle. Do you feel that you lead a creative life now? What feelings and images does this phrase evoke for you? Is a creative lifestyle very different from the one you lead now?

2. In the list of strategies on page 18, which one most intrigued you? Which one do you feel you are least interested in exploring? Now that you have identified a preference and an aversion, put them aside. Allow yourself to be open to all the possibilities every strategy has to offer.

3. Finally, think for a moment about your reasons for reading this book. Why do you want to be more creative? What goals do you think you might reach more easily or quickly through creative avenues? Do you want to be a better artist or writer? To invent something? To get a better job? What aspects of your life do you hope might change after you finish this book?

You may wish to write down your thoughts on these topics. You will find that by clarifying in advance what you hope to get from this book, you will enjoy reading it more and derive more usable information from each chapter.

Next Steps

Before you read about the ten strategies, three important issues are covered in the next three chapters. "You *Do* Have a Creative Strategy" examines the myth of the creative personality in order to liberate you from any doubts or fears you may have about \ learning to become more creative. "Tapping into the Creative Process" explains the nature of the creative process and suggests how you can find inspiration and develop new ideas by using the ten strategies. "Mastering the Techniques of Idea Capture" discusses how to capture your ideas so that as you read the chapters and implement the suggestions, you will not risk losing your new thoughts and breakthrough ideas. All three topics are critical in helping you maximize the creative rewards that can result from reading *Aha!*

Further Readings

The Courage to Create by Rollo May (New York: Bantam Books, 1975).

Growing Up Creative—Nurturing a Lifetime of Creativity by Teresa M. Amabile (Buffalo, N.Y.: Creative Education Foundation Press, 1989).

Imagineering: How to Profit from Your Creative Powers by Michael LeBoeuf (New York: McGraw-Hill, 1980).

Lateral Thinking: Creativity Step by Step by Edward deBono (New York: Harper & Row, 1970).

Paradigms: The Business of Discovering the Future by Joel Arthur Barker (New York: HarperBusiness, 1993).

The Woman's Book of Creativity by C. Diane Ealy (Hillsboro, Ore.: Beyond Words, 1995).

You <u>Do</u> Have a Creative Personality

In the workshops and seminars I present, I often hear comments like "I just don't have a creative personality," or "I'm not the artistic type," or "I am a left-brained [logical] person, not one of those right-brained creative types." The problem is, comments like these lead people in the wrong direction when thinking about creativity. This chapter explores the creative personality question from several angles and shows how you can develop four critical qualities to boost your creativity.

Is There a Baseline Creative Personality?

Try this test. Read the following list of characteristics and circle all those that you think belong to a creative person. Circle as many as you want. Don't look ahead to page 24, where I've shown the answers.

- absentminded
- adaptable
- adventurous
- aloof
- assertive
- confident
- confused
- critical
- curious
- cynical
- determined
- disruptive
- dynamic
- energetic
- enthusiastic

- excitable
- flexible
- humorous
- idealistic
- impulsive
- independent
- industrious
- insightful
- intelligent
- intolerant
- introverted
- inventive
- moody
- obsessive
- open-minded

- original
- perceptive
- persistent
- playful
- preoccupied
- rebellious
- resourceful
- risk tolerant
- sensitive
- skeptical
- spontaneous
- stubborn
- tense
- unpredictable
- versatile

Which traits belong to the creative personality? Well, here's a surprise for you. Any and all of the traits you circled belong to creative individuals, or, more appropriately stated, any combination of characteristics can result in creativity.

We're all familiar with the stereotype of the "creative genius," the rumpled, forgetful visionary too caught up in deep thoughts to be bothered with the mundane details of daily life. Contrary to popular belief, no special personality is a prerequisite for creativity; any and all traits and temperaments will do. You can be a conservative sophisticate who wears three-piece suits and prefers life to be ordered and well organized, or you can be a bearded bohemian artist who lives life impulsively and spontaneously—or anything in between. Whatever your personality, you have as much capacity to be creative as anyone else.

Creative people come in all sizes and shapes, and they are found in every profession. In fact, history is full of examples clearly demonstrating that brilliant ideas and masterpieces of art emanate from a wide spectrum of individuals. If you were to examine the personality traits of the greatest thinkers and artists of the world, from da Vinci to Shakespeare to Spielberg, you would find an enormous range of qualities and characteristics fueling their creative output.

MINI WORKSHOP

BUSTING YOUR MISCONCEPTIONS AND LIMITING BELIEFS
In addition to widespread misunderstandings about the so-called creative personality, I commonly hear many related misconceptions. See if you identify with any of these:

- **MISCONCEPTION 1: Creativity cannot be learned; either you're creative or you're not.**
- **MISCONCEPTION 2: I'm a logical-type person; logic and creativity can't coexist.**
- **MISCONCEPTION 3: I have never produced a "masterpiece," therefore I am not creative.**

All these views reflect preconceived notions and prejudices that can severely stifle your creative development. They are all "limiting beliefs" that cause you to abandon learning and trying. In some cases, these limiting beliefs are based on doubts from childhood or early adulthood that continue to haunt you. In other cases, the limiting beliefs are based on our society's strong "product" orientation, which causes people to give up their creative work unless they can make something others will like or buy. The problem with any type of limiting belief is that it essentially puts the cart before the horse. It makes you think, *before you even try to create,* that your efforts will fail.

What, if any, limiting beliefs or misconceptions about your creativity do you have? Do you feel that you cannot learn to be more creative because you weren't creative as a child? Do you think of creativity in terms of a specific kind of accomplishment, such as a commercially successful commodity or a technically accomplished artwork? Do you let fear of criticism or rejection keep you from flexing your creative muscles?

Reflect on any doubts that block your ability to develop and expand your creative spirit. Abandon these fears and let yourself begin with a clean slate.

Creative Seven Ways

Related to the myth of the creative personality is a deep-seated belief that creativity is a reflection of intellectual ability. Too many of us think that "true" creativity is the birthright of the gifted.

However, these too are limiting beliefs that can undercut your creative potential. In fact, research has shown that each of us has the power to be creative in many ways. According to Dr. Howard Gardner of Harvard University in his book *Frames of Mind,* and popularized by Thomas Armstrong's book *Seven Kinds of Smart,* we are endowed with not one kind of general intelligence but rather seven kinds:

- **Verbal/linguistic: the ability to manipulate words in their oral or written form**
- **Mathematical/logical: the ability to manipulate number systems and logical concepts**
- **Spatial: the ability to see and manipulate patterns and designs**
- **Musical: the ability to understand and manipulate musical concepts such as tone, rhythm, and harmony**
- **Bodily-kinesthetic: the ability to use one's body and movement, such as in sports or dance**

- **Intrapersonal: the ability to understand one's feelings and to be reflective and philosophical**
- **Interpersonal: the ability to understand other people and their thoughts and feelings**

Each of us is usually dominant in one or two of these intelligences, but each of us has a unique combination of all seven that we can explore and tap into throughout our lives. Most of us severely limit ourselves, however, because as children we are encouraged to focus on only one of our intelligences—typically the verbal/linguistic or the mathematical/logical because they are the ones commonly emphasized in our educational system. As a result, we draw the conclusion that we don't possess abilities or potential in any other areas when the only real problem is that we have not had the proper chance to develop our other intelligences!

Gardner's pioneering theory of multiple intelligences is central to the field of creativity. Once we recognize that intelligence is not an all-or-nothing proposition, we are free to pursue our creative interests according to our unique mix of intelligences, whatever they may be. In seeking to be creative only in a narrow way (as an artist, writer, businessperson), or in attempting to be creative to achieve success as defined by other people, we do our creativity a disservice and limit our possibilities.

Whatever narrow visions you may have had in the past about your intelligence and creative potential, it is time to expand them and give yourself permission to experiment and find new ways to use your mind. As you read through the chapters discussing each of the ten strategies, don't limit yourself to imagining how they apply to work you *already* do. Think in terms of all your seven intelligences. Get up the courage to play on a much larger field and to pursue your inspiration wherever it may lie. If you are a scientist, you may very well discover that the ten strategies can help you explore your desire to become a watercolor painter or musician. If you are an executive, you may find that the ten strategies allow you to learn how to tap into your intuition and become a stronger problem solver. There is ultimately no limit to how you can use the ten strategies to achieve a more creative lifestyle.

WHAT ARE YOUR CREATIVE SMARTS?

To date no one has developed a scientific test to evaluate your multiple intelligences, but you can rate the areas in which you feel you excel. Rank them from 1 to 7, with 1 being the area in which you believe you are most gifted and 7 the one you consider to be your weakest. Don't be embarrassed about either your strengths or your weaknesses. Each of us is usually dominant in only a few intelligences — and weak in a few as well.

_____ verbal/linguistic
_____ mathematical/logical
_____ spatial
_____ musical
_____ bodily-kinesthetic
_____ intrapersonal
_____ interpersonal

1. Think about how your strongest intelligence relates to your job. Does your profession reflect your area of strength?
2. What hobbies or creative pursuits do you have and how do they relate to your intelligences?
3. If you could pick one of the intelligences you currently ranked low to develop, which would it be?

Owning Your Creative Spirit

The thrust of this chapter so far has been to help you identify and eliminate misconceptions about creativity that arise from stereotypes, preconceived notions, and definitions imposed by others. The more you liberate yourself from external limiting beliefs, the more you can focus on expanding your creativity from its only true source: inside you. Your creativity must ultimately arise from the unique blend of personality traits and intelligences that define you. To learn how to enhance and expand your creativity, you need to begin nourishing and developing *your own creative spirit*.

What is meant by the term *creative spirit*? We have already seen that creativity is not solely a function of intellectual ability or a specific skill such as musical or athletic aptitude. But this is not to say that the creative spirit cannot be defined, quantified, and nourished, or that there is no way to tell *which* qualities of the many that make up our personalities most foster creativity. In my view, there are four fundamental elements of the creative spirit. I call these four qualities your creative C.O.R.E., which stands for

C URIOSITY
O PENNESS
R ISK
E NERGY

These four elements are the heart of your creative spirit. Unlike the ability to create a ballet or solve a physics problem, they are inherent in all of us. Without these qualities, it is difficult, if not impossible, to be creative or to lead a creative life.

Here's how each quality plays a role in fueling your creativity.

Curiosity: The Questioning Force

A creative spirit first and foremost requires curiosity. Without an interest in what the world has to offer, what makes things work, what ideas others have, you have little reason to be creative. Curiosity is what prompts you to investigate new areas or look for a better way to do something. Curiosity drives your urge to invent, to experiment, and to build. As author and business philosopher Charles Handy aptly put it in *The Age of Unreason,* "Necessity may be the mother of invention, but curiosity is the mother of discovery."

As a child, you were perpetually curious. You questioned everything and answered your own questions with explanations you invented or imagined. In adulthood, however, your curiosity has probably been dramatically reduced. The phrase "idle curiosity" suggests that such speculation and exploration is an indulgence, a pointless pastime with no real purpose, as opposed to useful knowledge. Your curiosity may also be tempered by resignation—"Oh, I'll never understand how computers work"—or by time constraints—"I'd love to learn to cook, but my spouse does it so well, I'd do better to direct my energies where they'd be more useful." And fear, masquerading as "good sense," may hold you back from jumping into new situations or places.

Little by little, most adults draw lines around how far they are willing to go to keep learning. We unconsciously construct a "comfort zone," an area in which we feel safe but beyond which we feel threatened and rarely if ever choose to explore. It becomes harder and harder to go outside our comfort zones, and the boundaries of our lives eventually become firmly established. Our comfort zones translate into the routines of our lives—specific sets of acceptable people, places, things, and ideas that become our territory.

In losing curiosity, though, you lose a large part of your ability to create. A life in which every event is routine does not generate the new ideas that nourish your creative spirit. A routine life does not present you with occasions to meet new people or to hear about new concepts. It also does not provide you with new information that might eventually contribute to your next brilliant idea.

Imagine the world, for example, if the following people had not channeled their curiosity into creativity:

- If Newton had simply thought to himself, "What was that?" when he observed an apple fall from a branch, would the theory of gravity have developed in his century?
- If Scottish bacteriologist Alexander Fleming had simply washed them instead of wondering why the laboratory petri dishes containing bacteria failed to show growth when mold blew in an open window, would penicillin have been discovered yet?
- If chemist Roy Plunkett had accepted the explanation of others when a gas he was working with seemed to evaporate in its sealed container, would Teflon have been invented?
- If Edwin Land's curiosity had not been piqued by his three-year-old daughter's impatience to see their vacation photos, would instant photography exist?
- If Peter Hodgson had agreed with all the famous scientists that had told General Electric there was no apparent use for their unusual silicon substance, would the world know the joy of Silly Putty?

- If Percy L. Spencer had simply thought, "Better take these pants to the cleaner," when a chocolate bar melted in his pocket as he stood in front of a radar set power line, would we have been deprived of microwave technology?
- If U.S. Navy engineer Richard James had not noticed what happened when he dropped a torsion spring, would generations of children ever have known the fun of Slinky?

It helps to understand curiosity using the following visual of a funnel:

What you don't know you don't know

What you know you don't know

What you know

Flowing from the neck of the funnel is the body of information you have accumulated over your lifetime. It has already filtered into your mind and is available to you when you need it. Call this *What you know.*

In the hopper, or large part of the funnel, is all the information you know is out there but you have yet to assimilate and add to your personal knowledge base. Call this *What you know you don't know.*

Above the hopper, and extending into space, is a vast store of information that you are not even aware of. This is all the knowledge and wisdom available in the universe. Call this *What you don't know you don't know.*

Curiosity is the process of exploring whatever exists above the neck of the funnel. In being curious, your goal is continually to pour more information through the funnel so that you can feed your creative spirit.

Openness: Flexibility and Respect for the New

Like curiosity, openness is a vital quality of the creative spirit because it is by being open that you are able to accept new ideas and incorporate them into your thinking. If you subscribe only to your tried-and-true beliefs, you never challenge yourself to look outside or go beyond.

Creative people open themselves to new notions, people, places, and things. Creativity blooms when you build on the insights of others. If you shut out, ignore, or ridicule the ideas of others, you do not leave your comfort zone to discover the larger world beyond.

It's ironic that many people seem to have a harder time being open than they do being curious. They are willing to explore, but as soon as they encounter a new idea they don't like, they close up and criticize it; they reject it rather than assimilate it into their hearts and souls. New ideas are like bad dreams: They can be difficult to understand and they may go against the grain of our belief systems and thus frighten us. In most businesses, it takes only an average of ten seconds before people begin to come up with all the reasons why a new idea won't work (or so they think).

Think about the last time you met someone new, tried a new ethnic cuisine, or visited a new place. Did you fully accept the experience—or did you turn it away because you were unable to accommodate it into your comfort zone?

Openness also pertains to being aware of and "tuned in" to the coincidences of life. A closed mind shuts out the chance meetings and events that often become opportunities for discovery and invention (see the next chapter for more on the power of synchronicity).

Risk Tolerance: The Courage to Leave Your Comfort Zone

A creative spirit also demands risk taking. In fact, without the willingness to take risks, most creative ventures would never get off the ground. Writers take risks when they allow their work to be printed and bound and put onto bookstore shelves;

artists, when they exhibit their paintings; and actors, when they appear before an audience on stage or screen. Businesspeople risk their capital and their reputations when they start new projects or ventures.

Risk taking is tied to your comfort zone. If you are tolerant of risks, you give yourself permission to leave your comfort zone to encounter new ideas, people, and information that can enhance your creativity. If you are risk averse, you stay within your comfort zone, forsaking the potential challenges that might inspire you to new ideas and experiences.

Creative risks can be grouped into many categories, including the following:

• **Leaping into the dark risk.** You feel this type of risk instinctively, at the gut level. It arises from activities that get your adrenaline pumping, including physical adventures (such as skydiving and white-water rafting) and certain kinds of social activities (such as public speaking).

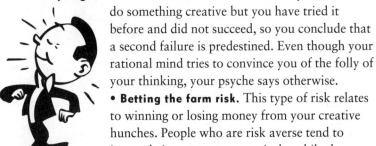

• **Tempting the fates risk.** You feel this risk when you want to do something creative but you have tried it before and did not succeed, so you conclude that a second failure is predestined. Even though your rational mind tries to convince you of the folly of your thinking, your psyche says otherwise.

• **Betting the farm risk.** This type of risk relates to winning or losing money from your creative hunches. People who are risk averse tend to invest their money conservatively, while those who are more tolerant of risk tend to be more willing to gamble for high stakes.

• **Becoming a laughingstock risk.** This type of risk is related to the fear of ridicule or rejection by others. Many creative ventures require you to make your work and ideas public. Risk-tolerant people are willing to do this, while risk-averse people shy away from it.

Organizations can also be affected by risk tolerance. Apple Computer, for example, earned a reputation for risk taking by designing an innovative new system that went against conventional wisdom. However, Apple later became equally famous for risk avoidance when it refused to allow its Macintosh operating system to be cloned by other manufacturers. Unfortunately, Apple's desire to protect its system motivated Microsoft to develop a competitive operating system, Windows, which now dominates the personal computer market.

Energy: The Fuel to Work and the Spark of Passion

The last quality your creative spirit requires is energy. Energy is the spark that ignites you. Without sufficient *mental* energy, your creative pursuits suffer from flaws, caused by faulty logic or short-term thinking, that can prevent them from being implemented. Without sufficient *physical* energy, your creative ideas don't get put into motion or remain in the closet to gather dust. In a sense, all creativity begins as pure energy because the ideas that compose your creative thinking are nothing more than electrical impulses in your brain. Without the energy of your brain waves, creativity is impossible.

The term *energy* also relates to the degree of passion you bring to everything you do. When you are fascinated by a project, or personally invested in a subject or task, you feel charged and exuberant. You are able to summon up as much energy as it takes to complete the job because the energy you invest is repaid by results and positive feedback. The more you love something, the more energy you will have to dedicate to it, and so the more creative you will be. When you are not energetic, the whole process may seem like a struggle, and your creativity will take a dive.

Dr. Mihaly Csikszentmihalyi of the University of Chicago has identified a state of high energy as a critical element in intellectual and creative success. Through extensive research, he has shown that people are more successful at their tasks when they are able to achieve what he calls *flow*. When people are in flow, their energy level is high and their mental acuity and concentration surge. They seldom need to pause or hesitate, and their minds are so tuned in to their work that they act almost instinctively.

Think of something you've mastered: it might be a sport, the ability to speak in public, an artistic or musical talent, or anything else you choose. You've entered the flow state when you are engaged in the subject of your mastery and are able to respond and react to everything required without conscious thought or reflection.

Getting into flow is also an important element of creative work. It's as if you become one with your endeavor, and so you become fully engaged in the task, you make fewer mistakes, and you are much more productive and insightful.

CHARTING YOUR COMFORT ZONE
How do you assess your creative spirit and creative C.O.R.E.?

PART I. ASSESSING YOUR C.O.R.E.
• CURIOSITY. On a scale of 1 to 10, how curious do you feel you are? A score of 1 would indicate a low level of curiosity, and 10 would indicate that you are curious about a wide range of subjects. Write your answer here:

_____

_____

• OPENNESS. On a scale of 1 to 10, how open do you feel you are? A score of 1 would indicate that you feel you are not open, and 10 would indicate that you are highly receptive to new people and ideas. Write your answer here:

_____

_____

• RISK TOLERANCE. On a scale of 1 to 10, how much of a risk taker are you? A score of 1 would indicate that you avoid risk as mush as possible, and 10 would indicate that you welcome risk as an agent of change. Write your answer here: _____

• ENERGY. On a scale of 1 to 10, how energetic do you feel you are? A score of 1 would indicate that you do not feel particularly energetic, and 10 would indicate that you pursue all activities in your life with a high degree of energy. Write your answer here: _____

_____

PART II. DRAWING THE "BOX" YOU NEED TO GET OUT OF
The following grid will enable you to chart and visualize your creative CORE as a box. From the center box, there are four diagonals—each numbered from 1 to 10. Each diagonal exits from a corner that represents one of the four qualities—curiosity, openness, risk tolerance, and energy. Put an X on the number in each diagonal corresponding to the number you gave the quality in Part I. Now, draw lines connecting the four X's.

You may have heard that, in order to be creative, you need to "get out of your box." The shape you have just drawn is a loose representation of your current box, and the purpose of the strategies in this book is precisely to help you get out of it.

If you have a very small box, it indicates that you need to work on enlarging your creative C.O.R.E. which you can do with the ten strategies. You are

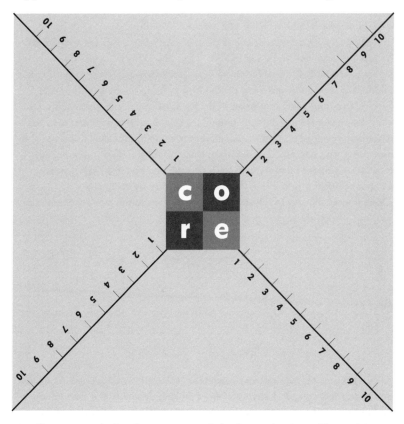

spending too much time in your own safe harbor and not reaching out to challenge. This may explain why you don't feel creative or wish you could be much more so.

If you have a very large box, it means that you already have a strong creative spirit, and the strategies will serve you well as you sail off into the wider world, seeking creative opportunities and challenges. But however large your comfort zone is, it can always get larger, and each advance will increase your level of creativity correspondingly.

Like many people, you may have a skewed box (sort of a rhombus shape) that extends far out in one or two quadrants but dives back in for the others. Perhaps you are very curious but have no ability to tolerate risk. Or you may have loads of energy but are not open to new ideas. In this case, it helps to learn to balance your creative C.O.R.E. Without balance, you will feel frustrated or exhausted because the four sides of your creative spirit are moving in different directions or battling one another.

PART III. EXAMINING WHERE YOU WANT TO GO

• CURIOSITY. Are you as curious as you were when you were a child? Do you feel you know all you need to know to get by? What can you do to increase your curiosity and facilitate your creative growth? For example, can you identify a passion you have always had to learn about a topic, place, or person? If so, make a commitment to begin spending some time each week using the strategies in this book to explore this area. If the idea of learning something new invokes unpleasant thoughts of being back in school, or is in some other way onerous or uninviting, think about a different manner of learning that might be more enjoyable to you. The ten strategies will show you that satisfying your curiosity does not need to be dull or dry.

Take a moment now to list three things you are curious about, and one or two ways you might satisfy this curiosity:

1. _____
   _____
2. _____
   _____
3. _____
   _____

• OPENNESS. Are you open to new ideas, concepts, and people? Or do you shun them? If you tend to shy away from new ideas, using the ten strategies can help you develop a more receptive mind-set. For example, consider these ways to expand your openness this week:

1. Read a magazine or book that contains ideas you know are contrary to your beliefs.
2. Engage in a conversation with someone you know whose views differ from yours.
3. Spend some time on the Internet exploring the great diversity of people and companies that are participating on the World Wide Web.

Can you think of other ways to open yourself up to new ideas and people as you use the strategies in this book?

• **RISK TOLERANCE.** In general, are you willing to take risks? If not, identify what you most fear about risk taking: embarrassment? being criticized? losing money? physical injury? How can you develop your tolerance of risk? Here are some ideas:

1. Talk to people you know who are risk takers. Ask them how they overcome the concerns you have.
2. Go to a bookstore and browse through the many books that address your specific fears.
3. Sign up for a course or activity you have always wanted to pursue. Many undertakings feel less risky when you face them with other people.

• **ENERGY.** Are you a high-energy or a low-energy person? If you are in the latter category, examine why your energy is lacking. Are you too stressed? Trying to accomplish too many things at once? Depressed? Bored? In need of exercise? Sleep deprived? Once you identify the specific cause or causes of your low energy, you can often find a way to eliminate the problem and increase your energy. Make a commitment to enhancing your energy this week.

Your Creative Spirit and the Ten Strategies

Developing your creative spirit depends on your ability to expand your creative C.O.R.E. The more aspects of life you approach with curiosity, openness, risk tolerance, and energy, the stronger your creative spirit will grow.

The relationship between your creative C.O.R.E. and the ten strategies in this book is synergistic, with each one fueling the others. The more you use the ten strategies, the more you will enhance your creative C.O.R.E. The more you seek ways to expand your C.O.R.E., the more reason you will have to apply the ten strategies to various parts of your life.

With time, creative synergy will infuse both your personal and professional lives. As you approach your endeavors with more curiosity, openness, risk tolerance, and energy, your creative lifestyle will reverberate through you, leading your creative spirit to seek further opportunities and challenges. This is the creative life cycle:

This synergy explains why creative people seem never to run out of ideas. Each experience leads them to new inspiration and new opportunities to further their quest for innovation and original work.

To become part of this world, all you need to do is jump onboard, like mounting a moving merry-go-round.

Further Readings

Creating Minds: An Anatomy of Creativity Seen Through the Lives of Freud, Einstein, Picasso, Stravinsky, Eliot, Graham, and Gandhi by Howard Gardner (New York: Basic Books, 1993).

The Creative Attitude: Learning to Ask and Answer the Right Questions by Roger Schank (New York: Macmillan, 1988).

Creativity—Flow and the Psychology of Discovery and Invention by Mihaly Csikszentmihalyi (New York: HarperCollins, 1996).

Flow: The Psychology of Optimal Experience by Mihaly Csikszentmihalyi (New York: Harper & Row, 1990).

Frames of Mind: The Theory of Multiple Intelligences by Howard Gardner (New York: Basic Books, 1983).

Seven Kinds of Smart: Identifying and Developing Your Many Intelligences by Thomas Armstrong (New York: Plume, 1993).

You Don't Have to Go Home from Work Exhausted! A Program to Bring Joy, Energy, and Balance to Your Life by Ann McGee-Cooper (New York: Bantam Books, 1992).

Tapping into the Creative Process

While the image of a lightbulb going on over one's head is a popular metaphor for the birth of an idea, in reality new concepts come into being in stages. This chapter explains the basic four-stage model of the creative process, as well as three other methods that have become increasingly acknowledged as sources of creativity. You may be surprised at how easy it is to tap into your mind's natural inclination to be creative.

The Four-Stage Creative Model

The path the mind takes to originate a new idea has long been studied by researchers and scientists. There are several models of what happens, the most widely accepted of which originated in the late nineteenth century with the German physiologist and physicist Hermann von Helmholtz; it was expanded and popularized by the American psychologist Graham Wallas in his 1926 book, *The Art of Thought.* Much of Wallas's work is based on studies he performed on the thinking processes of well-known scholars, scientists, and mathematicians.

In Wallas's model, creativity occurs over a four-stage process, as follows.

Preparation

In the preparation stage, your mind collects information and data that serve as background or research for a creative issue you are working on.

To some extent, your entire education, general background, and life experience contribute to your preparation for creativity. The broader and more diverse your experiences, the more prepared you are to meet creative challenges. But in Wallas's model, preparation refers to a task-oriented stage in which you do specific research on your project through reading, interviewing people, traveling, or other activities to help you gather facts, ideas, and opinions. For example, actors who are trying to create characters frequently visit the locales of their plays or films to study the real-life people who live there. Similarly, entrepreneurs seeking ideas for new businesses read relevant trade publications and visit stores or restaurants to study what others have done.

Incubation

The incubation stage is commonly known as the time-out phase, the period when you store the information you have gathered and cease to focus on it or consciously think about it. Although it feels like you are wasting time or even shirking the hard part of the creative process, this phase is crucial. During this apparent downtime, your unconscious mind takes over the information, caring for it in ways that the term *incubation* suggests.

It is often said that the key function of the unconscious mind during this period is connecting ideas. Creativity is the result of your mind's ability to link ideas, producing something new and different. In connecting ideas, the mind is actually performing a variety of processes, including the following:

- **JUXTAPOSING: taking one idea and pitting it against another; from the contrast a new idea arises**
- **BLENDING: borrowing characteristics or aspects from two ideas and merging them to form an altogether new one**
- **PYRAMIDING OR FUNNELING: joining many ideas to form a synthesis at the top or bottom, a sleek new idea that combines the best elements of all**
- **ENCIRCLING: starting with a fuzzy picture of a new idea, then narrowing the choices and options to find the one central concept that works**
- **IMAGINING: using imagination and fantasy to produce a new idea from an old one**

How does the mind know when to move from preparation to incubation? In general, whenever you begin to feel stressed, tired, distracted, or bored, your mind is telling you to take a break and let incubation begin. Many highly creative people say they actually sense when their minds want them to abandon preparatory work; they intuitively know that they have collected enough information and that the time for conscious creative work has come to an end.

The most important characteristic of the incubation stage is that it must happen on an unconscious level; the creative work of this phase is not subject to your mental control. You cannot tell your unconscious mind which processes to use or what data to consider. This phase is often compared to cooking in the sense that your mind is like a simmering caldron of ingredients that will not gain full flavor until they have made soup. Although you are the chef, you must learn to step out of the way and let the concoction cook on its own.

Many people think of this unconscious time of incubation as "getting out of your own way," affirming that this phase of the creative process arises from deep within your creative spirit.

Illumination

The illumination stage is best known as the eureka or aha! experience, the moment of inspiration when, seemingly out of nowhere, a new idea surfaces in your mind to answer the creative challenge you have faced. The surge of energy you get when this happens is usually so powerful that it hits you like a brick, and you recognize immediately that this flash is precisely what you had been seeking.

Oddly enough, illumination often occurs when you are doing something quite unrelated to your creative work, such as showering, driving, staring into space, listening to music, or being involved in another type of activity. Researchers believe that illumination is the point at which new ideas pass from the unconscious to the conscious mind, and that it is most readily reached by being relaxed and unstressed.

History is full of famous examples of illuminating moments. René Descartes was playfully watching a fly on the wall when he invented analytical geometry. The German chemist Kekule von Stradonitz discovered the ring structure of benzene, which led to a transformation of molecular chemistry, while riding atop a bus and having a momentary reverie. The French mathematician Henri Poincaré discovered Fuchsian functions while stepping onto a bus after fifteen days of concentrated preparation and seeming failure. Richard Wagner was in the midst of a fallow period when the theme to his opera *Das Rheingold* came to him in a dream. The Russian chemist Dmitri Ivanovich Mendeleyev conceived the periodic table of elements after getting a vision of it in a dream although he had struggled with the concept for weeks. And Albert Einstein's inspiration for the theory of relativity came to him during a "thought experiment" that was almost like a daydream.

The importance of relaxation or distraction to encourage incubation and illumination is now so well recognized that creativity experts highly recommend that you allow yourself sufficient downtime for these processes to occur naturally. Obviously, it's impossible to say how much time is enough for you, but experience helps most people recognize when they are too stressed or tired for their creative juices to flow and should let their unconscious minds take over. The lesson to learn about illumination is therefore *patience;* if you feel pressure to find your answer or new idea, you may be better off giving your mind a break so it can do its creative work. It will notify you when it's ready!

Implementation / Verification

Most books refer to this stage simply as verification, but I call it implementation/verification because this is the point at which you give form to your new idea to make sure it works. Now is when the writer sits down to write; the fund-raiser, to plan an event; and the businessperson, to test out his or her new project or business idea.

You can have one of two experiences in this stage. In some cases, the new ideas you receive in illumination are so perfect that you can implement them exactly as you conceived them. Some people refer to this kind of experience as *channeling:* you frantically write, draft, sing, or do whatever your mind tells you. Such experiences are indicative of the flow state of mind mentioned earlier, those moments when you are able seamlessly to transpose thought to action.

In most cases, however, the ideas are not delivered from your unconscious in perfect form, so you must work to refine and polish them. Your unconscious provides only the seed you need to get started, and it is up to you to help the seed grow to a healthy plant. This is where your abilities and thinking skills must come into play, as well as your passion and sense of joy.

For example, the writer who sought an idea for a new screenplay may get an illumination yielding a great plot but no dialogue. He must therefore use his love of writing to craft the manuscript. Similarly, a fashion designer may find an exciting new direction for her collection, but she still must realize it in fabric, cut, and construction.

In the implementation/verification stage, some ideas come to fruition very quickly, while others take months or years. Many great composers, like Mozart and Bach, are known to have written entire symphonies and sonatas in one sitting after hearing the themes "pop" into their minds. In contrast, many great artists, like Michelangelo and Leonardo da Vinci, and writers, like Gustave Flaubert and O. Henry, had to work years to bring their creative visions to life.

Tapping into the Creative Process

You have probably used this four-stage creative process many times without being aware of it. Most of us have had experiences in which ideas seem to appear in our minds from nowhere, ideas that helped us make a business decision or know what steps to take next to solve a problem.

But what is most exciting about understanding this model is that you can intentionally increase your creativity by consciously tapping into it *whenever* you want to generate a new idea or pursue a vision. You simply need to be aware of these four steps and allow them to happen automatically and naturally rather than feel pressured to get an idea immediately. Learn to give yourself preparation time to read, study, conduct interviews, or undertake whatever activities help you gather information; then let go of your thinking and allow your mind to perform its magic during the incubation stage. Trust that illumination will eventually bring you an answer. This is your mind's natural path to creativity.

Discovering Creativity in Serendipity, Synchronicity, and Chaos

In addition to the creative incubation process, I believe in three other powerful methods by which creative results occur. Your awareness of these processes can increase your creative output.

Serendipity

Serendipity is a creative process that involves fortunate and unexpected discoveries *by accident*. The word was coined by Horace Walpole in 1754 in a letter to Horace Mann, based on a fairy tale about the three princes of Serendip, who "were always making discoveries, by accidents and sagacity, of things which they were not in quest of."

People who are creative through serendipity are those who recognize, in the events of their daily lives, the seed of an idea or an insight that can help them in their work. History is filled with examples of serendipitous invention and discovery:

- **Marie Curie — radiation**
- **Wilhelm Conrad Röntgen — X rays**
- **Louis Pasteur — pasteurization**
- **Louis-Jacques-Mardé Daguerre — photography**
- **Clarence Birdseye — frozen foods**
- **Robert Augustus Chesebrough — Vaseline**

Many successful entrepreneurs get their start when they notice a seemingly trivial or inconsequential item and realize that the world needs it. A few typical issues of business magazines chosen at random, for example, yielded the following stories:

➤ Gail Frankel founded Kel-Gar, Inc., in Dallas, Texas, after going shopping with her two small sons and running out of places to put things. When she couldn't find a product on the market, she invented the Stroll'r Hold'r—a plastic device that clips on strollers and has drink holders and clips to hold purses and bags. Her company's sales are in the millions!

➤ Tomima Edmark went to see *When Harry Met Sally* in a Seattle theater in 1989 and saw a woman in the audience with a ponytail done in a French twist. She tried to duplicate it but came up instead with her own design and turned it into one of the most amazing "infomercial" successes, Topsy Tail. At last report, her company's annual sales had reached over $5 million.

➤ Dan Hoard and Tom Bunnell founded the company Mambosocks when Dan, in "an unbridled pursuit of fun," lopped off a pant leg and put it on his head in August 1989 to help cope with the heat in Australia while on vacation. His ridiculous hat creation caught on, and by their second year in business, they had sales of $1 million. They have recently gone over $3 million.

The intriguing aspect of serendipity as a creative process is that it does not follow the same laws as the incubation model. It is an immediate form of inspiration that is not preceded by preparation and incubation. People who generate ideas serendipitously don't consciously plan to discover something, nor are they unconsciously incubating an idea in their minds. They are simply open and available to life, and can discern the value of whatever they find by being aware and tuned in.

In whatever manner serendipity occurs, though, it is a creative "trigger" that you can learn to harness by strengthening your creative spirit (in other words, increasing your curiosity, openness, risk tolerance, and energy). You need to be aware so that you can see serendipity when it graces you. As Louis Pasteur said, "Chance favors the prepared mind."

Synchronicity

Synchronicity is closely related to serendipity, but I distinguish the two concepts in the following way.

- **SERENDIPITY refers to accidents and random coincidences that trigger an idea or concept when you are not looking.**
- **SYNCHRONICITY refers to those times when you *are* looking for an idea or answer, and you unexpectedly experience an event or a string of events that perfectly solves your problem.**

In other words, serendipity is stumbling upon a diamond buried in the garden, whereas synchronicity is losing the diamond but finding it because you happened to go out to the garden that morning to pick some flowers.

Carl Jung, the great psychologist, focused extensively on the concept of synchronicity and gave it its name, and perhaps its most simple definition—"a meaningful coincidence." He wrote, "Meaningful coincidences are unthinkable as *pure chance*—the more they multiply and the greater and more exact the correspondence is . . . they can no longer be regarded as pure chance, but for the lack of causal explanation, have to be thought of as meaningful arrangements." In this sense, synchronicity is a spin-off of the four-stage model. It occurs because you have done some preparation and perhaps partial incubation, but rather than your mind delivering the answer, it comes from an outside coincidence.

Both serendipity and synchronicity are examples of creativity that we usually ascribe to dumb luck, or as many people say,

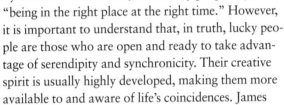

"being in the right place at the right time." However, it is important to understand that, in truth, lucky people are those who are open and ready to take advantage of serendipity and synchronicity. Their creative spirit is usually highly developed, making them more available to and aware of life's coincidences. James Redfield's best-selling book, *The Celestine Prophecy,* proposes the intriguing concept that the universe is full of synchronistic and serendipitous events that we can tap into once we learn how.

Chaos

This last creative process was only recently recognized formally. Its origins in the scientific community started with the meteorologist Edward Lorenz. A weather phenomenon is often used to explain chaos: A tornado that occurs in Texas may actually originate when a butterfly flaps its wings in Rio de Janeiro, setting in motion a chain of events that ultimately leads to the twister.

Chaos is the universe's trickster. It makes the inexplicable and unpredictable happen without our being able to account for them. In terms of creativity, chaos is what might be seen as inexplicable synchronicity, a new idea or insight we generate by a seemingly unrelated or even bizarre set of events.

Many creative people tap into all these methods, not just the four-stage model. Some ventures can only be explained as the result of a combination of methods. An excellent case study is the story of the noted businessman and author Paul Hawken, who founded the two successful enterprises, Erewhon Foods, and Smith & Hawken. While traveling in England one year, Hawken began talking by chance with a gardener who was using an extremely well-constructed spade. Hawken contrasted it to the broken tools he had noticed the farmers using two years earlier when he was touring fields in Texas, where crops for his food company, Erewhon, were grown. He wondered why American tool companies made such poor tools.

When he returned from England and thought about the excellent spade he had seen, he suggested to several companies that they begin importing the English-made tools. No one was interested, so Hawken eventually began importing them himself, thus founding Smith & Hawken.

An analysis of these events suggests that unconscious fermentation, serendipity, and synchronicity all contributed to Hawken's ability to turn his creative idea into an entrepreneurial success. Between his noticing the broken American farming tools and coincidentally discovering two years later the English gardener and his well-made spade, it also seems that chaos had a hand in the story.

MINI WORKSHOP

TAKING STOCK OF YOUR CREATIVE DISCOVERIES

1. **Can you think of a creative experience you've had that follows the four-stage model? What were you trying to create? Where were you or what were you doing when the illumination hit you? Have you ever consciously tried to use the incubation process to get a new idea? Has it worked? If not, what do you think went wrong?**

2. **Have you ever had a serendipitous or synchronistic experience? Where were you? What happened and what did you discover? Do you think other people are in the right place at the right time more often than you are? Do you think you could be more open to "cues" that help you tap into serendipity and synchronicity?**

How the Ten Strategies Aid the Creative Process

As you might have guessed, the ten strategies directly facilitate creative work and breakthroughs. First and foremost, they help you nourish your mind when you are consciously seeking new ideas, projects, or solutions to problems. They introduce you to the rich fields of life where you can gather ideas, information, and data as part of your preparation for creativity. With continued attention, they can even assist you during the incubation, illumination, and implementation/verification stages. Using the strategies frequently as part of a fully creative lifestyle also expands your opportunity to encounter synchronicity and serendipity—or to challenge chaos. Rather than remaining within your old comfort zone, the strategies encourage you to go out into the world to strengthen your creative spirit and enlarge your creative C.O.R.E.

Further Readings

The Alchemist: A Fable About Following Your Dream by Paulo Coleho (San Francisco: HarperSanFrancisco, 1993).

The Art of Thought by Graham Wallas (New York: Harcourt, Brace, 1926).

The Celestine Prophecy: An Experiential Guide by James Redfield and Carol Adrienne (New York: Warner Books, 1995).

Creating by Robert Fritz (New York: Fawcett Columbine, 1991).

The IdeaFisher: How to Land That "Big Idea" and Other Secrets of Business Creativity by Marsh Fisher (Princeton, N.J.: Peterson's/Pacesetter Books, 1995).

Secrets From Great Minds by John H. McMurphy (Dallas: Amaranth Publishing, 1995).

Serendipity: Accidental Discoveries in Science by Royston M. Roberts (New York: John Wiley, 1989).

Synchronicity: The Bridge Between Matter and Mind by F. David Peat (New York: Bantam Books, 1987).

Synchronicity—Science, Math, and the Trickster by Allan Combs and Mark Holland (New York: Marlowe & Company, 1996).

Mastering the Techniques of Idea Capture

When was the last time you had a great idea? Perhaps you have developed a design for a new and improved popcorn popper, the plotline of the next great American novel, or a better way to do your job. Maybe you offered your employer an idea that would save $50,000 over the next year or found a way to eliminate two time-consuming steps of a complex process at your company. Or you might have thought of a way to provide child care during school vacations for working parents in your community.

If you're like most people, that idea came and went quickly. Unless you were motivated to stick a piece of paper into a company suggestion box or had the good fortune to share your idea out loud with a colleague or spouse, chances are it got lost in the hustle and bustle of your daily routine. Maybe you were too overwhelmed with the demands of family to flesh out the design for a new popcorn popper. Or an unsupportive boss made you think it was a waste of time to drop that money-saving thought into the company suggestion box.

Then, the nightmare happens. You're walking through the housewares section of a department store and you see the exact popcorn popper you envisioned a few years earlier. Or you discover that the quiet guy two offices down the hall has won your company's Innovator of the Year award (along with a $10,000 bonus) for a concept nearly identical to the one you thought of last year.

So what separates the people who experience the exhilaration of having their ideas come to life from those who sit back and continually wonder about what might have been? In many cases, it is simply a matter of the discipline to document their ideas and a method for doing so. The fact is, ideas that sit rusting in our minds are like cars in an automobile graveyard—eventually they become unsalvageable. If we try to rescue an idea two hours—or two years—later, we almost always fail. And even if we do remember, the idea always has lost some of its original excitement and luster. The worst case is an idea whose time has passed; it would have been successful at one point, but no longer.

MINI WORKSHOP

REMEMBERING THE IDEAS YOU LOST
Can you think now of a good or great idea you once had? What happened to it? Did you ever get it implemented? Why or why not? How were you distracted from implementing your idea? Do those barriers still exist? If so, how can you remove them? What were the consequences of not implementing your idea? Has the idea been implemented or developed by someone else? If so, how does it make you feel to see another person reap the benefits of your idea?

Preventing the Loss of Good Ideas

It doesn't take much thinking to realize that ideas in progress should be caught. Not surprisingly, the greatest minds in history have all realized the wisdom of capturing or documenting their ideas. Creative thinkers ranging from the inventors Thomas Edison, Benjamin Franklin, and Leonardo da Vinci to the novelist Virginia Woolf, the psychologist Carl Jung, and the naturalist Charles Darwin all have used journals and notebooks to record their ideas and inspirations. These people understood that new ideas often come from combining many disparate pieces of information or concepts over an extended period of time. The only effective way to track your ideas and synthesize them is to document them as soon as they bubble up in your mind.

Capturing an idea makes it more real, more tangible. Whether you act on it within the next six months or the next six years isn't important. Nor is it important whether the people around you deem the idea impractical, or incredible. Simply writing it down for yourself is an intelligent course of action. When you decide to implement the idea at some later date, your written record may be your only source of reliable information.

Here are several idea-capturing techniques that you might want to practice before you read the strategy chapters. These techniques can help you record not only the ideas you get from reading this book but also all the ideas that will pour in once you begin using the strategies in your daily life.

The Idea Journal

One of the easiest and most effective ways to record your ideas is to start a personal "idea journal." By keeping this journal near you at all times—on top of your desk, in your briefcase or purse, on the kitchen counter, on the nightstand by your bed — you can record ideas that flash through your mind during the day and even at night.

You don't have to invest fifty dollars or more in a leather-bound notebook. Select a journal that makes sense for you; choose a format that interests and engages you, or develop one of your own. If crafting your own cloth-covered book will motivate you to document ideas regularly then by all means do it. But you must impose some order; if you try to keep track of your ideas by scribbling them in pencil on the backs of grocery receipts, credit card slips, and business cards, you'll have a much harder time retrieving the information you need.

Those accustomed to working with computers can use a personal information manager (PIM), which allows you to enter information on a keyboard. Or you may choose an electronic notepad such as Apple's Newton, which lets you write with a penlike stylus. You can also try professional planning books (organizers) published by companies like Franklin Quest, File-Fax, Day Runner, Day-Timer, and Covey Leadership Center. Some of these are available in both paper and electronic versions.

After trying several formats, I've settled on an artist's sketchbook with blank eight-and-a-half-by-eleven-inch sheets of white paper. The book's hard binding minimizes my chances of losing it accidentally or throwing away individual pieces of paper. Although this notepad is slightly bulky, I carry it with me wherever I go. When I'm working in my office, I keep it close to my computer. When I'm watching television, I keep it on a table adjacent to my favorite chair. At night, I make sure it's resting on my bedside table. If I have a creative brainstorm or experience a particularly evocative dream in the middle of the night, I wake up and document it immediately.

What goes in an idea journal? Thoughts, examples, illustrations, jokes, anecdotes, analogies, metaphors, and quotations. You may choose to paste in clippings that have particular relevance to whatever you wrote or thought about on a given day.

I recommend you review your ideas once a week or at the end of each month and create several sentences or paragraphs that synthesize your experiences. This type of review helps you perceive trends and themes in your entries that you may not have noticed before.

Whatever form your journal keeping takes, the most surefire way to murder your impulse to use it is imposing a set of meaningless rules or guidelines. For example, don't feel that your journal is worthless if you don't write in it every day, or if you don't use full, grammatically correct sentences. This is nonsense; it can be just as valuable if you write in it only a few times every week, or if you write in incomplete sentences or, on some days, just a few words. My own journal keeping improved dramatically when I abandoned the daily one-page-or-else rule. As soon as I surrendered rigid, lined paper for the more expansive, blank sketch pad, I discovered that my ideas flowed freely. Now I'm inclined to write any way I desire—even in circles—and in a variety of colors and handwriting styles. Sometimes I'll draw nothing but pictures. At other times, I'll write in long paragraphs, sentence fragments, or even lists. I gave myself the freedom of space, design, and language, and this has allowed me to expand my thinking.

If you already have experience writing in a journal, consult Julia Cameron's *The Artist's Way: A Spiritual Path to Higher Creativity*. Cameron recommends a specific technique that she terms "Morning Pages." She asks that, upon awakening every day, you write three pages in your journal. No other rules, no requirements, no subject — just three pages on whatever you want to write about. While you may feel three pages is more than you can commit to on a daily basis, Cameron's concept of making an entry at the start of each day is a powerful one and well worth trying.

The Focused Journal

Another type of journal you might want to consider is a focused one, in which you devote your pages to a specific topic, invention, or realm of your life. For example, a teacher might want to develop a journal focused on a new course to teach, while a parent might want to develop a journal that chronicles the birth and growth of a child. Similarly, an engineer might want to shape a journal around a new invention. (Note: A focused journal is also useful if you need to document the idea for a patent; however, you should consult an attorney to learn the special legal requirements of this process.)

The Visual Journal

Although the visual journal is typically used by people with artistic talent or training, don't let a lack of perceived skill or training stop you from dabbling with this intriguing tool. Some people create a visual journal by putting together a collage focused on a specific theme, such as innovation, personal power, or success. Your collage can be made from pictures cut out of magazines or with line drawings you do yourself. Even if you have no artistic training, the act of drawing or doodling may help you capture the ambience or significance of an event.

A photographic journal is another type of visual record. Just about everyone enjoys looking through an album of family photographs, and no matter how different we may have looked in high school, thumbing through a yearbook brings back a rush of both happy memories and regrets. You can exploit the same technique by developing an album collecting your life's experiences. Photographs are especially powerful when you're trying to recall the significance of particular events, scenes, or people. For example, an artist painting a sunset is able to study his or her subject for only a few moments. A photograph can capture the sunset's beauty. Photographs can work the same way for you. By studying a photo, you can recall the meaning of an event and the feelings associated with it, leading you to form connections that can be the trigger for your next new idea.

The Create-Your-Own Journal

Use whatever journaling method works for you. One of the best methods I've heard about was developed by a manager at Boeing who wanted to track ideas he had while traveling. He carried preaddressed, stamped postcards with him on which he wrote ideas as they hit him. Then he mailed the cards back to his house. I also know people who call their voice mail boxes and leave themselves messages. And tiny tape recorders that will capture a spoken line or two are available inexpensively. There is no end to the clever (and creative) ways you can record and document your ideas. Think of several ways you can create a journal that are appropriate for your lifestyle and that you will really *use*.

MINI WORKSHOP

DON'T UNDERESTIMATE THE POWER OF A JOURNAL

Do you have a preconceived idea about journal keeping? For example, have you ever had a diary that you felt obligated to write in every day because its pages carried dates? Do you feel obliged to write in straight lines, on lined paper, or in complete sentences?

One way to free yourself from any doubts you may have about keeping a journal is to visualize your own journal. What does it look like? What would you put in it? Would you tend to write long paragraphs or short tidbits of information? What would you tend to include? Quotations? Statistics? Jokes? News items? Stories about work or your personal life?

Can you see yourself recording your ideas about the following?

- An exciting or interesting thing that happened to you
- Something you learned
- A particular accomplishment
- A difference you made in somebody's life
- An impression left on you by a person or occurrence

Your journal can be as unique as you choose. A wine connoisseur I know keeps a wine journal. He was once asked to look up how he enjoyed the nose on a particularly expensive bottle of wine he had consumed. He replied that he kept track not of the wines but of the experience — who he shared the bottle with, what they ate. He used the journal to remember how he felt when he drank the wine, not how it tasted.

So develop your own idea for a new kind of journal, and begin using it. Choose a topic that intrigues or compels you. Center it on a new concept or invention, a relationship, or a personal problem or challenge. Use it as you go through the rest of this book to record any inspirations you get from the strategies chapters, as well as to record any and all of your creative ideas and insights related to your own endeavors.

Parting Words

You are now ready to move on to Part 2. As you read the details about how each strategy can support your creative work, keep in mind the two important concepts presented in this part. First, you are naturally creative and are not subject to any required personality or intelligence limitations; your creative spirit can grow by virtue of your ever-increasing curiosity, openness, risk tolerance, and energy. Second, you can tap into your natural creativity by consciously utilizing the incubation model of generating or finding new ideas, as well as by living a more creative life.

Further Readings

The Artist's Way: A Spiritual Path to Higher Creativity by Julia Cameron (Los Angeles: Jeremy P. Tarcher, 1992).

At a Journal Workshop: Writing to Access the Power of the Unconscious and Evoke Creative Ability by Ira Progoff (Los Angeles: Jeremy P. Tarcher, 1992).

The Creative Journal: The Art of Finding Yourself by Lucia Capacchione (North Hollywood, Cal.: Newcastle, 1989).

The New Diary: How to Use a Journal for Self-guidance and Expanded Creativity by Tristine Rainer (Los Angeles: Jeremy P. Tarcher, 1978).

Sark's Journal and Playbook: A Place to Dream While Awake by Sark (Berkeley, Cal.: Celestial Arts, 1993).

Part 2
10 strategies for creativity

Connect with People

Think of a time when you've been with other people at a class, workshop, conference, or meeting. Picture one of those moments when all present start to talk with animation and excitement as they share ideas or analyze a problem together. You can sense energy in the air, and everyone appears charged. Such uplifting and mutually beneficial sessions are a perfect illustration of why connecting with other people is a strategy that can enhance your *own* creativity. When it comes to sources for idea generation, inspiration, stimulation, and observation, talking to and being with other people cannot be beat.

In my seminars, I illustrate the creative potential of connections with other people with a simple visual demonstration. I take colored balls of yarn and give them to about a tenth of my audience; and then I ask each person with a ball to throw it to someone else he or she knows in the room. I then ask those people to throw the balls to people they know. And so on. Soon the entire audience is connected by a crisscrossed network of brightly colored strands of yarn. The most amazing aspect of this, however, is that, in most cases, after less than a minute of tossing every person in the room can trace a line from himself or herself to any other person in the room.

Keep this image in mind as you implement the strategies in this chapter for connecting with other people for all your creative endeavors.

CONNECTING WITH THE CREATIVE PEOPLE YOU KNOW

1. **Identify the three most creative people you know. In what sense are they creative: Artistic? Entrepreneurial? All-round lifestyle? Do *you* interact creatively with these people? Do you share your ideas with them? Do you**

seek them out to help you explore and develop your creative work? Do you make yourself available to them so they can share their ideas with you?

2. **Call one of your creative acquaintances. Find out what he or she is doing right now. Get inspired from the sharing. If possible, set up a time to visit while you are reading this book to discuss your ideas on creativity.**

Making Contact Through Synchronicity

Perhaps the most powerful way to enhance your creativity through people is to heighten your awareness of the amazing opportunities embedded in every meeting and conversation you

have. You are like a ball in the pinball machine of life, continuously bounding from one encounter to another. Each person you come across has the potential to send you in a new direction, which can spark your next great idea or lead you to new insights about your work. Some people inspire you directly, while others help you accidentally, through a nonchalant comment that you realize is valuable to your creative challenges.

Many entrepreneurs have gotten their start from synchronous or serendipitous connections with people although they had no plans to go into business. A new business in New York City began when Bill Zanker, also the founder of the Learning Annex, was visiting a San Francisco park one day and saw someone selling massages for a dollar a minute. Zanker thought he could make a business out of the concept, so he sold the Learning Annex and opened the Great American Backrub, which now has many locations and sells back-related products such as ergonomic car seats. Bob Langkamp started his company, Gemini Fiberglass Products, Inc., in Golden, Colorado, because when he was selling pools and spas in his previous business, someone called him to ask if the pools could be used for salmon hatching. Langkamp got inspired, and now his sales of over $1 million to the aquaculture industry account for about 50 percent of his business.

I met my colleague Deanna Berg at a professional conference where we discovered that we both had bid on the same consulting contract, so we decided to team up and offer some of our seminars together.

Many of the world's most renowned artists have likewise been greatly influenced by chance meetings. Lillian Hellman met Dashiell Hammett, author of *The Maltese Falcon* and other detective stories, at a Hollywood restaurant, helping propel her career as a playwright and screenplay writer.

John Lennon met Yoko Ono at a London art gallery and was drawn to her as a soul mate. Their work together completely changed Lennon's career.

By opening yourself to the prospect of synchronicity, you too can find more chance encounters leading you to creative rewards. One day it might be a person you happen to speak to in an elevator who turns out to belong to the association you were hoping to join. Another time it could be a phone call from a parent at your daughter's school who ends up telling you about a gallery opening she is about to sponsor just when you were looking for a place to display your watercolors.

To benefit from potentially synchronous encounters, you must learn to develop your powers of awareness and observation, what psychologist Ellen Langer calls mindfulness in her book of the same name.

In *Mindfulness*, Langer outlines three changes we can make to become more aware:

➤ **Stop living on "automatic pilot,"** the kind of routine behavior all of us easily get into by dwelling in our comfort zones. When you exist on automatic pilot, you stop noticing what's new around you. For instance, have you ever driven the same route for many years and suddenly noticed a museum or gallery you've never visited? Have you ever been at your job and realized that a new person started working there a month ago? Have you ever gone to a neighborhood in your city and discovered a new restaurant you had never seen before? In each of these cases, you were operating on automatic pilot, paying little attention to your routine until something made you sit up and take notice.

➤ **Be flexible in how you categorize life's experiences.** Many events in your life can be interpreted differently, but you keep seeing and understanding them in the same way. By doing so, you completely miss the novelty factor, the opportunity to learn something and open yourself to a new experience. The bore you met at a party last week might be a brilliant entrepreneur who was exhausted from a week's worth of travel, but if you are not willing to recategorize her the next time you meet her, you may never find that out. The saxophonist playing on the street may not be the second-rate musician you think he is; if you take the time to listen and get to know him, you may discover the next jazz superstar.

➤ **See everything from perspectives other than your own.** Being able to see life from more than one perspective makes you receptive to synchronous encounters with other people because you become more willing to tolerate opinions that diverge from your own.

When I was writing this section of the book, through my own synchronicity I happened to read a perfect example of how a heightened awareness led to a creative success for two people. Nicholas Callaway, a producer of high-profile illustrated books, was in a toy store when he saw some wonderful illustrations on the box of a child's pull toy. Rather than thinking "nice packaging," and dismissing it, he was able to recategorize the art and see it as inspiration for a book. He contacted the toy manufacturer, David Kirk, and offered him a contract to develop a children's book based on his art. Kirk eventually wrote *Miss Spider's Tea Party,* which has now sold hundreds of thousands of copies and generated a line of toys of its own.

A wonderful ancient Turkish tale encapsulates the sense of mindlessness that can prevent you from reaping the rewards of synchronicity. In this story, a man of little talent and success decides that if he is to make anything of his existence, he must travel to find Fate, who will tell him how to solve his problems. He begins his long journey and later that day meets a wolf. "Where are you going?" inquires the wolf.

"I seek Fate, who will tell me how to end the problems that have plagued me all my life."

"Fate is quite wise; when you find him, will you tell him that I have suffered for years from a headache, and ask how I can put an end to it?"

The man agrees and continues on his journey. He soon meets a watchman in the town where he has decided to spend the night. "Where are you headed?" the watchman asks the traveler.

"I seek Fate, who will tell me how to end the trouble I have with not being able to find a job that yields me more than failure and despair," the weary man responds.

The watchman tells the traveler that he too has had poor luck with work, and that his job has brought him long hours and meager pay. "Brother," says the watchman, "when you find Fate, will you ask him how I may obtain the things in life that I really want?"

The traveler agrees, rests for the night, and resumes his trek the next morning. He reaches the banks of a river, where a fish greets him and asks him where he is headed. He tells the fish his story. The fish says, "All my life, I have not been able to shut my mouth. Promise me that when you find Fate, you will ask him how I can close it, and I shall carry you across the river on my back." The traveler agrees, and the fish carries him to the other bank.

The man finally reaches Fate's house. There sits Fate, spinning his wheel. The traveler tells Fate his tale of woe, about his inability to make a living and lack of talent. Fate spins his Wheel of Fortune for the traveler, and then asks, "Good man, were there any others whom you encountered on your trip seeking my assistance?" The traveler suddenly remembers the fish, the watchman, and the wolf, and recounts their troubles.

Fate responds, "For the wolf there is but one remedy. He must devour the head of the stupidest man in the kingdom and his headache will leave forever. The fish cannot close its mouth because there are two valuable stones inside. If you remove the stones, the fish will be able to close its mouth. The watchman will find that if he goes to the northwest corner of the wall around his house, and if you help him dig, you will find two large jars filled with gold."

Returning home, the man first meets the fish. He reaches into its mouth and removes two beautiful emeralds. "Thank you," says the fish. "Please take the stones, for they are emeralds and have great value."

"I don't need the stones," says the man, tossing them into the water, "for Fate has spun his Wheel of Fortune for me."

Next, he meets the watchman and tells him of the jars of gold. They dig up the jars and the watchman offers the traveler half the gold, but the traveler refuses, telling the man that Fate has spun his Wheel of Fortune for him.

Finally, he meets the wolf, who asks about his journey. The traveler tells the wolf that to cure his headache he must devour the head of the stupidest man in the kingdom. "Did Fate tell you how I will know this man?" asks the wolf.

The traveler admits that he forgot to ask. He then tells the story of his encounter with the fish and the watchman. Finally the wolf jumps up and chases the man. "You turned down the fish's emeralds, and rejected one of the jars of gold, all because Fate spun his Wheel of Fortune for you. You had your answer from Fate. You failed to take advantage of the opportunities. No man could be more stupid than you!" And with that he devoured the man's head and cured his headache.

Remember this story. In the box on pages 64–65 are some ways that you can begin to be more aware of your creative opportunities through synchronicity.

Creative Communities — Join One or Form Your Own

You can also tap into the power of people by joining a creative community. Creative communities are not a recent invention or fad. Their roots actually extend far back in history. In the Middle Ages, for example, crafts guilds functioned both as the equivalent of unions and as schools in which apprentices learned their chosen crafts from experienced masters. Once an apprentice developed sufficient skills, he could become a journeyman and sell his services.

Many of the greatest names in Renaissance art, from da Vinci to Botticelli, learned their craft by working in a master's studio. The preimpressionist Barbizon school was a loose community of painters including Rousseau, Millet, Dupré, Corot, and others. In mid-nineteenth-century America, the famed Brook Farm community of Transcendentalist thinkers included Nathaniel Hawthorne, Henry David Thoreau, and Margaret Fuller. The Parisian apartment of Gertrude Stein and Alice B. Toklas was the center of an informal community that helped fuel the creativity of Ernest Hemingway, Thornton Wilder, Pablo Picasso, Henri Matisse, and F. Scott Fitzgerald, among others. These historic examples are proof of the intellectual and artistic benefits community members gain by being together and sharing ideas.

Today's creative communities are just as useful to people who share business or artistic interests. Some communities are loose and free flowing, meeting on an ad hoc basis and open to whatever discussions come up. Others operate more formally, with required meetings, goals and objectives, officers, and dues. Still other communities, such as the famous artists' colony Yaddo, are completely unstructured, simply providing a nurturing environment in which creative people can work and talk free from external distractions. Any of these communities can serve your creative needs, depending on the amount of time you are willing to commit.

One way to find a community is to ask at stores and educational centers that serve as loci for people in your field, such as art suppliers, music stores, meetings of professional organizations, specialty bookstores, pottery and craft centers, cooking supply outlets, small business associations, and so on. Many stores and centers sponsor their own creative groups or hold special events such as art openings, reading or discussion groups, and training sessions. Taking a class at an adult education school like the Learning Annex or through a community college in your city can also be a good way to find or start a community.

One of the fastest growing courses or support groups being formed in many cities today is based on the book *The Artist's Way,* by Julia Cameron. Written for "artists" of all kinds, this book offers a twelve-week personal workshop in developing creative self-esteem and overcoming common blocks that artists face.

Another type of "community" is the MasterMind Alliance, a concept outlined in the 1930 self-help classic *Think and Grow Rich,* by Napoleon Hill. Such alliances are highly effective groups of people who meet to accomplish a specific purpose. One organization I've worked with that has pursued Hill's idea is The Executive Committee (TEC). One of TEC's activities is to organize groups of twelve to fourteen CEO's or senior executives who are neither competitors nor suppliers to each other. They get them together every month for a daylong meeting so they can

HEIGHTENING YOUR AWARENESS OF SYNCHRONICITY AND SERENDIPITY

1. Begin paying attention to the synchronous or serendipitous events that happen to you for one month as a result of meeting people. These events can include coincidences as trivial as meeting someone and discovering that you have a friend in common, finding out that you share a client with a colleague, or coming across a magazine profile of a person you were just thinking about. Noticing such small events marks the beginning of your greater awareness of synchronicity. At the same time, start collecting stories from people you encounter or articles you read that recount a synchronous event that occurred in your community.

   Keep a journal or a "synchronicity scrapbook" to record your own synchronous happenings and stories about others. The more you become aware of synchronicity around you, the more likely you will be to experience it yourself.

2. As you develop your skills of observation and awareness, begin applying the potential for synchronicity to your creative projects. Start by making a list of your projects or problems. Then each day stop and ask yourself the following questions:

   • What have I seen, read, or done today that relates to another idea or theme in my life right now?
   • Who have I met today and what have I learned from this person?
   • How can I apply what I've learned from the people I've encountered today to something I am already working on?

Make an effort to talk to people who are out of your comfort zone — the person behind you in line at the bank or grocery store, the pizza delivery boy, the cabdriver who takes you to the airport — anyone with whom you would not normally strike up a prolonged conversation. You may find that ideas offered by these people, or connections they may have to other people, will be of tremendous value to you.

learn from one another. These meetings are facilitated by a chairman, and each participant has an opportunity to discuss business issues with the other members. Thousands of leading CEO's are now members of this organization.

If you cannot locate a creative community that fits your subject of interest or schedule, consider starting a group of your own. You can take out a classified ad in your local paper or post announcements in stores or community colleges indicating that you are seeking people for a creative share-and-support group. Have the meetings in a restaurant or café until you know the prospective members better and feel comfortable inviting them to your home.

If you are joining a community or starting one of your own, seek out people who can offer you both new knowledge and constructive support for your work. Don't judge people by the fame they have already achieved or by their financial success. Such factors are not necessarily indicators of compatibility and helpfulness in a creative community. What is likely to be more useful is a person's creative C.O.R.E., because these four factors show you how respectful and supportive he or she will be with other group members.

EXPLORING YOUR CREATIVE COMMUNITY OPTIONS
Spend this weekend browsing through newspapers or going to bookstores, gardening centers, art supply stores, or education centers to see if you can locate a group focused on your creative interests. It doesn't matter which interest you select; find one available to join. You might focus on finding a breakfast club or association where you can meet other people in your professional field. Alternatively, think about one of your leisure interests. Locate a group and then either phone the leader to ask about the group or go to a meeting to get acquainted with the members and determine if you want to join.

Find a Mind to Mentor You

The word *mentor* is derived from the name of the Greek character Mentor, who was Odysseus's trusted adviser and, under the guise of Athena, became the guardian and teacher for Odysseus's son, Telemachus. Technically, a mentor is someone who teaches, but a mentoring relationship requires more than a college professor or boss you admire. A true mentoring relationship involves care, concern, criticism, and compassion. A mentor provides guidance and develops your talent while teaching you the tricks of the trade that he or she has firmly mastered.

Many of the world's greatest artists learned from other more experienced or talented individuals via mentoring relationships. Leonardo da Vinci studied under Andrea del Verrocchio, J. S. Bach had German composer and organist Dietrich Buxtehude as his mentor, Ludwig van Beethoven learned from Franz Joseph Haydn, and Paul Gauguin and Paul Cézanne from Camille Pissarro, to name but a few of the best-known mentor relationships in the arts. Mentoring is also common in business today. Many companies of all sizes have formal programs that team junior managers with senior executives to help them increase their business knowledge and decision-making skills. And in Fortune 500 companies, many CEO's are mentored by their prodecessors. Schools and colleges have artist-in-residence programs that attract renowned poets and painters to mentor students. Many business associations are now adding formal mentoring programs to the services they offer their members.

If you have a personal hero or teacher who is a master of your creative activity, why not try to set up a mentor relationship that allows you to ask questions and have your creative work reviewed? If you enter into a mentor relationship, remember that you must use your entire creative C.O.R.E. to make it succeed. If you are not curious and don't have the energy to implement the suggestions your mentor offers, you will gain little from the experience. If you are not able to take risks and change your style, whatever your mentor teaches you may go wasted. And if you are not open to caring criticism, you will completely miss the point of the mentoring.

Alternatively, becoming a mentor to someone seeking your expertise can also be a valuable way to expand your creativity. Having a protegee often makes you realize how much you know and gives you confidence in your own skills. You can even benefit from the questions an apprentice asks, because they frequently lead you to recognize your thoughts or develop creative ideas that take your own work to a new plateau.

In all, the dynamics of a mentoring relationship can be stimulating to every aspect of your creative C.O.R.E. Whether you are receiving knowledge or giving it, the sharing and commitment inherent in mentoring can lead to more creative results than in any other relationship.

MINI WORKSHOP

FINDING A MENTOR

Can you identify a person in your area of interest who would make a good mentor? Write a hypothetical letter explaining why you want a mentoring relationship and why you feel you would make a good student for this person. If you feel satisfied with your letter, go ahead and mail it. If you don't get a response, either try again with a follow-up letter or phone call or identify another possible mentor and try to contact that person.

Form a Creative Partnership or Collaboration

One of the most powerful ways to tap into the power of other people is to form a formal partnership or alliance with one or more individuals to work on a specific creative endeavor. Creative partnerships are common in the arts, but they also exist in business. Envision the world without the talent and inventiveness of the following collaborative teams:

- **Fred Astaire and Ginger Rogers**
- **Lucille Ball and Desi Arnaz**
- **Chet Huntley and David Brinkley**
- **Stan Laurel and Oliver Hardy**
- **George and Ira Gershwin**
- **Orville and Wilbur Wright**
- **Ben & Jerry**
- **Paul Simon and Art Garfunkel**
- **Bill Gates and Paul Allen**
- **Steven Jobs and Steve Wozniak**

Unfortunately, the emphasis on competition so many of us encounter as children teaches us to work against others rather than collaborate with them, and this behavior lasts through adulthood. In the business creativity workshops I conduct, we often put cans of Play-Doh on the tables. Oddly enough, the audience members rarely touch the cans before we tell them to. Then we ask them to fashion creations of their own choice. They stare at their individual containers for a few minutes as they think of what to make; then they all automatically decide to work independently. They rarely ask someone else to share colors or offer their own colors to others. Some people even refuse to share when someone else has the courage to ask.

My colleague Deanna Berg and I always found this lack of sharing an interesting statement on collaboration. Deanna had a chance to observe how different the results were when she conducted the exercise in Japan. The Japanese participants all opened their Play-Doh and began to sculpt before the seminar started. As they sculpted, they shared ideas and even added clumps to one another's creations. They combined colors and created dozens of works of art in the same amount of time that most Americans would take just to examine the outsides of their containers. The reason is clear: Collaboration is highly valued in Japanese culture. Japanese businesspeople approach problems by working as teams.

The fact is, each of us has certain strengths but also certain weaknesses. You are seldom complete in all respects. As a result, you can often accomplish more if you allow yourself to work with someone who complements your strengths and fills in your weaknesses.

The Hopi Indians have a legend that captures the value of partnering. Centuries ago a Hopi tribe was forced to abandon its village suddenly because of a fire. In their haste, the tribe left behind two young boys—one blind, the other unable to walk. The boys realized they would perish if they remained at the abandoned village, but neither was capable of escaping on his own. So they combined forces and developed a plan. The blind boy hoisted the other boy onto his shoulders. With the sighted child guiding they way and the able child walking, the two found their way to the rest of the tribe. The tribe created a kachina doll to celebrate their victorious escape.

Managing Collaborations

 In the past several years, I've conducted portions of my business by developing creative alliances with others, and I've even had more than one collaboration going on at the same time. The factor that has contributed to the success of all these relationships was investing time in developing agreements covering how we would work together. In my experience, when collaborations crumble, it's usually because of a dispute over how one person approached a problem, made a decision, or spent money because no prior agreement was made. Following are five guidelines to ensure the success of your collaboration:

1. *Define the vision of the alliance or collaboration.* What is the scope of your alliance? How long will it last? Develop a definition that each participant can accept.
2. *Make sure that each person contributes not only resources and ideas but also benefits.* When one person in a relationship is forced to carry the economic or emotional burdens, he or she quickly becomes angry and resentful. Structure your partnership so that each person has an opportunity to benefit and contribute.
3. *Don't abandon structure.* Creativity usually isn't the natural by-product of a highly structured environment, but some structure will help to focus your work together.
4. *Deal with problems as they develop.* The quickest way to destroy a collaboration is to allow negativity, distrust, or anger to develop. Get issues that are starting to divide people on the table and resolve them immediately.
5. *Put it in writing.* A partnership agreement is important even if you have very little expectation of making money, or even if your partner is your best friend.

WHO'S A POTENTIAL PARTNER OR COLLABORATOR?

Think about which of your creative efforts might benefit from working in a collaborative arrangement. Consider your strongest areas of knowledge. What are the five things you know a great deal about? Technology? Manufacturing? Cooking? Art? Baseball? Interior decorating? What are your strongest skills? What are the five things you do reasonably well or extremely well? Editing? Carpentry? Organizing? Acting? Parenting? Driving race cars?

Now think about what you want or need to know. What skills do you lack for realizing your creative goal? Do you know someone who has those skills? Make a list of two or three people with whom you might be able to work.

Decide which person on your list you might approach to work with on a specific creative venture. You can pick something business oriented with a profit motive or a hobby that you do solely for enjoyment. Make an agreement with the person to work together for a test period ranging from two to six months to see if your relationship benefits both of you. If it does, continue the venture or expand it to include other people. If your enterprise runs out of creative steam, you can end it by a mutual agreement. Whichever route you take, profit or pleasure, focus your efforts first and foremost on expanding your mutual creative C.O.R.E.'s.

Expanding Your Network of Connections

You may have heard of the concept of "six degrees of separation," which suggests that you can create a direct line to virtually anyone in the world by exercising your contacts, who in turn exercise *their* contacts; according to the theory, by the sixth round you will have found someone personally acquainted with the object of your search. Networking is the process that taps into this concept. Among salespeople, small business owners, entrepreneurs, and home-based workers who need to expand their client lists, networking is a crucial part of a fully creative lifestyle. Networking is using your people skills—your interpersonal intelligence—in pursuit of your creative goals.

Seeking and finding other people to share your ideas can produce enormously valuable results. Consider all the following benefits you get from talking with others:

- Information to update or correct your knowledge or ideas
- Insight into new ways you can think about a problem
- Reality checks or "grounding" when you think your ideas have become weird or out of focus
- Inspiration for new ideas
- Motivation to try again
- Approval or feedback to validate your ideas
- Compliments and encouragement
- Criticism and/or constructive suggestions for change
- Connections to other people who might be interested in what you have to offer
- Wisdom and philosophical understanding that you did not have
- Leads to a new job, new business opportunity, or new romance
- Skills and knowledge that compensate for your weakness
- Brainstorming power to help you break through blocks
- Psychological support and encouragement
- Financial assistance

Networking is an especially effective way to meet others when you want to get involved with increasingly "higher level" people in a field. The songwriter needs to network if he hopes to meet the record producer or rock star; the enterpreneur needs to network if she is to build her business. The adage "It's not just what you know but who you know" is especially true for creative endeavors.

MINI WORKSHOP

BUILDING YOUR NETWORK

Identify places where you can network. If your priority is business, begin by contacting trade or professional associations in your area to see what meetings they sponsor, such as breakfasts, luncheons, or seminars. Many chambers of commerce and local business associations host networking sessions as well.

To network among creative circles where you might get a chance to be introduced to publishing executives, screenwriters, song producers, and other high-level arts professionals, begin by seeking out the various professional associations for people in your artistic area. At the regular meetings of these

groups you can often meet people who have access to the power brokers who can help you.

If you prefer, ask someone you consider a good networker to accompany you to your next event and provide tips on networking.

Knocking Down Roadblocks Between You and Other People

While many people say they recognize the value of meeting new people, joining a creative community, and networking, few prod themselves to do these things. Some people have difficulty out of shyness or embarrassment. Some can't muster the courage to approach strangers or people who they feel to be more important than they, even if they are interested in the same field. Many people dislike networking because it makes them feel manipulative or phony. But learning to benefit from the knowledge of people and making a commitment to tap your connections is a critical part of leading a creative lifestyle.

Here are four suggestions to help you work through some of the most common roadblocks to connecting with others.

1. Reframe Your Perspective

Reframing means looking at your actions or your purpose in a different way. There are always many perspectives from which to view any event, but some are more positive than others. There are several ways you can reframe your perspective on a situation in which you are feeling anxious about sharing your creative thoughts or asking others for advice and counsel.

First, you can remember that creativity is a lifestyle. By reframing your creative pursuits as *your* lifestyle, you give yourself permission to explore your ideas. Emphasizing your creative C.O.R.E. reduces the pressure you may feel to have your creative pursuits accepted by others.

Another way to reframe your perspective is to recognize that other creative people appreciate and respect those who lead creative lives. Rather than thinking that you have nothing to offer, remind yourself that your ideas and questions might very well inspire *them*—they may even thank you or credit you at a later date. In other words, frame your quest not as a one-way street but as an exchange of ideas from which you both can profit.

Finally, the most powerful way to reframe a situation is to think about the *opportunity* that awaits you. Instead of worrying that you may be rejected or criticized, think about the stroke of luck or good fortune that lies at the end of the path. Thomas Edison is one of the greatest examples of reframing. He was famous for telling people that his thousands of unworkable attempts to invent the lightbulb were not mistakes but rather tests that helped him understand which methods didn't work. You too can reframe any situation from a negative or pessimistic view to a positive one. If your request for an exchange of information is not well received, then you simply haven't yet found the right source. Keep looking.

2. Overcome Fear and Low Self-esteem

Fear of rejection or concerns that others will find your ideas unworthy can be serious detriments to living a creative life. They limit your ability to mingle with other creative individuals and prevent you from getting valuable feedback.

To combat these barriers, remember that other people are just that: people. They have no power over you, and you risk little by talking to them or sharing your ideas. The worst they can do is tell you they are not interested in looking at your art, trying your fund-raising scheme, or reviewing your invention. Think about it this way: Every meeting or conversation you have is an encounter between two comfort zones. If someone says no to you, it simply means his comfort zone is not ready to meet yours. Even the Beatles were turned away early in their career by a shortsighted producer at Decca Records who told them that "guitar groups were on their way out."

3. Become a Better Networker

Improving your networking skills can help you overcome some of your difficulties. Networking is a skill, like public speaking, that anyone can learn. Follow these steps to become a better networker.
• **Interact first.** Take the responsibility for meeting others. If you're tormented by the fear of rejection, remember that the

worst thing that can happen if you try to connect with someone unreceptive is a polite but perfunctory rejection.

• **Cultivate your relationships.** Whether you use a Rolodex or a computerized database, keep basic information (address, phone number, fax number, E-mail number) so you can reconnect with people you've met while networking. Then set up regular appointments for breakfast, lunch, or coffee.

• **Maintain contact in good and bad times.** Continually reinforce your relationship with cards, notes, faxes, and calls. Send articles you find that might interest new contacts. Ask them to accompany you to a special event you both enjoy, such as a speech or a lecture in your field.

• **Become a network architect for others.** Introduce others to people you know. Make yourself a valuable "door opener" who can help others find the people they need.

4. Don't Get Stopped by Logistical Barriers

Some barriers are physical or logistical, such as trying to contact a high-level corporate executive or celebrity—all of whom tend to be well insulated. However, there are ways around such obstacles. The best way to get in touch with anyone is to find a common contact. Perhaps you both belong to an organization, trade group, or computer network that allows you to have direct personal contact. Nearly every industry and profession has an association for people in its field. (A listing of more than 50,000 associations in the *Encyclopedia of Associations,* published by Gale Research, is available in most libraries.)

On-line computer services also facilitate making contact with many people you normally couldn't reach. From the big national services like CompuServe, America Online, and Prodigy to thousands of small and local on-line bulletin boards, computer services make it possible to chat with a wide assortment of people. Many of the "forums" and special areas on the national on-line services are run by specialists who can help you contact people in your field.

When you are trying to reach a person who is only distantly

connected to you, your chances of connecting are augmented if you follow these rules:

- **Know as much about the person as possible.**
- **Don't insult or go around the door opener.**
- **Know what you want to ask before you call or visit.**
- **Be cordial yet persistent.**

If you have gotten nowhere after trying your best to overcome all obstacles, recognize that some connections were not meant to occur. When I cannot reach people whom I have been trying to get to share ideas or questions, I usually conclude that our inability to connect is life's way of letting me know that I was seeking the wrong person. As discussed in "Tapping into the Creative Process," many adventures in life require serendipity or synchronicity to move them forward. Meeting people can be likened to an economic process with buyers and sellers. For each person in search of someone with whom to share ideas, there must be a corresponding person who is willing to listen. When you cannot make a "sale" of your ideas to someone, it means she was not a "buyer" at that time. You just need to find another potential "buyer."

MINI WORKSHOP

TARGETING YOUR BEST CONTACT

Think of the one person with whom you'd most like to talk but who you have been afraid to approach. How might you reach this person? What are your fears or hesitations about calling him or her? If logistical problems are in the way, how can you get around them? Reflect on your dilemma or write in your journal about your fears and doubts. Consult some books on networking, overcoming shyness, and other topics that will help you. Ask a colleague or acquaintance you consider a good networker for some advice that will improve your ability to meet people.

Networking for Bottom-line Ideas

Most of this chapter has focused on how your creative spirit can be fueled in general ways, through the support, encouragement, and knowledge of other people. However, people are also the most relevant source of inspiration to ignite specific instances of entrepreneurial creativity. People and their needs have inspired every invention and propelled every discovery in the history of humankind. All business and commercial enterprises are predicated on creating products and services that will advance the quality of consumers' lives or fill a perceived need. If you are seeking to develop a new product or service, look first to your neighbors, friends, and acquaintances, who will undoubtedly give you insight into where there are voids in the market.

Begin by making yourself more observant of the challenges you and others face in daily life. Most inventions were consciously designed to solve a problem or fill a need that the inventor had. William Korzon invented the magnetic tape recorder because he wanted to hear himself sing in the bathtub and knew that many others would enjoy being able to listen to themselves talk or sing. James Spangler invented the portable vacuum cleaner to remove dirt from carpets because of his severe asthma. Ermal Fraze invented the pull-tab beer and soda can opening mechanism after going on an outing and losing his church-key opener.

Similarly, many of today's businesses—from the corporate giants to thousands of small home-based ventures—are predicated on the fact that someone recognized and understood a need other people had. Fred Smith, founder of Federal Express, recognized that people would pay a premium price in order to have their business documents delivered overnight. Jerry Yang and David Filo, two Stanford University students, noticed that with the growth of the Internet, people would need a way to find one location among the millions. They started the World Wide Web index service known as *Yahoo!* in their dorm room; today it is one of the leading businesses on the Web.

To trigger your entrepreneurial creativity, each day stop and ask yourself questions like these:

- **What activities do you see other people doing that can be simplified, made faster or easier?**
- **What hassles or pet peeves can I translate into problems looking for solutions?**

- **What techniques or strategies do others use in their everyday life that someone else might like?**
- **What would friends like the future to include that would make their life better?**
- **What have I heard someone complain about or wish for today? (Complaints often suggest a need for a new product or service.)**
- **What services or life enhancements are missing in my community?**
- **What aspects of people's environment could be made better?**
- **What knowledge do I have that can benefit others?**
- **What trends do I notice in my family, my community, or around the country?**
- **Is there something I saw someone use today that with slight modifications could also be used for another purpose?**

And so on. Note that the questioning process works best when it arises out of your authentic curiosity about and passion for things that are of interest to you. Only through genuine enthusiasm will you develop the energy to imagine solutions for the problems you recognize and then take action to implement your vision.

Connections That Count

It doesn't matter whether you intentionally and consciously connect with other people through the techniques of networking, partnering, or joining a creative community or you stumble upon a million-dollar idea through the serendipity of meeting someone who has what you need. What matters is that you recognize that connecting with other people—in person, by phone, E-mail, fax, or however—is one of the most powerful tools you have to find inspiration, get feedback, and receive training. So talk to someone new today and see if you don't immediately feel more alive—and more creative.

Further Readings

The Artist's Way: A Spiritual Path to Higher Creativity by Julia Cameron (Los Angeles: Jeremy P. Tarcher, 1992).

Connections by James Burke (Boston: Little Brown and Company, 1978).

How to Win Friends and Influence People by Dale Carnegie (New York: Simon & Schuster, 1936).

How to Work a Room: A Guide to Successfully Managing the Mingling by Susan RoAne (New York: Warner Books, 1989).

Mindfulness by Ellen J. Langer (Reading, Mass.: Addison-Wesley, 1989).

Peoplepower: 12 Power Principles to Enrich Your Business, Career, and Personal Networks by Donna Fisher (Austin, Tex.: Bard and Stevens, 1995).

The Pinball Effect by James Burke (Boston: Little Brown and Company, 1996).

Swim with the Sharks Without Being Eaten Alive by Harvey Mackay (New York: William Morrow, 1988).

Think and Grow Rich by Napoleon Hill (New York: Fawcett Crest, 1960).

Type Talk: The Sixteen Personality Types That Determine How We Live, Love, and Work by Otto Kroeger and Janiet M. Thuesen (New York: Dell Trade Paperbacks, 1988).

Design an Enriching Environment

The second strategy for nourishing your creativity is finding the type of space that gets your thoughts and energy flowing. It's easy to take your surroundings for granted. They completely envelop you, yet they often fade into the background of your psyche as you push through your days on automatic pilot.

But your environment is a much more important influence on your creativity than is generally acknowledged. It affects your mood and your entire outlook on life. It is a strong stimulus to new feelings, ideas, and insights into the people you meet and the events you experience. It also fuels the artistic or entrepreneurial spirit, providing the inspiration that prompts you to see a new vision for a painting, hear a new song, or invent a new product.

Your environment includes the microcosm of the room, office, or house in which you spend your days and nights, and the macrocosm of the city, state, and region in which you live. The two may affect you in different ways. For example, for many people, spending a day in a cramped work space in a drab office building with no windows and stale air would feel depressing and uncreative—it might even make you seriously ill in extreme cases of what is now known as sick building syndrome. If upon leaving that building, however, you found yourself smack in the middle of the Latin Quarter in Paris, the theater district in London, or the Soho section of Manhattan, you might suddenly feel reinvigorated and ready to create again.

Your environment also includes the entire psychological ambience around you. Do you live and work with people who help you feel creative and encouraged, or are they pessimistic and destructive? Some companies are loaded with people who naysay every idea or who constantly change the target you are aiming for, sapping you of energy and enthusiasm. Such people are often called crazy makers because they create havoc for others on a daily basis. Creativity and productivity dramatically tumble in workplaces where conflict and negative energy reign.

The effect of the environment on your health, happiness, and productivity is now recognized as so critical that a new field, environmental design, has emerged. Environmental design encompasses many areas of study because researchers have learned that designing one's surroundings for greater health and enjoyment means much more than adding pretty wallpaper and fancy furniture. Environmental design takes into account interior design, space planning, ergonomics, psychology, sociology, engineering, biology, chemistry, neurology, and even cultural anthropology—all the factors that influence how people feel in their work spaces.

As a strategy for creativity, understanding more about your environment and learning how you can control it to maximize your creative efforts can be of great value. There are many ways you can modify your environment to support your creative work, as well as many ways you can use the environment to burst through creative blocks or solve difficult problems. This chapter presents a variety of actions you can take to enhance your surroundings and make them a creative tool that works for you.

MINI WORKSHOP

TAKE STOCK OF YOUR WORK SPACE ENVIRONMENT
How much importance do you place on your environment? Think about these questions:

1. Do you wake up in the morning, look around you, and feel stimulated? Do you go to bed at night feeling you have spent your day in a creative location?
2. Does the aesthetic mood of your work environment foster creativity? Is it a nicely furnished, brightly lit, and fun place to be?
3. Does your work environment ever make you feel physically ill? Does the air smell bad or are there fumes, fibers, or unknown sources of contamination? Is it possible that you work in a place that has sick building syndrome?
4. If you work for a company, does its management pay any attention to the

environment as a determining factor in your and other employees' creativity?

5. When you are trying to be creative, do you ever wish you had a better place to work?
6. Are you willing (or allowed) to redecorate your office or work space?
7. Would you consider moving to a location that makes you feel more creative?
8. Are there people around you who make your mental environment uncreative? What could you do to avoid this negative effect on your creativity?

Managing Your Environment for Creativity

Each setting conveys a specific feeling or connotation that you either like or dislike. You might feel comfortable and productive working in one setting and completely turned off in another. Try the following exercise:

Picture the office, room, or studio in which you frequently work. In your mind's eye, take all the furniture out of the room and imagine the empty space, without the weight, colors, and textures of your desk, chair, couch, and shelves or filing cabinets. Now, one group at a time, imagine your work space as containing the following groups of objects:

- An Oriental rug, four or five pillows on the floor, and an incense burner in the center of the room
- A large oak rolltop desk with an oak chair and bookcases on all the walls filled with dusty volumes in leather bindings
- An eight-foot-long cherry executive's table, six plush velvet-covered chairs, an original Rembrandt framed in carved wood hanging on the wall, and a silver coffeepot filled with fresh-brewed coffee on a silver tray
- An X-shaped felt-lined partition wall that demarcates four cubicles, from which emanate the sound of clanging typewriters and the acrid aroma of stale cigarette smoke
- Two steel file cabinets topped with a slab of plywood to form a rudimentary desk, piles of books and old newspapers on the floor, and a large bookshelf made from cinder blocks and two-by-fours

Does one group of objects make you feel more invigorated than the others?

The point of this exercise is to show you one of the most fundamental principles of environmental design: Your environment is created by all the perceptions and impulses that come through your senses—sight, hearing, smell, touch, and taste. Although we tend to emphasize sight, the other four senses also provide mental and psychological cues that influence our behavior and moods. Each of our senses is actually a microenvironment that affects thought, feelings, productivity, and creative capacity.

Consider all the elements around you. When you set up your environment so that all your sensory perceptions are coordinated harmoniously, you will feel more inspired and productive than you will in an environment that produces a cacophony of sensory perceptions that annoy or traumatize you.

This is not to suggest that there is one ideal sensory environment for creativity, such as a pleasant, quiet room or a mountaintop. On the contrary, every creative person and endeavor is different and requires a unique environment that corresponds to your objectives. The key is to coordinate your surroundings with the mood *you* need to get your creative juices moving. Consider which of the following states of mind would be most productive for you:

- **Inspired**
- **Excited**
- **Stimulated**
- **Eroticized**
- **Thrilled**
- **Challenged**
- **Curious**

- **Relaxed**
- **Reflective**
- **Serious**
- **Brooding**
- **Melancholy**
- **Frightened**

All these moods are useful for creative work, but each is more conducive to a certain type of work. A novelist or screenwriter working on a thriller might intentionally seek an exciting and highly charged environment that allows him to feel the pulse of the words in his brain. A watercolorist working on a soothing country landscape may prefer a quiet, relaxed atmosphere that helps her capture the same sense of peace and harmony on her canvas. An executive trying to make a tough decision might wish for a warm, solitary place that boosts his confidence. A group of toy developers trying to invent a new game might seek out a brightly colored, childlike environment that excites their curiosity and whimsy.

I once consulted with a company that produces holiday crafts. To keep their inspiration flowing with new ideas, the crafters surrounded themselves with the proper seasonal accoutrements—even though they were developing ideas months in advance of the holiday itself. On an eighty-degree day in June, the designers entering their work spaces would be greeted by Christmas music, decorations—even a Christmas tree.

Given this principle of matching your environment to your creative needs, what sensory elements can you control or modify when you intentionally want to design your environment as a tool for your creative work? The rest of this chapter covers the seven major elements that can be manipulated to enliven a creative environment.

MINI WORKSHOP

WHAT'S THE MOOD OF YOUR IDEAL WORK SPACE?
In general, what kind of mood do you prefer to work in? Take a moment to imagine your ideal space. Close your eyes and picture in fine detail what it would look like, smell like, feel like, and sound like. There are no barriers, either physical or financial. Decorate and furnish the room any way that pleases your creative mind. Make a list of some of the most prominent elements — was there soft music playing? A large picture window with a stimulating (or tranquil) view? Baskets of brightly colored materials? Choose one or two elements and implement them now.

Factor 1: Lighting, the Natural Source of Creative Energy

Light is one of the most powerful sources of creative energy. In fact, bright sunlight has a direct biological connection to your body and mind. In *The Light Book*, the medical writer Jane Hyman points out that sunlight not only controls the circadian rhythm that determines your body's sleep-wake cycle but also strongly affects your appetite, mood, ability to heal, productivity, and even sexual desire. One strong indicator of the connection between sunlight and the body is that people who live in extreme northern locales, with long winter days and little sunlight, are prone to experience seasonal affective disorder (SAD), an illness that causes moodiness, lethargy, loss of concentration and thinking ability, withdrawal, and depression. The change in amount of sunlight you receive while traveling is also a significant factor in jet lag. A recent study by the Rocky Mountain Institute showed that increased sunlight resulted in fewer errors and reduced absenteeism among workers.

The connection between light and your physical and mental energy comes from the effect sunlight has on the pineal gland, which secretes the hormone melatonin. Melatonin affects the hypothalamus gland, which is part of the body's day-night pacemaker. Because sunlight represses the flow of melatonin, which reaches its highest levels in darkness, researchers believe that melatonin, as well as other body chemicals affected by sunlight, plays an important role in regulating our alertness and capacity for physical and mental tasks.

While it's not possible to control the amount of natural sunlight you receive in every environment and during every season, you can learn to notice your personal sunlight requirements. For example, if you work in an office without a window or if you frequently work under pressure of deadlines, you may find yourself feeling unproductive and lethargic when you don't have a chance to go out during the day. Rather than blaming it on work stress or on your boss, consider that your body might be letting you know that you need more sunlight to fuel your creativity. By taking a half-hour morning or afternoon walk in the sunlight, you can often regenerate your creativity and improve your productivity more than enough to compensate for the time you are away from your desk.

In general, anyone who works in an enclosed space is better off working by the light of the sun, even on rainy or cloudy days, than by fluorescent light. When natural sunlight is not available or not bright enough, overhead lighting that minimizes shadows and illuminates your work as clearly as possible is recommended.

You may also want to explore purchasing light bulbs that produce full-spectrum light, which reputedly duplicates the color spectrum of natural sunlight. These bulbs are available from catalogs such as *Tools for Exploration* (see page 256).

You may even find it amusing and profitable to work under "unusual" lighting conditions. Try writing with a blue bulb in your lamp, or painting with Day-Glo colors under a black light, or singing and dancing under a strobe, or using any number of other nontraditional lighting sources. The psychological cues provided by such lighting conditions can change your mood and inspire you to have new insights. Some types of lighting are powerful reminders of feelings and memories that can spark creative ideas. It's telling that the lighting at events like circuses or carnivals, fireworks displays, discotheques, school theater productions, or holiday parties stay in our mental imagery for years.

Another corollary to respecting your need for light is appreciating your body's natural rhythms. Some people tend to be "larks," or morning persons, while others are "owls," or night people. The difference is not purely psychological but may be related to your body's unique sleep-wake cycle, which affects your level of alertness and energy. When larks try to push themselves to stay up late, or owls try to get up earlier, they often disturb their natural cycle, which can then lead to insomnia and feelings of disorientation. Working more in sync with your natural body rhythms by getting up or going to bed when your mind tells you to can improve your creativity and sense of inner balance.

Another aspect of recognizing how sunlight balances your body's rhythms relates to watching sunrises or sunsets. As Jane Hyman reports, sunrises and sunsets provide important cues for regulating the body's circadian rhythms. Eskimos, for example, experience weaker twenty-four-hour rhythms in the winter months of total darkness (without any sunrises or sunsets), causing insomnia, mood changes, and inability to concentrate.

As unlikely as it may seem, watching a long sunrise or sunset may actually help you reset your body's clock and make you feel more creative—and not just because the event itself is so beautiful. In fact, one product on the market, the SunRise alarm clock (available from The Sharper Image), wakes you up by simulating a sunrise, gradually increasing the amount of light in your room.

If you find you are seriously deprived of sunlight or you feel constantly depressed or lethargic, you may want to consult a doctor about getting artificial light treatment, a technique used on people who suffer from SAD and other illnesses. According to Jane Hyman, in studies of artificial light therapy, "Researchers frequently use lamps that approximate the amount of light to which one would be exposed by looking out the window on a sunny spring day. This is five to ten times brighter than ordinary room lighting. The light is placed at eye level, and participants are instructed to sit about three feet from the light and engage in their usual activities. The timing and dosage vary widely [from two hours to six hours]."

As a result of light therapy, many research participants experience a sense of calmness and alertness under the lights, and they frequently feel a surge of energy after approximately twenty minutes. They also end up feeling more cheerful and energetic, they concentrate better, and they become more sociable. Hyman warns, though, that artificial light therapy must avoid light that contains ultraviolet A and B portions of the spectrum, which can harm the skin and eyes.

The simulation of light can be almost as effective as real light. Many people say they feel better simply by looking at posters, paintings, or photographs that remind them of natural sunlight. Triggering your memory with a photo of a sunny afternoon on a Caribbean beach, or a brilliant day on the ski slopes of Colorado, can be sufficient to release hormones that either relax you or spark your energy. Try performing a simple meditation in your office by staring at a sunny poster or photograph for ten minutes; you may find that you feel almost as refreshed and mentally alert as if you had gone outside for a walk.

Factor 2: Color, the Magic Mood Creator

Artists have long known that certain colors make us feel more energized while others have a calming effect. Likewise, today's designers are using color in much more sophisticated ways to create specific environments for learning, healing, sleeping, and many other activities.

There are several basic ways you can use color to establish a creative environment. First, apply colors to large areas of your work space to create the feeling you prefer. If you work best with a sense of excitement and stimulation, use warm colors, such as reds, oranges, yellows, and browns. These colors tend to increase heart rate and respiration. If you prefer to work in a calmer, more serene atmosphere, use cool colors, such as blues, greens, and grays. These colors tend to slow down the body, which helps you become more pensive and tranquil.

If you have no control over the colors of your office or work space, you can still obtain results by adding specific colored items—such as furniture, wall hangings, rugs, or objects—to your environment. In *Peak Learning,* the educational consultant Ron Gross cites the following useful color combinations:

- **ENERGETIC: orange/white, yellow/green, green/purple, gray/red, blue/orange**
- **DYNAMIC: red/orange, orange/blue, black/yellow, black/red, black/orange**
- **FRESH: yellow/green, blue/gray, blue/white, green/light green, green/white**

To optimize your creative work, you might also think about multiplying or varying colors to suit different moods and needs. For example, if you are an executive working on a new product idea, you might hang a poster that contains many "energetic" colors on one wall and on a table in another part of your office put a vase containing flowers emphasizing "fresh" colors. A multiplicity of colors stimulates different kinds of thoughts and feelings, which explains why most of us find a monochrome environment boring.

Factor 3: Environmental Art, Icons in Your Mind

The term *environmental art* refers to anything and everything you have on the walls, shelves, and surfaces surrounding you. It includes anything from posters, wall hangings, and framed photos to knickknacks, sculptures, and objets d'art.

Some people are strictly utilitarian when it comes to decorating their environments. Their offices are filled with the usual photos and framed certificates, perhaps a few posters or maps, some bookends, or a pen-and-pencil set. A worst case example was at a company where I once worked; all employees were told what they could put in their offices or on their desks according to their corporate rank. The problem is, purely functional items seldom offer the depth of meaning and inspiration you need to maximize your creativity, contrary to what many "time management" experts might say.

Instead of a utilitarian approach, consider sparking your creativity with a variety of items and gadgets that have deep connections to your spirit and psyche. Decorating your work space with meaningful objects and "curiosities" influences your mood, helps you break through creative blocks, and inspires you with new ideas. Imagine the impact of having some of the following in your environment:

- Souvenirs from places you've visited
- Statues and trinkets from far corners of the world
- Reproductions of famous statues, busts, or artwork
- Historic items like signed letters and documents
- Ancient coins
- Fossils
- First-edition books
- Original movie posters
- Craft objects from other cultures (vases, bowls, jewelry)
- Period art (e.g., 1920s, 1950s, 1970s)
- Models of cars and airplanes
- Mind-challenging puzzles and games

If you think I seem to be suggesting that you should turn your office or work space into a museum, you are absolutely correct

—and you are the chief curator. The more exciting and unusual items you add to your environment, the more connections to other types of thinking and attitudes you will get. Some items can remind you of past generations or your own family; some may recall trips and adventures you've had; others help you to put life in global perspective.

Stop for a moment and think about the homes of the most creative people you know or those of creative celebrities you may have seen in magazines. What you'll notice about nearly all of these people is that their spaces are invariably decorated with a wide variety of objects of all colors, textures, and time periods. The point is not that creative people have more money to buy exotic bric-a-brac but that they understand the value of surrounding themselves with objects that inspire their creativity.

You don't need to be able to buy an original Cézanne, Wyeth, or Hockney to enhance your environment. You can buy quality reproductions. The key is to find a variety of items that bring meaning and spirit to your work space.

Here are a few more objects that might stimulate your thinking or help you expand your creative C.O.R.E.:

- **Ethnic art can help recall your heritage and family legacy.**
- **Children's art can evoke a sense of lost innocence and playfulness.**
- **Posters can summon up favorite events — from a popular western drama of your youth to museum posters from a favorite exhibit.**
- **Photographs of the world's most impressive natural sites — Yosemite, Yellowstone, the Grand Canyon, the Himalayas, or the fjords of Norway — can help you appreciate the beauty and mystery of our natural environment.**
- **Photos of the earth taken from space can help you remember "the big picture."**

Select also some objects to represent the humor, joy, and whimsy of life.

- **A magic wand can remind you that anything is possible.**
- **A colorful toy can remind you of the child in us all.**

- **A clown doll or funny mask can remind you of the humor inherent in every situation.**
- **The Greek masks of comedy and tragedy can help you remember the duality of life.**

In my office, I have a number of objects that help me in different ways. For those times when I want to block outside stimuli, I have a blindfold and earplugs as well as a sound-and-light machine that flashes lights at specific wavelengths as I listen to tones played through a headset. These help me relax. My office has a large collection of my children's arts and crafts. I also have a small Zen garden, which helps me to clear my mind and puts me in a meditative state. For stimulation, I have a bag full of little toys, like magic wands, games, puzzles, stones, and balloons. To remind me of cultural diversity, I have an Amazonian headdress of beautiful colored feathers, a large amethyst geode from when I worked in Brazil, and a paperweight made from an ancient Greek coin.

In your search for items, check with your local libraries and museums, many of which have programs that allow residents to borrow paintings, posters, and sculpture for minimal fees or for free.

Your environmental art doesn't have to be perfect, nor does it have to last forever. Feel free to change your art or move it around your home or work space. As the old adage goes, "Variety is the spice of life." Nothing could be more true when it comes to nurturing the creative mind.

Factor 4: Surround Sound, Music for Your Mind

Some people prefer to work in silence, but many others use music or background sounds to stimulate their creative process. Music and sound accomplish two things:

1. On the one hand, research suggests that certain types of music

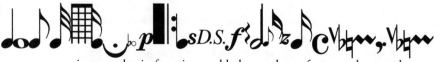

increase brain function and help you learn faster and remember
more. Experiments with children have shown, for example, that
listening to Baroque music while learning math increased learning speed and retention. Other studies have shown that some of
Mozart's music temporarily improves scores on traditional IQ
tests. Some theorists have suggested that the intertwining themes
of a Bach fugue cause us to grow larger neural networks connecting brain cells, literally increasing our intelligence.

2. On the other hand, the most powerful benefit of music and
sounds is that they have an indisputable capacity to affect feelings and mood, both of which are integral components of the
creative process. Music can make you happy or sad, hopeful or
despondent, excited or lethargic. It can soothe you to the point of
putting you to sleep, or it can awaken you and motivate you to
march or dance.

Music accomplishes exactly what you need to be creative,
transporting you out of your comfort zone into new thoughts
and feelings. So even if you're accustomed to working in quiet,
consider adding sound to your environment, if not all the time
then at least occasionally, when you need to break through a creative block or to change the tone of your work. As with color,
you can choose from many types of sound to create a variety of
moods or feelings:

- **Sounds of the natural environment, such as whales, dolphins, thun-
  derstorms, and rainfall, can reconnect you with the soul of nature.**
- **Classical music from the Baroque period or contemporary New
  Age recordings can relax you and help you focus on the present
  moment.**
- **Romantic composers like Chopin, Schubert, and Ravel can encourage a flowing "stream of consciousness" thoughts.**
- **Rock music or jazz can be useful when you need to recharge your
  batteries with a steady beat and lasting melodies.**
- **Music with thought-provoking lyrics can evoke new images and
  bring out your poetic side.**

Use whatever suits your creative needs of the moment. Experiment by listening to a variety of sounds so you can find one that matches your project or mood, and select your own music rather than listening to the radio. Some people pick out a composer or a song before beginning a project and then listen to it over and over because the music helps them get into a state of mind that works for that project. I find drum music is particularly effective for me because the rhythmic beat establishes a steady pace in my mind. However, if listening to the same music repeatedly tires you out, vary your sound environment from day to day, perhaps staying within a certain genre, such as world beat, salsa, tejhano, blues, choral music, or nature sounds.

In our visually oriented society, dominated by television and movies, it's easy to forget the value of music as a stimulus for your work. Take a break once in a while and go on a musical treasure hunt to rediscover your musical intelligence. Explore sounds you are not familiar with to get out of your comfort zone. If you generally listen to Frank Sinatra, try some new jazz or country-and-western. One particularly good source for ideas is ethnic music: Irish jigs, Hungarian folk dances, African tribal rhythms, and Aboriginal music played on didgeridoos. Ethnic music is a testament to the variety of human creativity and diversity and thus can prompt many images in your mind.

Factor 5: Aromas, Therapy for the Soul

If a scent has ever brought on a sudden rush of feelings or images for you, you won't be surprised to learn that experts have recognized the olfactory sense as a critical element in a creative environment. Neglected as the least important sense until recently, smell is now being discovered to directly stimulate an area of the brain—the limbic system—that is responsible for our most primitive emotions and memories. As a result, a single scent can dredge up a mountain of emotions and cause us to recall memories that extend back to our earliest years. For example, when I take a walk on a crisp December day with the smell of wood smoke in the air, I am invariably reminded of winter outings I had as a child, all bundled up and carrying my sled, followed by a warm fire and cup of hot chocolate. And when I enter certain kitchens with just the right combination of aromas, whatever the season, I immediately picture my family's ritual holiday setting, complete with the uncles, aunts, and cousins I haven't seen in twenty years.

The growing understanding of aromas has led to a resurgence of interest in the field of aromatherapy. While the ancient Egyptians, Greeks, and Romans all used fragrances and perfumes as part of their daily rituals and even to induce dreams, the term *aromatherapy* was coined in the nineteenth century by a French chemist, R. N. Gattefosse, who defined it as "the therapeutic use of odiferous substances obtained from flowers, plants, and aromatic shrubs, through inhalation and application to the skin." Aromatherapy has been popular in Europe since Gattefosse's time, and has gained a wide following around the world in the last decade.

Aromas have been shown to stimulate or relax the body, improve attention span and concentration, enhance learning ability, increase imagination, and so on. Here are some of the best-known scents and the therapeutic benefits ascribed to them:

- **Sandalwood — tranquillity**
- **Jasmine — passion and excitement**
- **Cedarwood — relaxation**
- **Ylang-ylang — calm**
- **Ginger — stimulation of the mind**
- **Cistus (rockrose) — mind expansion**
- **Clary sage (lavender) — antidepression**

According to Cynthia Watson, M.D., a noted expert in holistic medicine, certain negative mental and emotional states can also be improved by using aromas, as follows:

- **Insomnia — neroli (from orange blossoms), clary sage, sandalwood, basil, chamomile, lavender, orange, apple**
- **Nightmares — fennel, mint, rosemary, marjoram, orange**
- **Anxiety — basil, bergamot, coriander, hyssop, mint, rosemary, heliotrope, patchouli**
- **Depression — angelica, lemon, ginger, eucalyptus, neroli, parsley, patchouli**

- **Lethargy** — rosemary, ylang-ylang, eucalyptus, lemon, pine
- **Stress** — rose, tarragon, vervain
- **Inability to concentrate** — carnation, bergamot, coriander, jasmine, lemon
- **Stale or toxic air** — basil, peppermint, pine

Many aromatherapists mix unique combinations of scents from herbs and flowers, selling them under various names. Aromatics can be used in several ways. Pure essential oils should be placed in an aromatizer, a small machine that diffuses tiny particles of the oil into the air, scenting the entire room. Diluted with a base of vegetable oil, skin cream, or massage oil, essential oils can be used on the body. Most aromatherapy ingredients are available at health food stores and increasingly in perfume boutiques and mail-order catalogs.

You can also scent your environment with natural flowers and fruits, potpourris, or candles. Even peeling an orange or a lemon, or drinking a strongly scented tea, will give your brain an aromatic boost. Baking bread, sautéing onions and garlic, even being near turpentine or sawdust, are powerfully evocative for some people. If you want to experiment with this sensory element, begin by noting the different smells you encounter in your environment over the course of a week. Close your eyes and reflect on the feelings evoked by these smells. Are they positive or negative? Do they transport you mentally to any particular place or time of your life? Then experiment with different types of scents. Notice what effect each has on you: Does it make you feel more peppy or reflective? Then choose a scent that helps you feel the most creative and productive. Needless to say, smoking generally nullifies the effects of aromatherapy.

Factor 6: Touch, Comforting and Stimulating the Body

Touch can also be an important element in establishing a setting and mood in your work space, through the furniture you select, the items on your desk or work area, and other objects you encounter during the day. The textures you surround yourself with can make you feel comfortable, cheery, and confident—or stiff, confined, and unimportant. Some people, especially kinesthetic learners, absorb information and listen better when they have objects to touch and toy with.

When setting up or changing your work space, it is important to take into account the element of touch and the many ways texture influences your mood and sense of creativity. There are a number of ways to do this:

• **Use touch to establish physical comfort and relaxation.** Being able to relax and be comfortable in your environment is as important as being able to work effectively in it. Daydreaming and even conscious idea generation sometimes work best when you have access to furniture that lets you feel comfortable and completely relaxed. When you are stressed, sitting in a chair that invites you to sink deep into its recesses relieves tension, allowing you to think clearly again. But comfort is not just a matter of softness. The look of a chair or couch, the quality of the covering material, the depth of the cushions, and even the smoothness of wood or metal trim can change the sense of comfort that a piece of furniture imparts to you.

• **Use touch to calm and achieve tranquillity.** The objects around you can provide opportunities for balancing your thoughts or calming yourself. Some people find tranquillity in rubbing a small, smooth stone or playing with metal balls swinging on string. In Middle Eastern cultures, people use strings of beads called worry beads to focus their attention and reduce their stress.

• **Use touch and movement to provide stimulation.** Objects can give you energy and stimulation for your ideas and feelings. The executive who gets up from his desk in the middle of a big decision to swing a golf club is not simply practicing his game; muscular action can help focus thoughts and spur creative energy. This is another reason why it is useful to have environmental art around your office, including objects you can pick up and play with. Some people sarcastically call these toys, but fun objects let you fulfill your need to touch as part of the creative process.

𝓕𝒶𝒸𝓉𝑜𝓇 7: Taste, Food for Creative Thought

Food is also an important part of a creative environment under your control. Many people pay little attention to their diet but still expect themselves to be creative and productive. There is now a vast literature demonstrating that what you eat influences your mental and emotional state of being.

According to Judith Wurtman, author of *Managing Your Mind and Mood Through Food,* there are three critical nutritional principles to remember:

1. Carbohydrates make you sleepy, which means that eating an overstuffed sandwich or a hearty dish of meat and potatoes for lunch may reduce your creative energy.
2. Protein increases alertness while fats dull mental acuity.
3. The best diet is one that emphasizes fresh fruits and vegetables, and avoids processed foods, artificial ingredients, sugar, starch, caffeine, and alcohol.

MINI WORKSHOP

DESIGNING YOUR CREATIVE ENVIRONMENT

If you believe that changes to your environment will not pay off in your creative work, you are likely correct. A negative mind-set negates the significant benefits you can reap by having a positive, reinforcing environment wherever you work. But if you make an effort to surround yourself so that all your senses are stimulated, pleased, or excited, you will find that your inspiration will likely increase.

Given the seven environmental factors, begin designing or remodeling your environment so that it inspires your creativity rather than drags you down. Take a close look at your home and/or work space, and analyze it to see if it is the right space for your personal creative style. Look at the chart on pages 98–99 and, using its questions as a guide, note what you need more of and less of in your environment.

Creative Mind Triggers

An intriguing psychological principle that you should also consider in selecting the colors, furnishings, and even smells around you comes from the concept of neurolinguistic programming. It

LIGHT Evaluate the quality of light in your home and office. Do you have natural lighting available? Is the lighting comfortable and relaxing? Do you need more lighting, or need to change the positions of the lights? Can you experiment with different types of lighting and find an arrangement that works best for you?

Are you getting enough sunlight? Do you feel you are in sync with your natural body rhythms?

I NEED MORE

I NEED LESS

COLOR Evaluate the color palette that surrounds you. Is it warm or cool? Do you have patches of color to energize you and provide diversity from a monochromatic environment? If not, consider adding color in any way that you can afford and circumstances allow. Buy some flowers, repaint the walls, rearrange your furniture, hang some posters, and so on.

I NEED MORE

I NEED LESS

ENVIRONMENTAL ART What objects do you have surrounding you and how do these objects make you feel? Do they expand your creativity or dull it? How could you enhance your environment if money were not a factor? How can you adapt these ideas in ways you can afford?

I NEED MORE

I NEED LESS

SOUND Reflect on how — or if — you use music to motivate you to accomplish certain kinds of tasks. Could you use music in your environment now? Would you be able to listen to music while working? What kind of music do you find most stimulating? Do certain types of music work better at certain times of the day to inspire you?	**I NEED MORE**
	I NEED LESS
AROMAS Determine if your present environment is remarkable for either pleasant or offensive odors. Eliminate what you don't like by exploring aromatherapy and using its principles to help your creative needs. Buy some scents to surround yourself with soothing or stimulating smells.	**I NEED MORE**
	I NEED LESS
TASTE What is your diet like? Which foods do you need to eliminate or add to your diet in order to enhance your energy and alertness?	**I NEED MORE**
	I NEED LESS
TOUCH What can you touch in your work space? Do you need to buy new furniture that helps you relax or feel more comfortable while working? Are there some "toys" you can bring to your environment to use when you take a break or focus your thoughts?	**I NEED MORE**
	I NEED LESS

is known as a creativity trigger, a cue that automatically reminds you of a time when you were in the flow state of mind, producing your best work with ease. Just as the smell of mulled cider reminds some people of a wonderful ski vacation, or the sound of a marching band gets them thinking about their triumphant year on the football field, a certain sensory perception may trigger a specific memory of your peak creativity.

I realized that a heavy percussion beat was my trigger, probably because it reminded me of my days as an executive with Donnelley Marketing, where I had the habit of tapping a pencil during the meetings I had with my team. Since this realization, I have used a drumbeat to help me reenter my flow state whenever I am seeking to be creative. I wrote this book to the accompaniment of music like Paul Simon's *The Rhythm of the Saints,* Mickey Hart's *Planet Drum,* and a variety of great rhythms by Babatunde Olatunji. These works make extensive use of the drum and somehow appeal to my creative spirit more than any other technique I've ever used. Henry David Thoreau certainly understood this sensation when he wrote the famous words, "If a man does not keep pace with his companions, perhaps it is because he hears a different drummer. Let him step to the music which he hears, however measured or far away."

Environment to Go:
Creative Support When You're Not at Home

If you travel frequently, you may need to figure out how to keep yourself from becoming dulled and depleted by energy-draining environments like airports, hotel rooms, and drab offices. Here are six tips to help in these circumstances:

1. Bring your own music or sound environment. In today's age of portable radios, personal stereos, and CD players, it is easy to surround yourself with inspiring music when you travel or work elsewhere. The comfort and familiarity of your favorite composer or song can re-create the ambience of your regular environment. Or buy a recording of natural sounds like ocean waves, gently falling rain, a waterfall, or soft winds. The Nature Company sells many such tapes. Sharper Image and Brookstone sell a device that looks like an alarm clock–radio and contains a memory chip that plays several prerecorded nature sounds such as ocean waves, wind, and rain. You can put the machine on your bedside table in a hotel room or in your office and then relax as it eliminates annoying background sounds.

2. When you feel unproductive or stressed, try using a black eyeband and earplugs while meditating or relaxing quietly for twenty minutes in a comfortable chair. New headsets called noise busters eliminate low-frequency noise and are great for eliminating the loud noise on planes.

3. Bring an aroma diffuser with you or smooth lotion scented with essential oils on your skin to give yourself an aromatherapy session.

4. Take a bag full of polished stones or small objects that have special meaning for you. Rocks and other natural objects are symbolic of the vastness of time and help put daily events in proper perspective. Family items might remind you of your spouse, children, or parents. Whatever you choose, the objects can be a way to link your thoughts with the environment in which you are most comfortable.

5. Be sure to go out for walks during the day, especially when traveling. Jet lag occurs because your normal circadian rhythms, which are cued by light, are thrown out of sync. Walking and taking in sunlight after a long flight and several hours of time difference can help your body reset its clock.

Is Your Psychological Work Environment Creatively Healthy?

Your physical work space is not the only aspect of your environment that influences your creative spirit: Those with whom you work or live can also have a significant impact on your success. Some companies foster the creative spirit of all their workers by encouraging and supporting initiatives—and rewarding creative output. These companies also are not punitive when a creative idea fails to produce the desired results. Such a nurturing environment for the creative spirit invariably provides an extremely positive long-term return on investment for the organization.

FENG SHUI: THE CHINESE APPROACH TO THE PROPER ENVIRONMENT

If you are truly inspired to reconfigure your environment, consider exploring feng shui, the Chinese practice of arranging a room to maximize the harmony of its space. Feng shui has existed for thousands of years and brings a spiritual dimension to environmental study. The practice focuses on creating an environment that has the best "energy" — one through which *chi*, or what can best be translated as the life force, or life energy, can flow properly. The Chinese characters for feng shui translate literally, "Wind and Water."

Modern-day feng shui masters use a combination of ancient rules for the placement of objects and furniture to create harmony and a feeling of peace, tranquillity, and comfort. This idea is reflected in many Chinese concepts that you may have heard of: tai chi and chi kung, are based on the concept of *chi* flow. The rules of this ancient art are complex and have much to do with open space, directional positioning of buildings and furniture (north, south, east, west), and energy forces projected by objects. For example, on the advice of a feng shui master, the original structure of a forty-seven-story Hong Kong and Shanghai Bank building in Hong Kong was changed to face the sea with a hill at its back, a position that is thought to be wealth enhancing.

If you have ever wondered why many Chinese restaurants feature a bubbling fish tank near the doorway, feng shui provides the answer. According to its rules, bubbling water near the entrance of a commercial establishment provides good fortune.

Feng shui is attracting increasing interest in different parts of the world. Today many interior decorators work with feng shui practitioners to help plan the elements of homes and offices. You can locate a feng shui practitioner in your area by contacting environmental consultants and architects, who frequently work with feng shui masters.

Unfortunately, other organizations go to great lengths to construct rules and restrictions that cast a pall over creativity. Your creative spirit immediately plummets when you have a boss or co-worker who greets your ideas with statements like these:

- **We tried that before.**
- **It costs too much.**
- **It's too radical a change.**
- **We don't have the authority.**
- **That's not our problem.**
- **You're two years ahead of your time.**
- **It's not practical.**
- **I can't imagine where you dug up that idea.**
- **It's never been tried before.**
- **Let's put that one on the back burner for now.**
- **I don't see a connection between your idea and our business.**
- **We've always done it this way.**
- **Quit dreaming.**

The negative environment created by such statements not only discourages creative thinking, but in many cases ultimately drives the most creative people out of the company. And what may save a few dollars in the short term can often lead to the organization's downfall over the long run.

If your creative spirit is dampened by a negative work environment, it's time to consider your alternatives. You may be able to transfer to a different department, change jobs, negotiate with your manager for more leeway in your work, or hire a creativity consultant to help redesign your environment. But you need to begin to identify your possible solutions and to commit to doing something about your situation rather than live on automatic pilot in your comfort zone.

CRAZY MAKERS AND IDEA STOPPERS IN YOUR ENVIRONMENT

Reflect on what or who interferes with your creativity in your office or work environment. Do you feel you are trying to be creative but your manager or company rules are obstructing your ideas? What practices or procedures does your company have that might be squelching the creativity of every employee? What about yourself? Are you your own crazy maker? What changes might you propose? _____

_____

_____

_____

_____

What options do you have for extricating yourself from this negative creativity environment? _____

_____

_____

_____

_____

Can you discuss your views on creativity with your manager or boss? _____

_____

_____

_____

_____

Can you change jobs? _____

_____

_____

_____

_____

Further Readings

Bodyrhythms: Chronobiology and Peak Performance by Lynne Lamberg (New York: William Morrow, 1994).

Brain Boosters—Food & Drugs that Make You Smarter by Beverly Potter and Sebastian Orfali (Berkeley, Cal.: Ronin Publishing, 1993).

Feng Shui Step by Step by Raphael Simons (New York: Clarkson Potter, 1996).

Interior Design with Feng Shui by Sarah Rossbach (New York: E. P. Dutton, 1987).

Organizing for the Creative Person—Right-brained Styles for Conquering Clutter, Mastering Time, and Reaching Your Goals by Dorothy Lehmkuhl and Dolores Cotter Lamping (New York: Crown Publishers, 1993).

Zen Rock Gardening by Abd al-Hayy Moore (Philadelphia: Running Press, 1992).

Get out of Your Box Through Travel

Venturing beyond your geographic comfort zone invigorates your creative spirit. When you go somewhere you've never been before, your brain comes alive, and you become more acutely aware of your surroundings. You notice things you might not observe at home, and even the most common-place objects—road signs, store fronts, telephone booths, coins—are intriguing. Travel serves up a continually changing kaleidoscope of colors, textures, smells, and tastes that heighten all your senses and compel you to think and react in new ways.

When you stay in one place, you can get into a rut. Following the same general routines every day, going to the same places, and seeing the same people, your thinking can become stale. Travel helps to interrupt the monotony of daily life and gives you the freedom to break away from your usual routines. There are no deadlines, no car pools, no taking your clothes to the cleaner. Even mundane tasks like going to the market or buying a newspaper can be opportunities to learn about a different culture or see the familiar in a new way. Travel jolts you out of your normal habits and gives you a renewed sense of excitement about the world that can refresh your creative wellspring.

Perhaps more than any other tool, travel feeds your creative C.O.R.E. and strengthens your intelligences. Each time you observe an unusual custom, hear a foreign language, listen to strange music, or walk an unfamiliar path, you inject your mind with data that build your intelligences. For example, through travel you

- **charge your visual intelligence through exposure to the different architectural styles found around the world;**

- **develop your interpersonal intelligence by learning to meet and chat with people in other locales about the rhythm of their daily lives (even if you don't speak the language, communicating through gestures alone is a real test of your interpersonal abilities);**
- **sharpen your bodily-kinesthetic intelligence by learning to navigate unknown city streets or traverse unfamiliar countryside;**
- **boost your spatial intelligence by studying the layout and landscaping of other cities.**

Family travel can also play a critical role in helping children develop their intelligences, particularly in the formative years between birth and age ten. It aids their self-confidence, opens their minds to alternative ideas, and, of course, stimulates their creative C.O.R.E. in the same ways that it helps adults.

The great advantage of travel is that you can usually have a creative experience regardless of how far you go or how much time and money you spend. When you are stuck on a problem or trying to generate a new idea, you can benefit from even a half-day trip to a nearby town, where browsing antiques stores or visiting a gallery might provide the inspiration you need. If you have more time, of course, getting away for a full weekend or a week can change your entire perspective and even provide the occasion for a serendipitous discovery.

In general, airfares have dropped in recent years, so transcontinental and intercontinental travel is no longer a luxury only the affluent can afford. But many of the world's most skilled and experienced travelers compensate for a lack of money with high levels of curiosity and motivation. Using salesmanship and ingenuity, they find amazingly inexpensive flights, make deals with tour agencies, take on freelance jobs as journalists, couriers, chaperones, or bike tour leaders for employers who underwrite their expenses, or recruit companions to share costs. So, if you're truly motivated to take a journey, there's usually an affordable strategy to make your trip possible.

Travel can serve many creative purposes, including the following:

- **Burst creative blocks**
- **Provide inspiration for life in general**
- **Reveal new points of view**
- **Teach you something**
- **Create excitement and adventure**
- **Deliver opportunities for serendipitous discoveries**
- **Open up business avenues for profit**
- **Help you relax and reclaim your inner harmony**

Many prolific artists resorted to travel when they needed inspiration and new ideas. Paul Gauguin moved to Tahiti, an act that changed both his life and his work. Henri Cartier-Bresson's experiences during a year spent in Africa convinced him to abandon painting in favor of photography. Ernest Hemingway went to France, Spain, East Africa, and Cuba, where his experiences served as the inspiration for his greatest works. The Beatles sought spiritual renewal by studying Eastern philosophy with the Maharishi Mahesh Yogi in India, changing not only the direction of their personal lives but also their music. Several periods of Paul Simon's greatest music developed from his travels to Africa and South America.

Many locations are almost universally considered inspirational because of their innate natural beauty. From the vast mountain vistas of the Swiss Alps to the supernatural landscapes of the Grand Canyon, certain places overwhelm us with inexplicable grandeur and majesty. These places act directly on the soul. For many people, the planet's natural environments inspire a profound sense of spiritual oneness with nature and give a creative inspiration unmatched by any other experience.

Other places provoke by their bustling activity, their intellectual vigor, or their historic significance. The intellectual and artistic ferment of great cities like London, Paris, and New York produces an adrenaline rush in many people. It is nearly impossible not to feel charged and exuberant when visiting these cities. Mihaly Csikszentmihalyi calls this the "mental environment" and states that it is what drew great artists and thinkers to Paris in the early 1900s.

Some places elicit powerful emotional responses because of the momentous events that occurred there. For instance, visiting Civil War battlegrounds, the Normandy beachheads, or a World War II concentration camp can stir tremendous feelings of sorrow and bring a visceral awareness of the human capacity for violence. Creativity can be kindled by visiting other historic sites, such as places where important treaties were signed, where famous trials were held (for example, Salem, Massachusetts, notorious for witchcraft trials), or conversely, where the human spirit triumphed (such as at the Berlin Wall).

Many people get ideas from touring the homes of literary, artistic, and political figures they admire, such as Theodore Roosevelt, Louisa May Alcott, Ralph Waldo Emerson, Ansel Adams, Frida Kahlo, or Martin Luther King. Others draw inspiration from viewing the evidence of ancient civilizations in places like Stonehenge, the Egyptian pyramids, or the Inca ruins at Machu Picchu. Such environments have the power to spark the imagination and put us in the mood to paint, write, sing, dance, or reflect on life's meaning.

Travel can also provide direct inspiration by giving you a chance to watch artisans at work. At a number of historic villages—like Williamsburg, Virginia; Sturbridge, Massachusetts; or Winston-Salem, North Carolina—you can watch costumed employees demonstrate the old techniques of shoemaking, metallurgy, spinning, coopering (barrel making), and candy making. In modern artistic communities like Laguna Beach, California; Cranbrook, Michigan; and Middlebury, Vermont, you can meet painters, potters, and crafters and learn from their creations.

But it's not just physical locations that provide inspiration. Encounters with people of all types can also conjure new images and ideas. Nearly every person you meet along your journey will have an interesting point of view, a remarkable history, or a fascinating story to tell. Whether it's a blue-haired punk in London, an Indonesian dancer, the concierge of a Parisian hotel, a taxi driver in São Paulo, or the owner of a taverna on Mykonos, the people you interact with when you travel contribute to the storehouse of information that feeds your creativity. You simply need to be open to the possibilities.

I once had a deeply inspirational time while traveling in New

Orleans. As my wife, daughter, and I strolled through the French Quarter, we noticed that an old woman dressed in colorful, eccentric clothes was following us. She told us she was an artist and wanted to sketch our baby daughter. We agreed and followed her through the narrow streets directly into an area that our guidebook had warned us to avoid. Opening a small gate, she revealed a beautiful courtyard filled with lush vegetation and a fountain. The walls of her apartment were covered floor to ceiling with primitive American art painted by her late husband, whose works hang in the Museum of American Folk Art in New York City. Over the next two hours, as she sketched our daughter, my wife and I were treated to remarkable tales of her life as an artist in New Orleans. This experience of connecting with another human being in such a creative and personal setting affected me greatly; in fact, this visit was one of my earliest inspirations for writing this book.

Caution: wherever you go, don't attempt to force inspiration; it isn't always immediately forthcoming or even evident. There may be times when a scene clearly prompts you to take a great photo or paint a painting, or when someone you meet inspires an idea for a specific character in your next novel. But many times you are not conscious of how an experience is expanding your mind or how it applies to your creative work. Years later, however, it may bubble up and give you new ideas that become part of your creative work.

MINI WORKSHOP

GETTING INSPIRATION FROM YOUR TRAVEL MUSE

1. If you had to identify one location in the world that you feel would most fuel your creativity at this time, where would it be? A natural wonder like Yosemite or the Himalayas? A cultural mecca like Rome, Vienna, or San Francisco? A place of serenity like a thatch house in Kenya or a quaint Japanese inn? How would you benefit by going there? What kind of inspiration might it provide for your creative work? What is stopping you from going there? Can you find the means to get there this year?

2. Begin planning a trip to the location you have chosen. From the travel section of a bookstore or library, select some guidebooks and magazines

such as *National Geographic, Condé Nast Traveler, Travel & Leisure,* or *Islands.* Invest some time browsing the pages and developing — for the pure fun of it — a travel plan even if you don't have the resources to make the trip immediately. Go so far as to select the best dates for travel, choose your companions, and detail an itinerary and schedule of activities. Would you rent a car once there, take public transportation, or walk? What would you see first? Where would you stay? Compile a folder of selected articles on your destination and its people and attractions.

When you are done, analyze the barriers in your way, if any. Can you knock these barriers down? Can you save each month so that you might accomplish the trip sooner? Can you find an alternative way to travel that is less costly?

3. Whether or not you make your ideal trip, pay attention to the way that planning the trip made you feel. Did you find yourself getting inspired about the prospect of travel? As you looked through the guidebooks or magazines, did you imagine the sights, sounds, and smells of your dream destination? Now, apply the excitement you felt about this trip to other aspects of your life or work. Apply the organizational effort you put into planning this trip to any of your creative endeavors.

Travel to Find New Points of View

As the saying goes, "Travel is broadening." It stimulates your mind by expanding your frame of reference and exploding your cultural bias. Unless you travel, you cannot understand that cultures differ in significant ways, from the overall "feel" they have to the many seemingly trivial assumptions that other people (and we) make about how life should be led. Some cultures feel relaxed, while others feel tense. Some cultures perceive time as fast, others see it as slow. Every culture has its own rituals and traditions that dictate when meals are eaten, what days children go to school, which holidays people celebrate, and many more of the details that shape our lives. And, although you can read about such cultural differences, you must personally experience them to truly affect your creative spirit.

Dr. G. Clotaire Rapaille has done extensive research on the profound effects of cultural programming. Rapaille believes that just as the computer owner loads his or her machine with software that completely determines how that computer works, each society loads its members with a unique brand of cultural software that influences every aspect of how they think and respond to life experiences.

For instance, having lived for thousands of years on the vast landscape of the Australian plains with few obvious landmarks, the Aborigines have highly developed spatial intelligence. One study documents that Aboriginal children outperform white Australian children by approximately three years on a test that measures the ability to remember complex objects and locate them on a grid. Yet these Aboriginal children struggle with standardized intelligence tests that measure verbal/linguistic and mathematical/logical skills. Similarly, scientists have explored the way Japanese children master their complex written language. Their conclusion: The Japanese learn their highly symbolic characters using the right hemisphere of the brain, whereas English-speaking children learn language using the left hemisphere.

If you allow it, every culture can teach you to think and feel in a completely different manner and could even help the way you deal with a problem because it changes your normal mindset. In Rapaille's metaphor, when one type of cultural software combines with other types, breakthrough ideas often develop that heighten your creativity or even alter your life. For instance, visiting a foreign country might give you a new perspective on how to solve a difficult business situation. Seeing the art and architecture of another land in person can open your mind up to artistic horizons that you had never considered.

When you travel, become a student of local customs. Don't conclude that another culture "does things funny" or "is backwards" compared with your own. No culture is inherently superior or inferior to another. The more varied your experiences of other cultures, the more points of view you'll bring to situations. The more options you have available, the better you'll be able to make creative connections.

NEW POINTS OF VIEW

The best way to find new points of view as you travel is to think of yourself as an *explorer* rather than a *tourist*. Explorers seek to understand the heart and soul of a place, whereas tourists merely skim the surface. Here are four suggestions on how to travel as an explorer:

1. GO FOR DEPTH, NOT BREADTH. If you're seeking new points of view, keep in mind that the true value of travel lies in quality, not quantity. Avoid those "eight countries in a week" tours that leave you feeling exhausted and confused, overloaded with new sensations. To challenge your point of view, it is better to spend at least a week if not two weeks in one country where you might be able to soak in more details about lifestyle and customs. By the same token you'll benefit more from an afternoon in a small gallery than a day spent racing from one end of the Louvre to the other.

2. GO UNDERGROUND. When you read travel books, look for those that give an "underground" view of your destination, going behind the scenes to showcase more than just the usual tourist attractions. The best travel books are those that initiate you into the social customs of people you'll encounter. And when you get to the location, avoid tourist-oriented areas that offer the same products and services you can find at home; thanks to the globalization of business, you can go halfway around the world without experiencing anything unfamiliar — if you so choose. Why not choose to eschew the known, seek out the new? For instance, it may be easier just to take the kids to the same fast-food parlor you frequent at home, but you'll be missing out on a valuable opportunity to expand their vistas if you do.

3. GET TO KNOW THE REAL STORY. If you must take an organized tour for whatever reason (some countries require that you follow a tour guide), make it a point to get to know some of the locals. One of the best ways to do this is to strike up conversations with tour guides, doormen, waiters, hotel concierges, shopkeepers, and other people you meet along the way. You'll find that they are rich sources of cultural information and terrific advice. Sometimes these people are so taken with a friendly, open attitude that they will show you to some out-of-the-way site, neighborhood, or vista most other tourists never have a chance to experience. (Obviously, you should use common sense.)

4. ASK YOURSELF DIFFICULT QUESTIONS TO PROMPT YOUR LEARNING. Keep yourself from making automatic comparisons that "prove" your own

culture is better or superior. Challenge your own perspective by asking questions about all your assumptions on life, such as

- What is the overall ambience of this country?
- What makes the people here happy? What makes them sad?
- What is this culture's attitude toward work? (Many cultures have a very different attitude toward work than we do.)
- What are the differences between daily life here and in my own country (e.g., mealtimes, holidays, family habits, parenting)?
- What is the most important new idea that I can learn from this culture?

Travel for Learning

Travel is one of the greatest teachers. Wherever you go, you can always learn something new about whole ranges of subjects— social and political history, geology, plant and animal life, architecture, and technology, to name a few. Whatever knowledge you acquire from your travels both nourishes your brain with data and increases your storehouse of possible connections.

There are many ways to learn while traveling. If you prefer going on your own, you can soak up knowledge by visiting sites rich with history and culture, such as Florence, Mecca, Jerusalem, or Allahabad. There are also many destinations famous for learning centers of special renown, such as

- Trinity College in Dublin, Ireland, and the Tuskegee Institute in Tuskegee, Alabama
- The Huntington Library in San Marino, California; the Truman Library in Independence, Missouri; and the Library of Congress in Washington, D.C.
- The Louvre and L'Orangerie in Paris; the National Gallery in London; the Guggenheim Museum and the Museum of Modern Art in New York; the Uffizi and the Pitti in Florence; and the Prado in Madrid
- The Tulur-Kcata Tjuta Aborigine Cultural Center in the Northern Territory of Australia
- Living history exhibits (the re-creation of a colonial town at Williamsburg, Virginia; Hancock Shaker Village in Pittsfield, Massachusetts; the Moravian Village in Winston-Salem, North Carolina)

If you prefer formal instruction, hundreds of universities, museums, and cultural centers offer special programs that take place either on their own facilities or in schools overseas. You can study drama with the Royal Shakespeare Company, watercolor painting in France, or ancient art in Peru. Many such programs are hands-on: You can take classes in fashion photography in Paris, dig at an archaeological site in Israel, or do carpentry at a workshop in Maine. You can also find many exotic tours

through travel agencies. Look in magazines or do a search on the Internet for these possibilities.

One special program called Elderhostel is specifically targeted to senior citizens. Elderhostel offers courses of different length in music, history, languages, religion, art, crafts, and many other topics at many universities around the world. Enrollees live nearby and are taught by professors who specialize in that area.

One interesting way to learn through travel is to develop a theme for your journey. Focus each trip on a specific topic to deepen your background knowledge for a project you are working on or simply to augment your creative lifestyle. Here are a few trip themes you might want to explore:

- **Architecture (a specific style)**
- **History (a specific period)**
- **Gardens**
- **Subways**
- **Amusement parks**
- **Folk arts**
- **Fashion**

THEMED TRAVEL FOR LEARNING

Pick one of the following themes and plan a trip to investigate it. Use the results of your trip in a creative way, such as writing an article about your journey, making a collage, or drawing/painting a picture.

- *Ethnic heritage.* Take a trip that captures your ethnic heritage. Whether you know your exact lineage or not, retracing your family's journey can give you a profound sense of roots.

- **HISTORICAL JOURNEY.** Travel back to a specific period in history. Ask yourself: What would it have been like to live in that period? How would my life have been different from what it is now?

- **POLITICS.** For example, take a civil rights tour. Walk the routes of the famous civil rights marches of the 1960s. Visit one of the Martin Luther King historic monuments.

- **A JOURNEY OF OPPOSITES.** Take a trip to experience something that contrasts with your normal life. If you're used to urban life, go somewhere backwoodsy or spend some time in the desert; if you're used to small towns, schedule some time in a big city.

- **THE MAKEOVER TRIP.** Arrange a trip in which you plan to change or make over at least two aspects of yourself. Your makeover might be physical (learning a new sport or changing your hair or clothing style), intellectual (learning a new skill), or spiritual (communing with a higher power).

- **FOOD.** Create a vacation to get in touch with the cooking and cuisine of a city, region, or ethnic group. Arrange to take a cooking class and visit local markets, bakeries, and butchers.

Travel for Adventure and Unique Experiences

Travel can significantly enhance your creativity by providing a level of stimulation, excitement, and novelty not encountered in your everyday environment.

Exotic adventures of all kinds are readily available today. These adventures can last a few hours or a few weeks. You can arrange to take a safari to Africa or spend several days in the outback of Australia; climb Mt. Kilimanjaro; scuba-dive among sunken ships in the Caribbean; eco-tour the Galápagos Islands; go llama trekking in New Mexico; raft the wild rivers of Chile; or survey California's wine country in a hot-air balloon.

Some touring companies specialize in organizing highly personal fantasy adventures. One Los Angeles firm, for example, will coordinate one-of-a-kind experiences, like a sleepover in the king's chamber of the Great Pyramid in Egypt, or a seventy-five-minute flight in a fighter jet. Such special-order adventures usually come with a hefty price tag. But for those on a budget, there are many inexpensive alternatives, from snow-boarding to riding

an aerial tramway to the top of a mountain. The point is to find
an activity that is offbeat and unfamiliar to provide that thrill of
newness—and risk—that can kindle creativity.

PLANNING A CREATIVE EMERGENCY TRIP
**Unfold a map of your town or city. Use a colored marker to outline the area
where you spend most of your time and label it "My Comfort Zone." Then
look at the areas outside the marked section. Have you ever traveled to these
areas? Divide them into four squares. Plan to visit one part of the map outside your comfort zone any time you feel blocked in your work. Go to an offbeat museum or historical preservation, eat in an ethnic restaurant typical of
the neighborhood, examine how the rhythms of this district differ from those
of your home turf: Are there more or fewer people on the streets? What are
the social centers and gathering spots? Is another language prevalent? How
does the area compare with your comfort zone, and with your previously held
perceptions and ideas about that part of town?**

Travel to Burst Creative Blocks

Travel is often an effective way to get unstuck from creative
blocks. There are three key reasons that travel helps produce
breakthroughs:

1. Sometimes your conscious mind gets tired. You need to set
your project aside and let your *unconscious* incubate ideas while
you are concentrating on other things.

2. Sometimes you spend so much time on one task that you lose
perspective or get the sense that you cannot see the forest
through the trees. Travel takes you out of your element, which
tends to refresh your perspective and reveal new insights or
approaches to your problem.

3. Sometimes you need more facts or examples to give your
project color, punch, or pizzazz. Through travel, you can
research, collect samples, take photos, or do whatever is necessary to fill your mind with new knowledge.

One company I have worked with, Hallmark Cards in
Kansas City, provides sabbaticals to keep its artists inspired with

new ideas in all of their product areas. The company provides time off and expenses for travel and exploration of other cultures. This program has resulted in many of their popular holiday offerings.

When you hit a creative wall, consider taking what I call a "creative emergency trip," a journey intended to help you find inspiration or insight, get reenergized, or locate information you need. The very spontaneity of this kind of trip can trigger the "Aha!" sensation you need.

For this kind of a trip you don't need to go far; even local travel can help you unblock. No matter how long you have lived in a city, the odds are there's a street, restaurant, park, neighborhood, or out-of-the-way historic location you haven't visited that might get your brain functioning again. If you have the time and the money to take a more distant trip, go to one of the places in the world where the greatest artists and thinkers have historically found creative inspiration. For example:

- **The hilltop known as the Acropolis in Athens, which is the setting for three of the finest monuments of Classical Greek architecture — the Parthenon, the Erechtheum, and the Athena Nike temple**
- **Florence, home to some of the great masters of Renaissance art and architecture, including Michelangelo and Brunelleschi**
- **The small towns of southern France, which inspired new visions of color and texture for many Impressionist artists**
- **The Lake District in England, which triggered the poetry of William Wordsworth**
- **The countryside of New England, which provided the setting for many of America's greatest writers, such as Emily Dickinson, Louisa May Alcott, and Robert Frost**

Many modern artists and craftspeople also identify a few other destinations where creativity seems to be especially heightened. These include

- **Delphi, Greece**
- **Kathmandu, Nepal**
- **Machu Picchu, Peru**
- **Maui, Hawaii**

- **Santa Fe and Taos, New Mexico**
- **Sedona, Arizona**
- **Stonehenge, England**
- **The Cotswolds, England**
- **The Great Pyramids, Egypt**
- **Yellowstone National Park, Wyoming**
- **Yosemite National Park, California**
- **Tahiti**

Whichever one of these destinations you choose, and for whatever reason, you will likely return with new insights, inspiration, and energy to bring to your project—and your life.

Travel to Experience Serendipity

Getting out of your routine to tour unfamiliar places often leads to those chance discoveries and unanticipated connections known as serendipity. The reason such so-called coincidences occur so readily when you travel is that leaving your comfort zone incites your natural curiosity and energy to explore, to ask questions, and to talk to strangers. It causes your senses to come alive, so you are more alert to unusual things.

Consider these serendipitous discoveries that occurred while their inventors traveled:

- **James Ritty, inventor of the modern cash register, was inspired to solve the pilferage problem at his Ohio restaurant while traveling to Europe via ocean liner. A mechanism in the ship's engine room gave him the idea for the counter used in early mechanical cash registers.**
- **Clarence Birdseye, inventor of the quick-freezing process that popularized frozen foods, realized the principle of rapid freezing while traveling in Labrador, where he discovered that duck and caribou frozen in the dead of winter tasted better than foods frozen in milder temperatures.**
- **Elmer Ambrose Sperry, inventor of the gyroscopic compass and automatic pilot for navigation, was thrown from his berth while traveling on a ship during a storm. He connected the balancing system of a gyroscope (long a children's toy) with the rolling of the ship and understood how the toy could be used for commercial purposes.**

- **George deMaestral, inventor of Velcro, was hiking in the Alps in Switzerland when he noticed burrs stuck to his dog's fur and his clothes. He thought about the sticking of fibers and realized it could lead to a new fastening system to replace zippers.**

Here are five suggestions to help you maximize synchronicity and serendipity as you travel:

1. Let life lead you. The key to reaping the serendipitous rewards of your travel is learning how to let life lead you rather than trying to control every minute. There is great value in what some may call going with the flow because, in abandoning control, you open yourself up to noticing life all around you and choosing to react to whatever pleases you *in the moment*. You also end up going places you've never thought to visit.

2. Listen to your inner voice. Wherever your destination, let your natural inclinations lead you to serendipity and synchronicity. Follow your instincts to cities whose names you like or go to parts of the world to which you are inexplicably drawn. As you will discover, there is often a deep-seated reason for your attraction to a particular location. It may be that your soul seeks peace and harmony there, or perhaps you will meet someone "by coincidence" who becomes a lifelong friend or business partner.

3. Take the back roads. Get off the expressways and travel on the small roads. You'll find hidden towns and villages in every state and country, and stumble across people and sights that inspire your creative thinking in different ways. Living in isolated locales seems to bring out many qualities that are not found in urbanites—qualities that help you expand your knowledge of life and lifestyle.

4. Forget the clock. To maximize your chances of serendipity, train yourself not to watch the clock— or to try to fit too much into your schedule. Give yourself permission to play in a mountain stream; study an elk, deer, or eagle; or browse in a country flea market. You'll never find anything you're not looking for if you're hell-bent on checking into a hotel by 6:00 P.M. or beating the rush-hour traffic to your next destination.

5. Look for connections. As the inventions listed earlier suggest, you need to keep thinking and making connections between what you sense and experience, and opportunities or unmet needs you have at home. Many of today's entrepreneurs got their ideas while traveling.

In some cases, you will recognize serendipity immediately—such as taking the wrong road and ending up spending the night in the most charming hotel you've ever found on the edge of a lake. However, other times it may take a while before the beauty of a serendipitous event becomes clear to you.

TAKE A SERENDIPITY TRIP
In the next month, make plans for a weekend excursion without an itinerary. Let whimsy and chance be your guides. Give yourself plenty of time to wander, explore, and even get lost. Pack some clothes and necessities, but avoid making specific plans about how you'll spend your time. Once you arrive, go in search of adventure. Be sure to talk to people you meet along the way and ask them to recommend interesting sites and local attractions. If you're having fun, extend the stay; if you're not, just move on. Keep a journal of your experiences.

Travel for Profit

Travel has one other potential creative purpose: developing ideas for a business from which you might profit. Many people fuel their entrepreneurial spirit by traveling to find new products. The booming import-export business in the United States depends heavily on creative people traveling overseas to find innovative foreign products to bring in—or foreign markets to which they can export American goods. Thousands of people who travel have discovered a desire to import wines, foodstuffs, tiles, ceramics, toys, clothing—anything they admire from artisans throughout Europe, Asia, and South America. A recent column by the noted business writer Jane Applegate featured two former Wall Street executives who were traveling in Imprunetta, Italy, with their families when they happened upon some beautiful pottery. Thinking that the American market might be attracted to the unique clay color and the notable Italian designs, they invested $4,000 to begin a sideline importing business. Within two years their company, Seibert & Rice, had sales of more than $100,000.

In addition to import-export, you can turn your love for a location into a business. Marjorie Shaw turned her personal love for her native Italy into a tour consulting business, Insider's Italy, which makes arrangements for people to rent a villa or house in the Italian countryside. Antonia Neubauer founded Myths and Mountains, Inc., in Haverford, Pennsylvania, after she visited Nepal and fell in love with it. She made several trips back, bringing other people with her. As her trips gained a following, she got the idea to start a business in 1988. At first she offered only six tours; now she has more than thirty.

CREATIVE PROFIT MAKING FROM TRAVEL
Think of the next trip you plan to take. Read the following questions and see if you can develop a creative plan to make your trip profitable.

1. Where are you planning to go?
2. What is the area known for?
3. Are there manufacturers, farmers, or artisans who might like to have you sell their product in your area?
4. Is the area interesting for any particular geologic, historic, or cultural reason that you could write about for a newspaper or magazine?
5. Are there contacts you can make in that location through your local networking that might help you expand your creative pursuits or business ventures in the area?
6. Would other people enjoy visiting this location with you as a guide?

There are many ways you can transform any journey into a creative business trip that might either make money for you as a future business or at least allow you to deduct the costs of the travel as legitimate business expenses while you explore a potential business idea. (NOTE: Be sure to check with your accountant before assuming that your expenses are fully deductible.)

Travel for Relaxation and Inner Study

Travel is usually synonymous with *vacation,* which *American Heritage Dictionary 3rd Edition* defines as "a period of time devoted to pleasure, rest, or relaxation." In general, though, many people see their vacations not as creative experiences but as time away from work to relax and avoid burnout.

A simple stay-at-home vacation devoted to pure relaxation can help your creativity in many ways. Quiet time and solitude allow you to engage in contemplative activities such as reading, writing, meditating, or walking, which in today's frenetic society can be difficult to do without unstructured time. Vacations provide a perfect opportunity to take life at a slower than normal pace, clear your mind, and let go of tension. Obviously, this goal is easier to accomplish if you stay in one place for a while rather than race from one attraction to the next.

A retreat is another time when creativity can emerge from stripping away all your usual outer possessions, goals, thoughts, and conceptions. Left with nothing, your inspiration comes from inside yourself—from your deepest thoughts and feelings, which slowly rise to the surface because nothing is in their way. With no telephone, television, or newspapers to distract you, your mind has a chance to refind its voice. Ultimately, the only conversations you have are with yourself—and therein lies your creativity.

If a solo retreat is too lonely for your taste, you can achieve relaxation at a spa or health resort, where your body can be pampered while you have some company with whom to meditate.

Something to Write Home About

You can significantly enhance the value of your travels by keeping a journal of each trip you make. Making entries in a journal prevents you from letting your travel lull you into the same humdrum routine as your daily life. Even while visiting a foreign country, it's easy to wake up in the morning and approach each day as if you were back in your home or office—feeling you need to think about the same things and accomplish the same tasks.

In the hands of gifted writers, travel journal can become spell-binding chronicles (if not best-sellers) on their own; think of John Steinbeck's *Travels with Charley,* William Least Heat Moon's *Blue Highways,* Peter Mayle's *A Year in Provence* and *Toujours Provence;* and, of course, Charles Kuralt's *A Life on the Road.* But even if no one ever reads your reminiscences but you, your travel can have far-reaching effects on the quality of your life—and your creativity.

Further Readings

Alfred Frommer's New World of Travel: Alternative Vacations that Will Change Your Life by Arthur Frommer (New York: Simon & Schuster, 1996).

Along the Edge of America by Peter Jenkins (Nashville: Rutlidge Hill Press, 1995).

Around the World in 80 Days by Michael Palin (San Francisco: KQED Publishing, 1995).

Falling off the Map: Some Lonely Places of the World by Pico Iyer (New York: Vintage Book, 1993).

Pole to Pole: North to South by Camel, River Raft and Balloon by Michael Palin (San Francisco: KQED Publishing, 1995).

Smart Vacations: The Traveler's Guide to Learning Adventures Abroad edited by Priscilla Tovey (New York: St. Martin's Press, 1993).

Transformative Getaways: For Spiritual Growth, Self Discovery and Holistic Healing by John Benson (New York: Henry Holt & Company, 1996).

Wild Planet! 1001 Extraordinary Events for The Inspired Traveler (Detroit: Visible Ink Press, 1995).

Be Sparked by Play and Humor

Almost all new ideas have a certain aspect of foolishness when they are first produced. — ALFRED NORTH WHITEHEAD

People do not quit playing because they grow old. They grow old because they quit playing. — OLIVER WENDELL HOLMES

Creativity is not all serious business. In fact, the ability to play is a vital ingredient in many creative endeavors. Play encompasses all forms of *having fun,* including games, toys, sports, jokes, puns, and what are sometimes referred to as childish pursuits, such as coloring with crayons and other seemingly unimportant activities. Whatever activity is involved, play also requires letting go of self-consciousness and guilt about having a good time.

Some people think that, as we grow up, we are supposed to replace our childish "play ethic" with the "work ethic." The prevailing wisdom is, if we are not working hard, earning money, paying taxes, or somehow contributing to society, we are being unproductive and lazy. This negative view of play can be seen in our culture's bias against "fun-meisters" of all ages, from youthful surfers who live purely for the joy of catching the next great wave to adults who enjoy playing silly games and horsing around. We tend to dismiss most of these people as unfocused, unambitious, or immature. Think for example of the class clown in your school who everyone loved because he was so much fun yet who was often the butt of jokes when he wasn't around.

But play is a vital component of the creative process. Play eases you into a state of mind that contains many of the elements you need to be creative—curiosity, imagination, experimentation, fantasy, speculation or what if, role playing, and wonder. Through play you open up your creative spirit to the fanciful mental processes that allow you to make new connections, see new images, and get new insights. In their book *Wake Up Your Creative Genius,* Kurt Hanks and Jay Parry sum it up nicely: "A person might be able to play without being creative, but sure can't be creative without playing."

Putting Your Inner Child to Work

Does this mean that to be creative you need to go back to writing with crayons and sitting in a sandbox? In many ways, yes—at least when you need a strategy to get your creative juices flowing. Whether you're writing a novel, designing a theatrical set, or trying to get a team of people to invent a new product, play facilitates the creative process in many ways.

First, play produces feelings of pleasure, which help you escape from two major creativity killers—stress and self-consciousness. When you experience physical or emotional stress from overwork or psychological pressure, you are seldom successful in generating new ideas or solving difficult problems. Stress closes down the mind and shuts off thinking, or it makes the brain work so fast in a "fight or flight" response that your unconscious mind doesn't have a chance to incubate ideas. Self-consciousness also blocks creativity. It often arises from perfectionism and self-criticism that stifle the free flow of ideas and thoughts. When people take their work too seriously, they stifle their creativity by being focused on the goal, not on the process. My business associate, Deanna Berg, calls the desire to be perfect "a spiritual flat tire" that prevents us from moving forward; we fear trying something new unless we know that we will succeed.

In contrast, playing around helps you loosen up. By making a game out of your work or allowing humor and laughter into an otherwise somber task, you can substantially reduce stress and make your efforts more enjoyable. Some types of play, such as exercise and laughter, even have physiological effects, causing your brain to release beta endorphins, your body's natural "feel good" opiates. These endorphins literally enliven you and raise your self-confidence.

When you do something in the spirit of play rather than work, you also become much less self-conscious about your creativity. Play lets you get lost in the moment, so you can forget those self-critical thoughts that interfere with inventiveness and experimentation. Thinking of work as play lets your healthy "inner child" —that is, the part of your mind that likes everything you do and does not criticize your imperfections—take over. When you create in the spirit of play, you give yourself permission to keep singing a new song in different ways until you find the sound you like, or to put a clump of green clay over here rather than there, or to let your imagination come up with outrageously wild ideas when you are trying to invent a new product.

Another benefit of play is that it stimulates your creative C.O.R.E. without the pressure to produce or the fear of making a mistake. Playing a game or indulging in a hobby teaches you to try something new and to test your hypotheses. Humor allows you to be more open to other people and ideas. Many sports, like hot-air ballooning, bungee jumping, mountain climbing, or sky-diving, stretch your concept of risk as well.

Play also prevents boredom and monotony from stifling the creative mind. A world of all work and no fun feels colorless and dull. Play adds variety to your life. People intuitively understand this, but when they are feeling pressured to create, they often forget to take fun breaks that allow them to enjoy the moment and feel alive.

Playing is also an important way to develop and expand your multiple intelligences. A step aerobics or Jazzercise class will refine your bodily-kinesthetic intelligence; a poetry class might develop your verbal/linguistic intelligence, sparking your ability to write songs and understand musical rhythm. And doing brain teasers and puzzles improves your mathematical/logical intelligence.

A further benefit of play is that it opens up communication channels, allowing people to share ideas and work creatively together. In many group situations, people tend to dilute the power of their collective creativity because they spend their time arguing and butting egos rather than working collaboratively. Organizational behaviorists have learned, however, that play helps build team spirit and a unified vision. Many companies now let teams play games or fool around before and during meetings to instill a sense of camaraderie, which helps the teams function together.

Finally, play leads directly to profitable ideas for many entrepreneurs and businesses. Playing a game or sport can be the impetus that pushes your imagination to develop a new toy or game. For example, think of the many inventions we see each year in the burgeoning field of play or sports, from the barrage of new toys and games every holiday season to inventive new exercise equipment. Entrepreneurs Bill Ritchie and Andrea Barthello's Binary Arts Corp. was founded as an outgrowth of Bill's love for brain-teaser puzzles. A family friend suggested he invent a few and today the company has sales of over $5 million.

The joy sparked by toys can also inspire any number of artistic pursuits. A. A. Milne's *Winnie-the-Pooh* is based on his son's beloved teddy bear, Tchaikovsky's *Nutcracker* ballet tells the story of a toy soldier, and Martin Handford made a fortune hiding a little man named Waldo in puzzling illustrations.

Go for It! Putting Fun Back into Your Life

How do you go about using play as a creativity tool? The first principle is to put fun back into your personal life—as much of it as you can each and every day!

Keep in mind that having fun is first an attitude, then a process. Some people have an easy time having fun because they look for opportunities to release their humor and sense of playfulness everywhere. They insist on starting meetings or conversations with jokes or funny stories; they play clown or court jester all the time; and they make off-the-wall trips and buy wacky gifts. Even the most serious of their ventures are not off limits to fun.

Sadly, many people spend their entire lives hearing messages like these:

- **"Stop acting like a little kid."**
- **"There's work to be done, so quit fooling around."**
- **"Grow up and pay attention."**

But people who are successfully creative know that if work isn't fun, it isn't worth doing. Creative individuals place a high value on fun because it enables them to soar in their other pursuits. So invigorating is fun to these people that they often schedule fun breaks into their days.

Fun people also have a profound impact on others and on the culture of their businesses or organizations. Their commitment to fun has a ripple or domino effect. By helping themselves to fun, they make fun and play legitimate goals. In their own way, they become leaders. People seek them out for a boost of encouragement, a joke, or a funny comment on a serious situation.

Here are some ways to add fun to your daily routine:

- Get some crayons and draw pictures expressing your happiness.
- Play a portable musical instrument like a harmonica or recorder.
- Engage in "walking sponge sessions," in which you take walks while trying to absorb as many new ideas as you can.
- Have a "toy box" in your office or work space, and when you get stuck in a project pull out a toy and see what new ideas it triggers.
- Jump rope, spin a top, or use a hula hoop.
- Spend some time thinking of new hobbies you can pursue.
- Design an imaginary tree house.
- Turn the music up loud and dance.
- Play with Silly Putty, Play-Doh, or finger paints.
- Rollerblade, ice skate, or go for a bike ride.
- Wear an unusual hat or costume, a funny tie, or wacky earrings.
- Read some joke books.

MINI WORKSHOP

REKINDLING YOUR FUN FACTOR
Fun is a matter of personal taste. This exercise can help you relocate the "fun factor" in your life.

PART I
Close your eyes and imagine yourself as a five- to ten-year-old. What kinds of activities made you feel like you were having fun? Did you build sand castles on a beach? Construct a fort from which you ruled your own world? Create a make-believe tea party for your friends and dolls? No matter what activity it

was, try to identify what brought you the pleasurable feelings of fun. List five things you did as a child that were fun for you:

1. _____
2. _____
3. _____
4. _____
5. _____

PART II

Now, as an adult, can you structure some time in your day to refind fun? If you're trying to boost and channel your creativity, are there activities that can help you recapture the pure joy and simple pleasures you felt as a child? Using the list of fun ideas on pages 132–134 — or any other suggestions you have — write at least five ways you can commit to having fun now:

1. _____
2. _____
3. _____
4. _____
5. _____

PART III

List at least five fun things you've always wanted to try. Let your imagination run wild — without regard for difficulty, cost, or time.

1. _____
2. _____
3. _____
4. _____
5. _____

Circle the one item on these three lists that's easiest to accomplish and begin it within the next twenty-four hours. Afterward, go on to another item on this list. Make a commitment to complete that item within a few weeks. Then continue with your list. If you think the cost of any one activity is beyond your financial means, try to accomplish it in a creative way. Post the list in a place where you'll see it often and can cross off completed items.

Ten Ways to Bring Fun to Your Workplace

Psychologists recognize that fun is a vital component of an effective work environment. A vast body of research shows that employees work faster and smarter when the organizational culture allows for some loosening up. For example, many companies now allow "casual" days on which employees can wear informal attire. Some companies take the concept a step further and encourage employees—even the most senior executives—to wear wacky clothes, including beanie hats with propellers on top or ties that look like bananas or fish. *Sunset* magazine published a photo of the company Christmas card showing twelve employees dressed like Crayola crayons standing inside a box.

A great example of a company that encourages fun in the workplace is Microsoft. During a visit to their corporate headquarters, I encountered employees engaged in an exciting game of miniature golf in the hallways. True to form, this was no conventional game, however; the way they played demonstrated the fabled creativity of Microsoft's people. The elevators were used to move the ball from the "tee" (on the first floor) to the "green" (on the second floor). Although there may not be a direct correlation between Microsoft's enormous success and the apparent fun enjoyed by its employees, it's easy to surmise that innovative ideas and products developed by Microsoft arise from its employees' ability to relax in the midst of difficult work and to be whimsical and playful during the day. In fact, Microsoft managers get a "morale" budget to spend on spontaneous fun in whatever way they see fit.

The best way companies can foster this kind of buoyant atmosphere is to continually reinforce the message that fun is allowed, encouraged, and rewarded. This principle applies if you're a CEO of a Fortune 500 corporation or the president of the local school council or a church singles' group. Robert Townsend, writer of such books as *Up the Organization* and former president of Avis Rent a Car, nicely captured the meaning of workplace fun when he said, "If you don't do it excellently, don't do it at all. Because if it's not excellent, it won't be profitable or fun, and if you're not in business for fun or for profit, what in the hell are you doing there?"

Here are a variety of suggestions to encourage creativity throughout your workplace. These can also be used to help generate ideas in specific situations.

• **Kick off or close meetings with a fun participatory event.** Many executives run meetings as if they were funerals while expecting people to originate new ideas and be creative. But creativity does not thrive in an environment in which people are afraid to talk or smile. I always suggest that meetings open with some kind of humorous content. When I ran FastData, I hired an actor who, in full military regalia, played General Patton to kick off the new sales campaign. The unexpected messenger defused the somewhat austere tone of the message to the salespeople to make their quotas; the sales reps enjoyed the meeting and absorbed the information much more readily.

Making events participatory invariably results in a more creative outcome. Have everyone attending the meeting come in prepared to tell a joke, or give everyone a sheet of paper and some crayons, and ask for drawings illustrating the problem you will discuss at the meeting.

• **Go to an arcade or carnival.** I recommend this technique from my own experience. In my last corporate position, my staff experienced an especially stressful workweek. I secured a couple of hundred dollars in quarters from petty cash and took everyone to a local arcade. When we arrived, I passed out handfuls of quarters and said, "Have fun." For more than two hours, executives, salespeople, secretaries, and clerks alike rode bumper cars, played Skee Ball, and socked balls in batting cages. Afterward, we headed to the local White Castle, the fast-food chain notorious for its teeny tiny thirty-nine-cent hamburgers known as sliders. The result: a reinvigorated, laughing staff returned to work that afternoon and, instead of bickering and complaining about their work, tackled problems with a fresher attitude. Productivity and morale rose dramatically, and people chatted nostalgically about the event for months.

• **Establish a room where employees can go to unwind.** Many businesses want their people to be creative but don't want them to disrupt the office environment. Why not designate one office space as a creativity room, where employees can fool around with musical instruments, electronic keyboards, a drawing board and easel, and all kinds of other creative materials? After only a few minutes in this room, employees will return to their desks feeling refreshed. Lucent Technologies has implemented this concept in a learning center called Ideaverse, and has even included beanbag chairs in the room for comfort.

This room can also be a place to post humorous business-related cartoons, jokes, and stories, or to hang silly but stimulating questions, such as "If our organization were an animal, what would it be?" "If our company were a movie, who would you cast as our CEO?" Such questions may seem absurd, but they can often provoke interesting ideas that can benefit the company. You might try the exercise author and creativity consultant Roger von Oech uses in his seminars: "Develop the worst possible slogan for your organization." My favorite from a group Roger shared with me was a slogan created by employees of a major bank: "You're never alone—until you need a loan."

• **Have a "Play Day."** Ask employees to bring their children to work or invite children in from a local school. With kids around, adults feel freer to experiment with toys and games and play make-believe. I've seen CEO's and senior managers play with Legos on the floor—such is the power of a seven-year-old child over serious-minded adults. When one large Texas power company tried this, a twelve-year-old came up with an idea that ultimately saved the company millions of dollars.

• **Use toys and games to make business learning more interesting.** The element of play can be critical to learning. In the seminars my company conducts, we ask managers and employees at all levels to play as part of the learning process. At some workshops, we teach participants how to juggle and spin plates in the best *Ed Sullivan Show* tradition. We also use a variety of "learning aids" —the politically correct business term for toys—to help participants remember the key points we made long after the dust has settled on the typical workshop notebook. For example, we hand out flexible magic wands to remind people to be flexible in their thinking. We throw around a Styrofoam rock that looks like it weighs thirty pounds to remind people not to be deceived by appearances. Because they're enjoyable, these exercises help the participants retain the information they convey painlessly.

• **Allow employees to wear costumes, masks, or other offbeat garb on special occasions.** *The Wall Street Journal* reported the story of a Northbrook, Illinois, accounting firm, Lipshults, Lavage and Lee, where the CEO dons a gorilla mask to amuse employees and keep their spirits up during the busy tax season. He also allows employees to play darts and other games in their offices. Apparently, the fun has paid off—economically and psychologically; the company's turnover is down and revenues are up.

• **Transform one employee into the VPF (vice president of fun).** Give someone in your office who enjoys merrymaking the responsibility for organizing special events and helping keep the office ambience lighthearted. Rotate the position every few months to make sure everyone gets a chance to use her or his creativity in planning fun events for co-workers.

• **Use unusual titles on business cards.** It's easy to fall into the trap of taking yourself too seriously. Show your creativity on your business cards. One salesperson I know has the title "Marketing Goddess" on her card, while the CEO of a consulting firm uses the title "Paradigm Shifter" on all his business stationery.

• **Give fun awards.** Establish a monthly or yearly awards celebration and honor the most creative people in your office. Name the awards after the people in your industry or company who've become infamous for certain behaviors. For example, if a manager has an extremely messy office, you might present the "[company name] Award for Environmental Excess." This kind of in-house humor is far more instrumental in helping people become productive and creative than costly, prefabricated service award programs purchased from outside consultants.

• **Send humorous E-mail messages and cards to colleagues.** The element of surprise significantly increases the thrill of a joke or a special event. Try sending an entertaining fax to a client, customer, or friend for no reason at all. Look for opportunities to bring laughter to all the people with whom you associate. You may find that they reciprocate by sending you an idea you can use in your next creative endeavor.

• **Write a parody.** Spoof your company newsletter, compose "typical" meeting minutes that gently lampoon colleagues's idiosyncrasies, or create a humorous—and *almost* credible—press release about a staff or policy change. But make sure it's really witty, or it will fall flat.

THIRTY DAYS TO A MORE FUN WORKPLACE

Whether you are a worker, a middle manager, or an executive, think about the opportunities for fun your company allows, using the following questions:

1. Does the company permit casual dress one or more days per week? If not, why not?
2. Does the company let people relax during meetings? How so? How could they feel *more* at ease?
3. Do you have toys and games in your office that relax your mind or help you be creative?
4. Who is the most fun person in your department or group? Is he or she encouraged to express his or her zany side at work?
5. Are you expected to be creative but not allowed to have any fun in the process?
6. Do senior executives recognize the value of fun in the company and foster a fun atmosphere?

If your assessment indicates that your company is stodgy, boring, or completely un-fun oriented, and you believe creativity is suffering as a result, take action. Implement your own thirty-day fun plan using the preceding list of suggestions and any other ideas of your own to see if people can become more confident, productive, and creative.

Alternatively, if, despite your best efforts, you cannot add fun in your workplace, perhaps it's time for you to look for another company, one that values the benefits of fun in the workplace. Not only will your job be less onerous, but your overall creative life will likely improve from the infusion of fun.

Turning Ha-ha into Aha: Using Humor and Laughter

Humor is a universal language; everyone can relate to funny stories, pratfalls, and crazy antics. But humor can also be used as a serious technique to spur creativity and to solve problems. In addition, humor contributes to healing and good health. Many noted books by authors like Norman Cousins, Dr. Bernie Siegel, and Dr. Carl Simonton have extensively documented how humor has helped cure or relieve cancer patients of their pain and even of their disease.

The sound of laughter shocks people out of automatic pilot so that they can become fully *aware*. Humor is often the starting gun that tells people it is OK to imagine fun, or weird, thoughts —exactly what you need to trigger an association or idea that breaks down a creative block. In fact, some of the most interesting ideas come from making connections between blips of thought and associations made after hearing a joke, story, pun, or odd twist on a situation or event. As Dr. Joel Goodman, director of the Humor Project, an organization based in Saratoga Springs, New York, that produces a major national conference on humor, puts it: "Comedy can turn ha-ha into aha."

Here are eight ways to integrate humor into your creative work:

• **Start a collection of your favorite cartoons** from the comic section or from magazines like *The New Yorker* or *Going Bonkers!* Keep them in a file, and when you're stuck for an idea, pull out the file and browse through them.

• **Initiate a library of your favorite comedy recordings.** Contemporary comedians and those of years past offer excellent humor breaks from tedious work and help you get your brain going again. Among my personal favorites are Bill Cosby's early recordings, Steve Martin, anything featuring Carl Reiner and Mel Brooks, and old radio broadcasts featuring the likes of George Burns and Gracie Allen. Play one when you need to recharge your mind or release tension.

• **Subscribe to a humor magazine or newsletter.** Such publications often have an appropriately wacky perspective that can start you thinking in new directions.

• **Go to a comedy club on a regular basis.** If you're ready to take a risk, go on an open mike night and try out your own material on the audience. If you can't make it to a club, watch comedy TV on stations like Comedy Central, an entire cable channel dedicated to humor and comedy.

- **Build a joke file on your computer.** I've created a large humor database using a program called InfoSelect (specialized database software that I describe more fully in Strategy 7). Browse through your file whenever you need to relax or if you feel stuck.
- **Take an improvisational acting class.** Improv gives you permission to be silly and helps you learn how to think creatively on your feet. Most major cities have improv clubs that offer ongoing workshops to anyone interested.
- **Start a daily joke exchange** on your office E-mail system.
- **Get a page-a-day calendar** with humorous sayings or cartoons.

Remember this technique: when the going gets tough, laugh! Find something—anything—that might help you burst through creative blocks using laughter.

MINI WORKSHOP

ASSESSING YOUR HUMOR QUOTIENT

Try this humor audit. Answer the following questions to assess the role humor plays in your life.

1. When was the last time you told a joke?
2. Can you tell a joke right now?
3. How frequently do you read the comic section in the newspaper?
4. What was the last humor book you bought?
5. What is your favorite comedy film?
6. Who is your favorite comic actor?
7. Where is your nearest comedy club, and when was the last time you went to it?
8. Do you encourage your family members and other people to laugh by telling jokes or reciting funny stories?
9. What radio stations in your area have a humor hour?
10. When was the last time you had a good laugh at your own expense?

If you cannot easily answer these questions, you may need to add more laughter and humor to your life.

Adding Fun to Your Environment

As suggested earlier, the effect of your personal work environment also shouldn't be overlooked. Wherever you spend your creative time should shout out, "Have fun" or "Be playful." For example, do you keep toys, games, or puzzles around to help take your mind off problems or give you ideas? The film producer and director Steven Spielberg has an office filled with video games and pinball machines. Writers, editors, and other creative types stock their offices with novelties such as rubber chickens, humorous buttons, and strange hats. These wacky items help highly creative people laugh at the world and boost their creative output.

In the 1980s, companies spent millions of dollars creating corporate Olympics or using ropes and ladders to encourage teamwork and introduce fun into the workplace, rather than allowing employees to define their own concepts of fun. Despite the best intentions many of these costly efforts failed to produce the desired results.

The truth is, fun that is generated by in-house teams is usually more effective at boosting morale and fostering a congenial atmosphere in which creativity can thrive.

Find interesting new things to enliven your space. If you haven't been to a toy store recently, visit one and see what new gizmos, games, and toys you are attracted to. And don't overlook stores such as the Sharper Image, Hammacher Schlemmer, Brookstone, or the Nature Company (all of which have mail-order catalogs) and software stores. You will be pleasantly surprised at the many creative items available, from 3-D puzzles of the world and kaleidoscopes to animated games that make you feel like a child again.

Remember that such toys need not be related to the work you do, but they should stretch your mind. Start the ball rolling by bringing in your own toys, or better yet, buy a selection of toys for the entire office and share.

CREATE A FUN BOX OR WACKY BAG

I recommend that you have a portable fun box or wacky bag you can use anywhere the urge strikes you to have some fun, release stress, or inspire your thinking. You can use a plastic toolbox or a colorful plastic or cloth bag. Include any or all of the following fun- and idea-provoking items:

- Slinky
- Miniature Etch a Sketch
- Silly Putty
- Crayons
- Play-Doh
- Kaleidoscope
- Superball
- Bubble maker
- Legos or other building blocks
- Kooshball

Take these to your office too. If you're having a meeting, dump the toys on the table and encourage people to play with them. Research has shown that some people learn and think better through movement and touch; they can literally think more clearly if they have something in their hands to manipulate or if they are able to move.

Fun Through Sports

Sports and exercise can help boost your creativity. Some sports not only release endorphins that make you feel exhilarated and clearheaded but also promote teamwork and strategic thinking. Consider these suggestions:

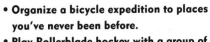

- **Organize a bicycle expedition to places you've never been before.**
- **Play Rollerblade hockey with a group of twelve-year-olds and look at the world through their eyes.**

Legal notice: The author strongly suggests that you wear a helmet and knee and elbow pads, and by reading this paragraph you agree to hold harmless and indemnify said author from any and all injury, damage, or pain suffered as a result of this activity. However, the author does take credit for any fun you might have in the process.

FAMILY FUN

A home in which fun reigns can also aid your creativity, especially if you have children to help you recapture your inner child. Your children's unconventional approach can often free you from your own restrictive thinking. If you're a parent, don't be afraid to get down on the floor — or even in the mud — with your children. Let them see you wearing funny hats and costumes — even if it's not Halloween. Use mealtime as an opportunity to tell stories and jokes. Once your children recognize that homemade fun is much better than watching television, they'll come up with their own ideas. The result is a happier, more creative family.

In my own family, the children decided early on that turkey basters were really

microphones. Since then, we've purchased a set of basters, so the whole family can sing along to our favorite songs. When my business associate, Deanna Berg, was raising her two daughters, she occasionally donned a crown and robe and told them that she was "Queen for the Day." As her subjects, they were required to do her bidding. For example, once she asked the girls to pour chocolate pudding on wax paper, create chocolate paintings for her kingdom, and lick their hands. Not surprisingly, the girls loved it.

How do you employ fun in your family life? Do you encourage other people and members of your family to relax and have fun? Or do you try to get them to fit your definition of the way things ought to be? Do you laugh, let loose, and play with your children? Or do you tend to separate yourself and act according to society's image of a serious, responsible adult? Do you greet silly behavior with a grin or a disapproving frown? Remember, you don't live any longer just because you decide to take life seriously. Check out magazines like the aptly titled *Family Fun* or any of the myriad parenting books on finding entertaining things to do with children to inject a bit of good, clean fun into your family time.

- **Enroll in a gymnastics, ballet, or jazz dance class.**
- **Take up yoga, tai chi, or another challenging relaxation activity you've never tried.**
- **Switch a sport's equipment. For example, try to play baseball with a basketball, or play tennis with boxing gloves.**
- **Organize a sandlot baseball game or stickball game for neighborhood kids and parents.**
- **Learn rock climbing in one of the new rock walls at some sports centers.**
- **Break up the day with a lunchtime visit to the gym or, better yet, racewalk through the downtown area to get a different perspective on your work environment.**

The Ageless Truth of "Party On, Dude"

Just outside Phoenix, Arizona, are two areas developed by the Del Web Corporation called Sun City and Sun City West. If you're like many people, these names probably evoke in your mind a sleepy rest home in the middle of the desert. In fact, when my parents told me they planned to buy a home there upon my father's retirement, I envisioned them sitting in rocking chairs in an air-conditioned sunroom.

But because the developers of Sun City understand the power of fun at any age, they've built what is actually a summer camp for adults. Residents can visit recreation centers to enjoy just about any type of fun imaginable—from tap dancing, aerobics, and computer classes to model railroading, theater production, and photography. Instead of being retired, these seniors are re-fired. They use every bit of their life experience as well as their newfound energy to pursue adventures, discover new talents, and get more enjoyment from each day. Needless to say, my parents love it. Their only problem is finding enough time to do everything they want to.

Why wait till you are fifty-five, sixty-five, or seventy-five, and ready for a move to Sun City? No matter what your age and where you live, have fun *now* to make yourself feel alive! Find the kind of play that invigorates you, and you will find too that the stresses of your career, marriage, or family seem to fade away while your creative C.O.R.E. grows stronger and more vibrant.

Further Readings

A Creative Companion: How to Free Your Creative Spirit by Sark (Berkeley, Cal.: Celestial Arts, 1992).

Laffirmations: 1,001 Ways to Add Humor to Your Life and Work by Joel Goodman (Deerfield Beach, Fla.: Health Communications, 1995).

Managing to Have Fun: Motivate Your Employees, Inspire Your Coworkers, Boost Your Bottom Line, and Have Fun at Work by Matt Weinstein (New York: Simon & Schuster, 1996).

Expand Your Mind Through Reading

The man who does not read good books has no advantage over the man who can't read them. — MARK TWAIN

Throughout most of our education, we are taught to read primarily for information rather than to discover how reading can influence our creativity. We were largely taught "power reading" instead of "reading power." In my view, one of the most important purposes of reading is to fuel your own ideas and creative work. The best reading is actually a life cycle with an author's ideas flowing into you, and your ideas then flowing back to the world in the form of things you create, works you do, and the people you affect.

The best kind of reading takes you out of your comfort zone and expands your creative C.O.R.E. It engages your curiosity by letting you venture into the diversity of human life; it enhances your openness to new ideas and views of the truth; it teaches you to take risks by enabling you to try on new ideas or explore provocative topics in the safety of your home; and it fires up your energy and passion when you delve into causes or ideas that are profoundly meaningful to you.

In 1851, the German philosopher Arthur Schopenhauer wrote, "Reading is equivalent to thinking with someone else's head instead of with one's own." By reading, you're able to enter the minds of other people and add their thoughts and experiences to your own. By assimilating their visions, values, motivations, and perspectives, you supplement the storehouse of ideas from which you fuel your creative work. Furthermore, the printed word is still the primary source of information for most of us. Written materials provide the basis for much of the information we get about our culture and community, our jobs and our professional growth.

Reading also has a direct and positive impact on the development of many of your multiple intelligences:

➤ Few creativity tools surpass reading in enhancing your verbal/linguistic intelligence. Reading boosts your vocabulary and knowledge of grammar and syntax. More important, reading introduces you to many modes of creative expression, thereby expanding your own linguistic sensitivities and expressive capabilities. Through reading, you learn about metaphor, implication, persuasion, tonality, and many other elements of expression—all of which are valuable to any kind of artist, businessperson, or innovator.

➤ Most kinds of reading push you to use elements of reasoning, order, and logical thought to understand a story line or solve a mystery, thus building your mathematical/logical intelligence.

➤ Many books and articles invite you to be introspective and ask yourself serious questions about your values, feelings, and relationships. Some books directly help you move closer to your deepest feelings and thoughts. But even romance novels, mysteries, or humor collections indirectly develop your intrapersonal intelligence, prompting you to think about your life and to review decisions about your direction.

➤ Reading triggers your imagination. A good book invites you to visualize an entire world with its events, scenes, and characters. The images you glean from each book or article you read stick in your mind, over time setting up a vast network of ideas and feelings that form the background for your own creative ideas. These images will eventually become the basis of the metaphors you write, the figures you draw, and even the decisions you make.

After high school or college, many people forsake reading completely or reduce their reading volume to make room for other information delivery systems. Television in particular has become for many adults the dominant source of news—as well as for any learning they may do beyond their formal education.

However, television compares very poorly with books and magazines in its power to provoke you to think or to be creative.

Media experts consider television a passive medium; it is not demanding because it floods the brain with visual images that appear to fill the "data gap" between what you don't know and what you want to know. It generally doesn't entice you to participate in learning or thinking creatively.

MEASURING YOUR CURRENT READING QUOTIENT

The following questions are intended to help you measure your current reading quotient and give you a "baseline" by which to gauge your progress after you read this chapter.

1. In the last three months, how many nonfiction books have you read?

   Score 3 points for each book. _____

2. In the past six months, how many fiction books have you read?

   Score 1 point for each book. _____

3. How many magazines do you subscribe to?

   Score 1 point for each subscription. _____

   a. What percent of the magazines you receive do you read or at least scan each month?

0	No points
1–33%	5 points
34–66%	10 points
67% or more	15 points _____

4. How many newsletters do you subscribe to?

   Score 1 point for every subscription. _____

   a. What percent of these newsletters do you read or at least scan each month?

0	No points
1–33%	5 points
34–66%	10 points
67% or more	15 points _____

5. How many newspapers do you subscribe to?

   Score 1 point for each subscription. _____

6. When you read a newspaper, do you (choose one of the following):
   a. Read only selected portions, such as the sports section, the home section, or the financial section?

   Score 5 points. _____

   b. Read everything in detail, front to back?

   Score 10 points. _____

   c. Scan the entire paper and read interesting articles in detail?

   Score 15 points. _____

   d. I don't have a particular methodology when reading the paper.

   Score 7 points. _____

7. In the past two weeks, how many publications (newspapers, magazines, books) have you read that are not part of your usual reading?

   Score 2 points for each publication. _____

8. In the past month, have you scanned or searched any on-line service or the World Wide Web for a publication or magazine?

   If yes, score 10 points. _____

9. Do you open and scan your mail, even advertising material?

   If yes, score 5 points. _____

10. Do you read the backs of cereal boxes?

    If yes, score 5 points. _____

11. Have you read any children's books (either on your own or by reading to a child) in the past month?

    If yes, score 1 point for each book read. _____

12. Have you visited a bookstore in the past month?

    If yes, score 2 points. _____

13. Have you visited a library in the past month?

    If yes, score 2 points. _____

14. Have you visited a newsstand and browsed through newspapers or magazines in the past month?

    If yes, score 2 points. _____

15. Do you subscribe to any books- or magazines-on-tape?

    If yes, score 5 points. _____

16. **Have you listened to an audiotape learning program in the past ninety days?**

If yes, score 5 points. _____

17. **Have you ever learned a method to increase your reading speed or fluency?**

If yes, score 5 points. _____

Total score _____

INTERPRETING YOUR SCORE

• *Score above 100.* You are providing your mind with diverse and healthy creative connections.

• *Score of 75–99.* You're on the right track, but you need to increase either the breadth of your reading, by including more subjects, or the depth, by reading more material in the same subject.

• *Score of 50–74.* You need some prodding to invest more time and energy in reading.

• *Score of 50 and below.* Your reading habits are weak; work hard to increase your reading every day.

Setting Up a Creative Reading Plan

If you would like to boost your creativity through reading, put yourself on what I call a creative reading plan. This serves many purposes, including the following:

It strengthens your commitment to read in support of your creative work. A reading plan is essentially a contract you make with yourself to read each day. Without this kind of commitment, it's easy to go for days at a time without picking up a book.

It broadens the diversity of your reading. With more than 50,000 books published every year, plus thousands of magazines and journals, deciding what to read can be a nightmarish proposition. You are probably familiar with the term "information anxiety," coined by information specialist and author Richard Saul Wurman to describe the distress many people have about the flood of data hitting them today. Having a reading plan is the antidote to information anxiety. In setting up your plan, you pre-think your goals about what to read, rather than making haphazard decisions. The larger the variety of writers you read, the more grist you add to your inspiration mill. All writers have different perspectives on life, which are evident in their writing styles, their moral stances, and the subjects they write about. Think, for example, of the difference between the midlife satire of writer Dave Barry, the moral lessons delivered by *Book of Virtues* author William Bennett, and the spiritual advice offered by best-selling authors Jack Canfield and Mark Victor Hansen in *Chicken Soup for the Soul*. Each of these authors presents the world from a different perspective.

It stimulates opportunities for serendipity and synchronicity. Because your reading plan commits you to reading every day, you increase the chances of "coincidentally" finding something of value or interest to your creative work. As I was researching this book, I constantly came across material that found its way into my writing or gave me new ideas to develop in my professional life.

Here are four steps you can take to develop your own reading plan.

Step 1. Agree to Read Creatively Every Day

Begin by making a contract with yourself. Use wording like the following:

I, _____ , IN PURSUIT OF BUILDING MY CREATIVE C.O.R.E., DO HEREBY AGREE TO READ A MAGAZINE, NEWSPAPER, JOURNAL, FICTION OR NONFICTION BOOK, OR OTHER PRINTED MATTER EACH DAY FOR THE NEXT _____ MONTHS. MY GOALS IN ESTABLISHING THIS READING CONTRACT ARE

    A) TO DIVERSIFY AND DEEPEN MY READING SOURCES;

    B) TO INCREASE MY KNOWLEDGE AND AWARENESS OF THE WORLD;

    C) TO BROADEN MY INTERESTS AND SATISFY MY CURIOSITY;

    D) TO DEVELOP MY ABILITY TO GENERATE IDEAS FOR MY CREATIVE WORK;

    E) *[fill in any additional goals you may have]*.

I WILL EXTEND THIS CONTRACT FOR AN ADDITIONAL PERIOD OF _____ MONTHS ONCE I HAVE COMPLETED THE INITIAL PERIOD AND FEEL THAT IT HAS BENEFITED ME TO MY SATISFACTION.

Hang your contract on the wall above your work space or in your bedroom as a constant reminder of your commitment. If you miss a day once in a while, don't fret. It happens to everyone. But anytime you begin to break the spirit of your contract by not reading, renew your commitment and get back on track.

A good way to ensure that you follow through on your agreement is to keep a reading journal or integrate your notes on reading into your creativity journal. If you keep a separate reading journal, you can use a spiral-bound notebook or a small, preprinted pocket calendar in which you record what you read each day. You may wish to make a small note about the content as a reminder in case you need to go back and find something you want to use in a project. For example, entries for a few days might be as follows:

Jan 15—TECHNOLOGY & INVENTION *magazine— Jan. 12th issue —scanned entire mag.—good article on submarines*
Jan 16—BON APPÉTIT— *Jan. issue—scanned—interesting piece on French desserts*
Jan 17—7 HABITS OF HIGHLY EFFECTIVE PEOPLE—*read 50 pages*
Jan 18—*browsed in a bookstore for 1 hour—scanned new fiction titles.*

And so on. Whether or not you keep a journal, use this exercise as an experiment to see if the self-contract technique helps you become a more creative reader. If you are successful, renew your contract for another few months.

Step 2. Read in Small Chunks

The main element in a creative reading program is to take several small reading breaks over the course of the day. Look for brief periods—just five to ten minutes long—when you can take a moment to refresh your mind. By reading in short stretches, you have a chance to experiment with a wide variety of materials, each offering something new and different. Don't feel that you need to finish any particular article or text. Enjoy whatever number of pages you can read in that period of time.

You can also read books or magazines as you already do for longer periods of time. But that kind of reading provides a different experience than these short reading breaks.

Step 3. Read from a Diversity of Sources

In your short breaks, read from as many sources as possible. Think of this kind of reading as snacking rather than eating one big meal a day. The more diverse your sources, the more you'll enjoy yourself and the larger your database of potential ideas and knowledge will become.

A wonderful way to diversify what you read is to let chance dictate your selection. Go to a newsstand and stand in front of the rack of magazines: close your eyes and grab whatever your hand lands on. The late Buckminster Fuller—author, architect, engineer, and famed designer of the geodesic dome—made a

 habit of purchasing whatever magazine was in the upper-right-hand corner of whatever newsstand he stopped at. In this way, he made sure he exposed himself to new ideas and perspectives, and unusual, offbeat information. In preparing this book, I found myself exposed to the following publications:

GOING BONKERS! Cute name; everyday psychology to live a better life; great cartoons
SKIN AND INK. The tattoo magazine that's more than skin deep
TRANSWORLD SNOWBOARDING. *The* snowboarding magazine
THE GUIDE TO WESTERN MEDITERRANEAN ARCHEOLOGY. Featuring an article on mystery mummies of ancient China
VOTRE MAISON. French magazine on home decorating featuring English text; great photos
THE STRADE. Classical music magazine featuring an article titled "Beethoven as a Fiddler"
ROUTE 66. The definitive magazine on winding your way from Chicago to LA on the Mother Road
THE CATALOG OF CATALOGS. A guide to catalogs on just about everything
HOMESCHOOLING. A magazine on teaching your kids at home

TRAVELER. **The guide to great historical destinations**
GUITAR WORLD. **Featuring an exclusive interview with Pearl Jam**
UFO'S ARE REAL. **A magazine featuring a UFO 900 hotline for reporting sightings**

Exposing yourself to magazines that you would otherwise have considered "fringe reading" contributes to your personal repository of cultural software and can assist you the next time you confront a crisis, problem, or opportunity. For example, the magazine *Going Bonkers!* provided several ideas for the creativity seminars I give for companies.

Build yourself a bookshelf, subscription list, and information resource bank with as much diversity as possible. Investigate every kind of publication imaginable. Diversity includes many "alternative sources" of information. Most people limit their concept of reading to books, magazines, and newspapers, but there is a wide range of other sources from which to charge your creative batteries, including the following:

- **BOOKS-ON-TAPE. A number of companies provide audiocassettes of edited books as well as audio newsletters. Audiotapes let you "read" while driving, exercising, or engaging in other activities.**
- **NEWSLETTERS. Thanks to desktop publishing, there are literally thousands of special-interest newsletters, covering every field imaginable.**
- **DIGESTS. You can multiply your reading by subscribing to a service that reviews hundreds of publications and prepares brief written summaries or audio digests. There are digests for fiction, nonfiction, business, and many other areas.**
- **ON-LINE CLIPPING SERVICES. An exciting development from several computer on-line services as well as on the Internet is a personalized reading service that searches through hundreds of publications and picks out articles in subject areas you have identified in advance.**
- **MULTIMEDIA REFERENCE WORKS. CD-ROM and on-line services are rapidly supplanting traditional print resource books like encyclopedias. For example, Microsoft's Encarta is a multimedia encyclopedia on CD-ROM that contains thousands of entries, many of which include photos, artwork, audio segments, and video clips. Many other companies produce multimedia CD-ROM disks containing a variety of reference materials.**

- **DIRECT MAIL.** Don't always toss out the direct-mail pieces that come to you before you've looked at them. A catalog might inspire you to develop new ways to package and market your own product. A brochure might have an intriguing headline that kindles an idea for promoting your own company.
- **FOREIGN MATERIALS.** Even if you aren't fluent in another language, you can pick up information about other cultures by looking at photos and flipping through headlines, articles, and advertisements.

Step 4: Apply What You Read to Your Life and Watch for Synchronicity and Serendipity

This is the heart of the creative reading plan, the point at which idea generation may occur. It consists of two separate but equally important exercises: prereading, questioning, and postreading reflection.

Prereading Questioning

Before you begin reading something, ask yourself out loud: "What am I doing or working on now that might benefit from a new idea?" Apply this question to your business problems, hobbies, artistic projects, and family and community life. Make a mental list of specific issues you are working on.

Framing this question consciously before you read makes you "mindful"; it helps you think about the creative challenges you may be facing and helps you recognize seeds of ideas that could be useful to you. Questioning also energizes your brain in advance of the reading process and puts "hooks" in place on which you can hang ideas you capture as you read. If you encounter valuable ideas, note them in your journal or a pocket notebook, or record them on a pocket recorder.

Postreading Reflection

Prereading thought is one part of the process. It is also useful after you read to spend a few moments reflecting on the reading experience, reviewing the new information to see if you may have missed any connections that could help you. Ask yourself these questions:

1. What is the gist of this article or passage?
2. What problem is the author trying to solve or what idea is he or she presenting?
3. How do the writer's ideas or solutions relate to my life?
4. Is there a method of thinking or a metaphor implied in this piece that I can adopt to solve a problem in my life?
5. Is there an opportunity for a new idea embedded in this article?
6. Does it leave questions unanswered?
7. Do I want to explore the topic of this article or book more deeply?

By maintaining a high level of awareness about your creative needs before you read and consciously assessing the relationship of the article or book to your life after you read, you can significantly increase your chances of making serendipitous or synchronistic connections. Even reading materials that have no apparent relationship to your creative challenges can turn out to contain inspiration or specific ideas that can help your work. All it takes is a single story, article, or report to "resonate" deep inside you, resulting in your own aha! experience.

YOUR CREATIVE READING PLAN

Set up your own creative reading plan. Spend a few days to a week taking small reading breaks. Arm yourself with a wide variety of printed matter, including the following:

- **Books you already own that you have been meaning to read for months or years**
- **Magazines from the stacks on your tables that you have not yet gotten to**
- **Books and magazines borrowed from your library or purchased at your local newsstand**
- **Audiotapes from a bookstore or audiotape rental company**
- **Direct-mail materials (catalogs, brochures, solicitation letters, and so on)**
- **Professional journals and newsletters**

Use this trial period to become comfortable with the idea of reading in short spurts without finishing what you start. Sample an assortment of materials, using the prereading question and postreading reflection techniques at every opportunity. Once you feel comfortable with this creative reading plan, commit to it for several months as stated in your self-contract.

"Deep" Reading

The creative reading plan doesn't mean that you should forsake reading novels, nonfiction books, or professional materials in their entireties. Reading deeply serves a vital purpose too in expanding your creative C.O.R.E. Some books need to be absorbed fully to be appreciated or understood. And your own intellectual or professional learning needs may require that you read certain books intensely from cover to cover.

Reading deeply also means that, whenever you find a topic of interest, you should check into supplementary materials on it. For example, if you are interested in American colonial history, you can approach it from any number of traditional history texts, but there are also historical novels, biographies, museum notes, original documents, newspapers, diaries, children's books, and other sources that would add to the depth and breadth of your understanding.

Which Reading Style Is "Right" for You?

In order to get the most from your reading, it's important to move easily between these two reading styles, rather than adhere to one or the other exclusively. The key is to recognize your goal in reading, which might be categorized by answering the following three questions:

1. Are you looking for a quick breeze of inspiration or for "seeds" of thought to help plant your own garden? If so, reading creatively in short bursts from a wide diversity of items might suit your need. In creative reading, you often stumble on ideas serendipitously, or by making yourself mindful you consciously connect ideas you read with your current creative problems.

2. Are you looking for in-depth information, many points of view, and expertise? If so, reading deeply is most likely what you need. Deep reading is useful once you've identified an idea and need to learn about as many facets of it as you can. And, of course, you cannot build expertise on a subject unless you read "vertically," meaning that you read everything from basic introductory material down to detail-oriented, in-depth volumes written by scholars and experts.

3. Are you looking for pure relaxation and enjoyment? For this goal, either method can be useful. Creative reading can give you a wonderful sense of accomplishment as you broaden your horizons and knowledge. Creative reading also removes the guilt you may feel about not finishing a book you've started—which may enable you to read something else. On the other hand, deep reading is one of the most enjoyable mental activities there is. People who get fully involved in an exciting novel find their cares recede into the background as they are transported out of their everyday world. They achieve a state of relaxation that is often just what they need to refresh their own creativity. A well-written, thought-provoking nonfiction book can be engrossing and illuminating, shedding a new light on your creative work. Both reading styles are important to make reading a productive creativity strategy for you.

YOUR READING STYLE

Think about the last six months. Have you done more creative reading or deep reading? Do you tend to read in bits and pieces, or do you mostly read entire books, one at a time and cover to cover? Whichever reading style you currently use, do you think that your creative work could improve by changing styles?

How might you better use this tool to enhance your creativity? Decide which of your creative interests you can develop through reading over the next few months. Visualize your reading habits and your bookshelf a year from now. Can you turn this vision into a reality?

Bookstores: Amusement Parks for the Mind

Checking out bookstores is a key ingredient of living a creative life. Few environments are more mind stimulating than a good bookstore. Many of the best bookstores encourage customers to browse and learn; if you see signs saying, "Please don't read the magazines before you've purchased them," you're in the wrong store.

Many people enter bookstores with a specific or narrow agenda that reflects their specialization. However, you can benefit by taking yourself on what I call a "creativity cruise" down the many unknown paths of your bookstore. Stop in sections you've never looked at before. I once facilitated a creativity session at a major chain bookstore to demonstrate this technique. I asked participants to tour the aisles for ten minutes and share an insight about something they had learned. The results of this adult treasure hunt were overwhelmingly positive. All the participants had noted something and were delighted with the new knowledge they had gained in a relatively short time. They left the store exhilarated by the possibility of exploring these new topics further.

Visiting a bookstore is also one of the best ways to encounter serendipity when you are seeking new ideas for a project or needing to break an impasse. By spending an hour browsing through a wide range of titles, you can often encounter a phrase or picture that contains just the information or idea you need. This might happen as you skim books related directly to your work, but it can also occur while you flip through books that have no direct relationship to your topic. The key is to leave yourself open to anything; take a walk around the bookstore and pick up books at random in every section: cookbooks, business, self-help, general nonfiction, even books from the children's area. As always with serendipity, you never know where or when an idea will hit you.

BOOKSTORE CRUISING

1. **When was the last time you went to a bookstore or a large newsstand? If it has been more than two weeks, go to a bookstore this weekend and see how different you feel as you peruse the aisles after reading this chapter. Did you feel energized and creative while visiting the store? Try to determine what aspect of the bookstore experience makes you feel the most creative.**

2. **The next time you are seeking a new idea or are blocked, take an hour off to visit a good bookstore. Go to any section of the store that attracts you. Give yourself free rein to enjoy browsing wherever you are drawn. As you pick up a book and flip through the pages, free your mind to make connections between what you read or see and your creative challenge.**

Finding Synchronicity via Library Angels

Like bookstores, libraries are critical in many creative endeavors. Not only are their resources free but through them you can access an infinite reservoir of information via shared information systems. Most contemporary libraries have on-line access to the catalogs of other libraries across the country, as well as on-line research services, CD-ROM's, and videotapes and audiotapes that may be too expensive for the average person to buy individually. Another big advantage of libraries is that they usually employ information specialists who know the latest technology and database searches. Having access to this type of professional is otherwise prohibitively expensive.

The noted author Arthur Koestler claimed that libraries have hidden synchronicity in the form of "library angels"—mysterious sources of assistance that find just what you need when you are looking for it. Koestler was amazed at how often he was guided to books that gave him exactly the right quotation or triggered an idea on a project he was developing.

Ode to My Creativity Colleagues

Another important way to use the reading strategy is to delve deeper into the field of creativity itself. Today dozens of excellent books can help you learn new thinking strategies or focus on specific strategies to generate new ideas and develop innovative solutions to your problems. Some of these books are for general audiences, while others are oriented to business concerns.

Among my favorite books in this area are the following:

- *The Artist's Way* by Julia Cameron
- *Conceptual Blockbusting* by James Adams
- *Creating* by Robert Fritz
- *Creativity* by Mihaly Csikzentmihaly
- *Higher Creativity* by Willis Harman and Howard Rheingold
- *The IdeaFisher* by Marsh Fisher
- *Imagineering* by Michael LeBoeuf
- *It Only Takes One* by John Emmerling
- *Jamming* by John Kao
- *Lateral Thinking* by Edward deBono
- *Mindmapping* by Joyce Wycoff
- *Thinkertoys* by Michael Michalko
- *Transformation Thinking* by Joyce Wycoff and Tim Richardson
- *A Whack on the Side of the Head* by Roger von Oech
- *What a Great Idea!* by Charles "Chic" Thompson

The more of these books you read, the more you will develop your knowledge of creative thinking strategies and idea generation techniques.

Increase Your Reading Pleasure — 1, 2, 3

If you do not like reading, or do not feel that you get as much out of it as you should, this section will give you some quick tips on how to make it a more enjoyable and fruitful experience.

1. Maintain awareness of your creative needs. This element is the key to making the most of any reading experience as a creativity tool. The more you are aware of your creative needs, the more adept you will be at making connections between ideas, concepts, and insights you read and the creative problems you are trying to solve in your mind. A higher level of awareness is what enables you to experience the flow state, in which your mind naturally seems to move in the right direction, grasping the best ideas and the correct answers at each and every moment. When you work in this flow state, nearly anything you read resonates in your brain. Inspiration and ideas practically jump out at you.

2. Set up a healthy reading environment. Your reading enjoyment is greatly dependent on your environment. For example, think of how uncomfortable you feel in a library with hard wooden chairs and low tables that make you lean forward.

Whenever you read, find an environment that enlivens and stimulates your brain while allowing you to be physically comfortable. The following suggestions can help:

➤ Make sure you have enough light. The best sources of reading light are the sun and full-spectrum lightbulbs. Do not focus the light right on the page you are reading while your surroundings are dim; diffused light from several sources prevents glare. Avoid high-intensity reading lamps because their brightness can cause eye fatigue.

➤ The best position for reading is seated at a table in a comfortable chair. You will find that your reading speed and comprehen-

sion, and your clarity of thought, will increase just because you sit in an appropriate posture. Keep your book on a table propped up about two or three inches, at a 45-degree angle, to decrease eyestrain and prevent stress on your neck and back. Lying down, lounging, or slouching may feel comfortable, but these postures are not conducive to alertness and concentration.

➤ Minimize distractions when you read. Whenever possible, do your reading in a place where you will not be interrupted and can concentrate as fully as possible.

➤ If you are doing deep reading, take breaks every forty-five to fifty minutes to refocus your eyes and prevent eye fatigue.

3. Develop your reading skills. If you read slowly and feel your lack of speed hinders you from getting the most out of the reading experience, don't give up hope. Millions of people have improved their reading speed by using a home-study book or course or enrolling in a speed-reading school. Reading is like any other skill and can be developed through practice. It is usually a question of finding an approach that works for you. Each speed-reading program is based on its own methods, so find one that feels comfortable and try it for a few months. Even a 10 percent improvement in your reading speed may be sufficient to help you get more out of the time you devote to reading.

Further Readings

How to Read a Book by Mortimer Adler and Charles Van Doren (New York: MFJ Books, 1972).

Levingers—Tools for the Serious Reader (catalog), 800/544-0880 or 407/276-4141.

Making the Most of Your Mind by Tony Buzan (New York: Linden Press, 1984).

Mastering the Information Age: A Course in Working Smarter, Thinking Better, and Learning Faster by Michael J. McCarthy (Los Angeles: Jeremy P. Tarcher, 1990).

PhotoReading Whole Mind System by Paul R. Scheele (Minneapolis: Learning Strategies Corporations, 1993).

Take up the Arts

Ask the average person to name a pursuit that requires creativity and he or she will likely think about painting or playing a musical instrument. In this chapter I will show that the arts and music can themselves be used as tools to fuel creativity in *any* endeavor, whether it's solving a business problem, developing a new idea for a product, or finding a way to be a better parent. (For clarity, when I use the term *art* in this chapter, I am referring to painting, drawing, filmmaking, pottery, and any other form of craft or visual expression. In addition, when I write "the arts," I am referring to art, music, theater, and dance.)

The power of the arts derives in part from their ability to take you out of your usual workaday world. They encourage you to think in a completely different way. The visual arts use images, shapes, colors, and space to convey a multitude of ideas in a compact space and short time. Music, especially music with lyrics, can arouse your sense of poetry and pace more than the speech patterns you hear from colleagues, friends, and family members.

However, the real power of the arts is that they speak directly and deeply to your creative soul. Your interaction with art and music rekindles emotions that you often leave untapped in your daily life. Art and music can be uplifting, thought provoking, amusing, annoying, heartwrenching, challenging, depressing, comforting, or surprising. The feelings that art or music produce can lead to creative breakthroughs in any area of your life.

Here's a fascinating example that demonstrates the power of art to spark creativity in business. Hal Rosenbluth, president of Rosenbluth Travel, once sent crayons to all his employees, asking them to draw pictures showing how they felt about where they worked. After receiving the artwork, he saw more powerfully than any memo might have conveyed some of his employees' negative feelings. This experiment inspired him to revamp his firm completely, and it has since become one of the nation's leading travel agencies.

In this chapter, I describe two ways you can benefit from the arts: by actively making or doing your own artwork and by observing other people's artistic creations.

Being Your Own Artist

Creating your own art or music is one of the most powerful tools you have to elicit your strongest creative feelings. You needn't attempt to be a professional artist, or even to produce something you can show to other people. The point is, by getting actively involved with one of the fine arts, you take a critical step toward living a creative life.

If you have not seriously tried your hand at the arts, or learned to play a musical instrument, consider the benefits they offer any type of creative work. The arts help you do the following:

• **Liberate yourself from "adult" constraints and return to your primal sense of fun.** Most artistic pursuits require you to abandon the rules of conduct that govern others areas of your life, such as order and tidiness. Some arts are messy, even chaotic. When you throw pots or work with oils, you get dirty, and everything around you may too. You end up abandoning decorum and giving in to your authentic creative impulses, however unlinear they may be. That allows you just to have fun with the process and stop worrying about things like how you look or what other people think. In other words, you get to act like a child again.

• **Learn to see things according to different perspectives.** When you create your own work, you see things differently. You realize that there are myriad ways to draw an object or play a piece of music—and that each person uses his or her choice of perspectives, colors, sizes, shapes, densities, and so on differently. Consider all the ways artists have portrayed the human body, or landscapes, or even bowls of fruit. When you step into the role of the artist, you meet endless possibilities for interpreting the world around you and learn which modes of expression have the most resonance for you.

• **Explore your fantasies, daydreams, and visions.** By doing your own art or music, you release your inner creative spirit. The colors, the sound, the feel of the material or instrument connect deeply with your soul. Art often arises from ideas and even bizarre images that come from your fantasies, daydreams, and visions.

• **Define your *own* style.** When you start painting, sculpting, or taking photographs, you realize that you're the one making the rules. If you want to sculpt a face with three noses or design a trapezoidal house, no one can stop you. As you experience the satisfactions of doing things your own way, you will gradually begin to reject convention and orthodoxy to find your own creative center. This center is what can guide your thinking in all your other endeavors.

• **Relax and eliminate stress.** Engaging in art or music can often be more relaxing than pursuits like reading or watching television. Through the process of making art, your mind clears itself of worries, and you surrender to the enjoyment of your work. Many famous entertainers—including Kirk Douglas, John Lennon, Anthony Quinn, Judy Collins, Tony Bennett, and Joni Mitchell—have painted for recreation as well as to inspire their creative thinking. Winston Churchill painted as a means of escaping the rigorous demands of his political work. Albert Einstein found diversion playing the violin. When he is not conducting high-level international diplomacy, former President Jimmy Carter writes poetry, and he recently began painting.

• **Clear away problems that interfere with your creativity.** Art often serves as a form of personal therapy, a way of working out vexing problems or dealing with strong emotions such as grief, anger, or confusion. In essence, you express your emotions through your art, and the ensuing release can lead to creative breakthroughs in your other work. Each artistic domain offers a different type of therapy. For example, you might find that playing the drums, or finger painting, or making a collage allows you to burn off anger, while weaving or pottery consoles you and sorts out confusion in your mind.

• **Acknowledge the importance of process, not product.** When you willfully engage in your own art, you permit yourself to do for the sake of doing, not to please others or to achieve a specific result. You become more process oriented, less goal oriented. Instead of drawing or playing music to create a beautiful picture or song, you learn to experiment, to test, and to rejoice in whatever you do. Your mind focuses on the actions, not the end result.

Sadly, many people avoid doing art because long ago they simply told themselves they couldn't. In most cases, their reluctance results from prior experiences in school, where attention is given to the output rather than to the creative experience itself. Most of us have had our artwork criticized, or have compared our own work with that of the greatest artists of all time and feel we could never do as well. But, as Julia Cameron says in *The Artist's Way,* "creativity lies not in the done but in the doing." And in the words of the professional artist and doodling teacher John Pearson, creativity "is not in the execution, but in the exploration."

My daughter Ashley had an unfortunate experience of how the educational system stifles our interest in doing art. As a second-grade student, she had to write a story about something that had happened in her life. She wrote about a recent vacation we had taken to Georgia, where she had seen some dolphins swimming directly off our beach. She also drew pictures of these beautiful creatures. When she took her "book" to the class assistant, the woman looked at her drawings and told her that they did not look like dolphins. She offered to show my daughter how to draw a dolphin the "right" way rather than accepting the creative output of a budding writer-illustrator.

If you've concluded from past experiences that you're not artistic, or you cringe at the thought of picking up a paintbrush or a musical instrument, you need to prevent that prejudgment from interfering with your natural desire to create in an artistic way. We are all born with curiosity and an inclination to do some kind of art with our hands, and you simply need to find one or more forms of artistic expression with which you are comfortable. The point is not to engage in an artistic pursuit to become a professional, or even to create something to sell or hang in your office. Instead, it is to immerse yourself in the *artistic process* so you can experience the joy and wonder that comes from creating with your hands. You do art for you.

Here is a three-step program to help you rediscover your natural artistic curiosity and joy.

Step 1. Doodling Your Way to Creativity

Doodling is a much maligned art form. But despite its tradition of using only simple, untrained lines, doodling is actually a wonderful technique to start releasing your inner critic and let your hands be free to draw. Doodling is like improvising in music; you just allow your natural feelings to flow into your fingers. You doodle in the moment, not knowing where you are going or what will appear. You follow the flow of one line, then another, without a preconceived notion about style, shape, image, or color.

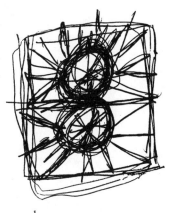

For years, I told people, "I'm not an artist. I don't even draw good stick people." Then, one day when I was attending an extremely dull computer symposium, I picked up my pen and absentmindedly began doodling. I had doodled on many occasions, but this experience was different. I began to draw my hand, and I just kept drawing a series of lines that crisscrossed every which way. I was elated by my doodle and suddenly realized how much I enjoyed drawing. It was the creative process itself, more than the end product, that excited me.

Doodling is a form of exploration that will help you begin your artistic pursuits. The next time you find yourself slowed to a creative standstill on any kind of problem, try the doodling exercises on the next page.

DOODLE MANIA

1. Get an eleven-by-seventeen-inch piece of white paper or newsprint and some colored pencils or markers. Sit down at your kitchen table or desk and find an object in the room that you would like to draw. Pick up a pen or pencil, put the tip on the paper, and begin drawing the object with a continuous line; don't raise your pen or pencil from the paper. Stay loose — do not attempt to draw the object accurately. When you are done, don't criticize your drawing but take pride in your artistry. Keep this doodle as a reminder of your natural creativity.

2. Doodle for five minutes each day to release stress. Your doodle can be anything — an object, word, or shape. Allow the images to begin in your hand and go to your head, rather than the other way around. Don't make doodling a form of work. Treat it as a doorway to creative ideas.

Step 2. Drawing the Right (Brained) Way

Many people who doubt the power of art and their own artistic abilities are often floored by what they accomplish using the drawing method developed by Betty Edwards. Before I introduce her breakthrough discoveries, a little bit of background is necessary.

One of the most important advances in the study of the brain occurred in the 1960s and 1970s when Roger Sperry of the California Institute of Technology led a team of researchers to a new understanding: that the human brain consists of two hemispheres, each of which controls different processes. Since Sperry's findings, for which he won a Nobel Prize in 1981, it has become widely accepted that the two sides of the brain have these distinctive areas of dominance:

LEFT	RIGHT
analytical	holistic
logical	intuitive
verbal	pictorial
sequential	simultaneous
temporal	spatial

In light of this research, the left side of the brain is often viewed as our logical, language- and math-oriented side, while the right side is seen as the seat of creativity and imagination. This division of labor between the hemispheres is clearly not cut and dried, but the two-sided model has served useful in understanding how our brain functions for different tasks.

This split-brain research has helped millions of people who never envisioned themselves as creative or artistic learn to draw. In what has become the best-known book on the subject, *Drawing on the Right Side of the Brain,* California State University Art Professor Betty Edwards presents a unique set of methods to teach drawing based on understanding how to shift into "right-brain" mode.

Recognizing that our left, logical brain interferes with our ability to relax and release our fingers to draw what we see, Edwards developed a variety of techniques, one of which she calls "*upside-down* drawing," in which you draw from an inverted image. According to her, inverting the image is necessary because our intransigent logical left brain gets stuck on recognizing and naming what it sees, so refuses or is unable to translate the information into the lines of a picture. To overcome the automatic interpretative power of our left brain, we must ignore the overall image and concentrate on the individual lines and shapes we see when the image is turned upside-down. As Edwards explains in her book:

> **Familiar things do not look the same when they are upside down. We automatically assign a top and sides to the things we perceive, and we expect to see things oriented in the usual way — that is, right side up. When an image is upside down, the visual clues don't match and the brain becomes confused. We see the shapes, and the areas of light and shadow. We don't particularly object to looking at upside-down pictures unless we are called to name the image. [Then] the task becomes exasperating.**

Whether or not you have had positive experiences with art, I recommend that you try your hand at the techniques detailed in

Drawing on the Right Side of the Brain to reinvigorate your natural artistic inclination. When I spoke with Betty Edwards in the course of writing this book, she was adamant about the value of doing art. She told me, "People cannot wait for art to happen to them. If they do, they will wait a lifetime." She also offered the following advice for anyone eager to discover the artist inside:

- **Don't fear risk.**
- **Persist.**
- **Practice.**
- **Have confidence that you will and can learn.**
- **Above all, keep your internal critic quiet.**

In my view, her advice applies to any creative endeavor.

UPSIDE-DOWN DRAWING
To do this exercise, forget everything you have ever learned about art. Take a sheet of paper and a pencil or pen and draw the picture on the facing page *without turning the picture right side up*. Do not be distracted by trying to right the image in your head; simply concentrate on drawing the lines as you see them. Take your time. Do not turn your sheet of paper or the image around until you are completely finished.

Step 3. Liberating Your Inner Artist

You are now ready to step further into art exploration. Begin to open your eyes to the world using your natural artistic interest. Let go of the end product you want; allow your creative spirit to dictate the direction you take, both in terms of which medium you use (pen and pencil, pastels, watercolor) and in regard to the colors, shapes, and style in which you work. Surrender to the process that arises from within you and be open to spontaneity. Finally, don't judge yourself or get frustrated with your results. Do it for you, not for the critic in you.

There is an ancient Chinese folktale that metaphorically describes the enormous power and magic of doing your own art. A poor young boy named Ma Liang grew up developing great

skill as an artist. He drew with twigs in the sand or with coal on flat rock. As much as Ma Liang longed to paint, he was so poor he couldn't afford a paintbrush.

One day an aged man rose out of the sea and gave Ma Liang a paintbrush. He told Ma Liang the brush was magic and would bring great joy and prosperity if it were used to help others. But it would bring disaster if he used it unwisely. At first, Ma Liang used his brush to paint animals. As soon as he put the last stroke on a bird, it magically came to life. Realizing the power of his brush, Ma Liang took it into the village with a roll of paper and painted things that would help his neighbors: a new fishing net for the fisherman whose net was full of holes, a plow for a farmer whose plow was broken, and rice seeds for a family whose food supply was diminished.

One day, an evil emperor learned of the boy with the magic brush; he ordered him to come to the palace, where he commanded Ma Liang to paint riches for him. The boy refused, telling the emperor that his brush was to be used only for good. The emperor had Ma Liang thrown in jail. Trying to use the paintbrush himself, the emperor painted so many gemstones that he almost drowned in them. Sensing the power of the brush, he asked Ma Liang to paint a peaceful scene and a tree of gold. The boy drew the tree on an island and then painted a boat so the emperor could travel to see the tree. Then the boy painted a gentle wind to carry both of them to the island.

The emperor became impatient and ordered the boy to get them to the tree faster. So Ma Liang painted a great storm. As the boat tossed about, the emperor implored Ma Liang to calm the winds, in exchange for which he would never make another request. The boy took his magic brush and painted out the entire scene, including himself. The Chinese say that the boy still wanders from place to place, helping those in need with his magic brush and the power of his art.

You too can have a magic paintbrush (pencil, pottery wheel, musical instrument, loom, whatever) with which to indulge your powers.

DO ART FOR YOU

Try these activities to stretch your artistic development. Select whichever one appeals to you first. Spend as much time on these projects as you like and repeat those you enjoy the most.

• PROJECT 1. REDISCOVER THE ARTISTIC FREEDOM YOU FELT AS A CHILD. Purchase a box of crayons or colored pencils. Put the box on your desk, table, or anywhere where you'll see it daily. Make a point of taking five minutes out of every day to open the box and draw something. If you let loose, you'll notice the emergence of a childlike creative freedom that carries over into the rest of your work. Some businesspeople I've worked with actually offer crayons and paper to people who come to their offices for meetings.

• PROJECT 2. STIR YOUR FEELINGS.
Buy children's finger paints or bold poster paints and some paper. Put on old clothes and, for an afternoon, give yourself license to dip into the paints and make the wildest designs you can imagine. Paint for the fun of it, for the intensity of the colors and patterns, for the emotions stirred in your heart and soul. What you paint and how it looks when you're finished does not matter.

A fun project is to paint about twenty-four letter-sized sheets of paper and then hang them side by side in a grid on the wall. You will be surprised at the beautiful collage you can put together.

When you're done, think about how the process made you feel. Was it stimulating? Relaxing? Can you turn this pleasure into a desire to explore doing some other type of artwork? Can you use this exercise again when you are stuck on a problem?

• PROJECT 3. EXPAND YOUR PERSPECTIVE.
This exercise helps you understand that there are many ways of seeing. Get a camera and take a dozen pictures of a familiar object, trying to make it look unfamiliar, funny, surprising, warped, taller than it is, shorter than it is, and other twists on how people normally see the object. Take your photos from different angles — below, close up, above, to one side, and so on. In each photo, create an emotional context or try to "make a statement." You will be surprised at how many creative ideas this assignment will engender.

• PROJECT 4. EXPLORE YOUR CREATIVE SOUL.
Make a collage to represent your creative soul. Select any items you want to express your innermost secrets and passions. Use natural objects or swatches of fabric as well as newspaper and magazine clippings of headlines and pictures. Glue them all to a large piece of heavy cardboard or posterboard. Any time you are feeling frustrated or blocked, use this collage to remind yourself of the beauty and power of your true creative spirit.

- **PROJECT 5. PAINT AWAY YOUR PROBLEMS.**

Pick a problem you have: conflict with your boss, stress from overwork, parenting issues, whatever. Get some watercolors or colored chalks and focus your feelings on painting or drawing your emotions about the situation. Take as much time as you need to express these feelings on paper, and use as many colors as you like to get the feelings out. You can the draw the people themselves, or shapes representing the problem, or whatever else helps you express the conflict.

Music of the Creative Spirit

Like art, the sound of music resides in our collective unconscious. From the moment of birth, we feel rhythm and sense melody. It's not surprising that nearly all primitive mythologies include tales about the power of music. In one Aztec myth that describes the beginning of creation, the people of the world were saddened because the great spirits had departed. Searching for the spirit of Tezcatlipoca, one man walked to the Eastern Ocean. There, Tezcatlipoca told the man to travel to the house of the sun and bring back singers and instruments so that people could make music in his memory. Tezcatlipoca arranged for the man to travel to the sun's house on a bridge created by a whale, a sea turtle, and a sea cow.

As the man was about to cross the bridge, the sun told the singers that a thief was coming. The sun counseled the singers that if the man called out to them, they were to ignore him. However, the man called out with a song so sweet that the singers could not resist following. Playing their instruments and singing their songs, they formed a parade behind him. From that point on, whenever people hold celebrations where they sing, dance, and play instruments honoring the spirits, the spirits descend from the sky to join in the music.

As this myth suggests, music brings spirits from afar to join in our creative expression and offer inspiration. Unfortunately, many people approach music in much the same way they approach art: hesitant, fearful, and overly critical of their own muse. These attitudes often begin in childhood, when music lessons focus not on enjoying making music but on learning the "right" way to play. Children unfortunate enough to be labeled musically inept are even sometimes discouraged from any participation or involvement in music. In worst-case scenarios, teachers advise children who can't carry a tune simply to mouth the words while children with more acceptable voices sing around them.

Like doodling and drawing, learning to play an instrument of any kind can boost your C.O.R.E. in many ways. Each instrument has a history and tradition that can arouse your curiosity. Each also has a character and emotional range that can speak powerfully to your deepest feelings. Some instruments are bold and brash, while others are soft or even melancholy. Practicing on an instrument can also be relaxing. And, as mentioned earlier, a variety of studies have indicated that playing or listening to certain types of classical music can even improve thinking skills. Understanding and seeing the relationships between notes in a composition appears to develop logical and mathematical abilities.

If you had a negative experience with music as a child, the impetus for moving beyond that experience rests with you. Exploring your dormant musical talent demands that you not only relish various types of music but also take up an instrument again. This time, however, do it according to your *own* rules. It's never too late. I started learning piano at age thirty-five, and I know several people who began violin and cello in their midlife years. Select your instrument, and find a self-guided music training program that emphasizes comfort with the music and the instrument, and personal enjoyment.

MUSIC FOR YOUR SOUL

Learning to play an instrument can take time. However, you can give yourself an accessible outlet by trying a simple instrument like a drum, tambourine, harmonica, electric keyboard, flute or recorder, bass guitar, or jaw harp, whose basics can be learned in as little as a few weeks. Even if you don't have time to practice much, you will enjoy the feeling of producing your own sounds, melody, and rhythms.

If you have more time, try an orchestral instrument like trumpet, clarinet, oboe, or violin, or an ethnic or folk instrument like a zither or bagpipe. Many instruments are available as rentals from music stores, and today many instruments such as keyboards are available for purchase in relatively inexpensive electronic forms.

Put a Museum in Your Head

Observing art inspires us to appreciate all aspects of life. From ancient Egyptian jewelry and Greek vases through medieval and Renaissance oil masterpieces to modern sculpture, the sheer number and variety of artistic pieces available for viewing at the world's fine museums are testimony to humankind's strong artistic spirit.

But observing art can also be a boon to your creative endeavors. First, art enhances your creative C.O.R.E., particularly your curiosity. Given the thousands of artists and the multiplicity of styles they've invented, you can spend a lifetime exploring the different periods and movements and still have more to learn. But above all, art teaches you to be open to myriad ways you can see the world. Consider how thousands of artists have looked at the same scenes or the human figure, yet have rendered them in countless distinctive ways. Every piece of art is a constant reminder that you can interpret life from many perspectives. This freedom of artistic expression is one reason we can feel so inspired or exhilarated after visiting a museum.

What is especially instructive in observing art is noticing how successive generations of artists reinterpret the prevailing traditions to create a new aesthetic. In the Western European tradition, for example, the Renaissance spawned several waves of masters, from Alberti and Bellini to Titian, da Vinci, and Michelangelo, who learned to use increasingly sophisticated linear perspective as well as rich colors and forms in their painting and sculpture. The Baroque period that followed broke many of these Renaissance traditions, with artists like Caravaggio in Italy and Rubens in Belgium emphasizing space, drama, and light. In the nineteenth century, however, the prevailing artistic aesthetic was again challenged and reconfigured, first by the movement we call Romanticism, which wanted above all to illustrate emotional intensity and a return to simplicity, and then by artists who sought to portray life in its true details, in the style we call Realism.

Since the mid-1800s, the pace of new artistic styles has accelerated wildly. Think of the steady stream of isms you have probably heard about or studied—Fauvism, Impressionism, Expressionism, Dadaism, Cubism, Surrealism, Futurism, Constructivism, Minimalism—all occurring in just 150 years. In our own time, American art has also undergone many revolutions, as artist after artist has created his or her own philosophy and vision, from the huge, energetic canvases of Jackson Pollock to the radical feminist sculptures of Judy Chicago and the avant-garde work of Christo, who wraps entire buildings and bridges in fabric.

This constant questioning of artistic principles and exploration of new media and methods can be truly inspirational for your own creativity. You can learn a great deal about creativity from any artist but especially from those who have burst barriers or intentionally challenged themselves—and us—to completely rethink art and life.

So, the next time you go to a museum or concert, don't simply accept what you see or hear. You will have a more creative experience if you bring all your faculties to the act of observing. Interact with what your senses take in; draw out of yourself as much as possible the feelings and thoughts the art inspires in you. When you stand in front of a painting or listen to a piece of music, for example, determine what emotions it arouses in you. Does it make you happy? sad? exuberant? annoyed? angry? surprised? Beyond your feelings, use the experience of viewing or listening to push your own creative ideas forward. Ask yourself the six journalistic questions—Who? What? Why? When? Where? and How?—to get thinking about what you see or hear. These questions will literally nourish your mind and stimulate you to seek out answers that may lead to a multitude of new connections applicable to your own creative work.

A story told by Tom Wujec in the book *Five Star Mind* illustrates a funny twist on the technique of active observation. Wujec recounts that when Rembrandt's famous painting *The Night Watch* was restored and returned to Amsterdam's Rijksmuseum, the curators devised a plan to attract greater attention to the masterpiece. They first asked a sampling of visitors to pose questions about the painting. Of the questions they received, some covered the usual territory that most people ask about: How much did the painting cost? Has anyone every tried to forge it? Did Rembrandt intentionally plant any mistakes in the painting? The curators also received questions focusing on deeper artistic issues such as, Why did Rembrandt choose to paint this subject? Are the identities of the people in the painting known? What techniques did Rembrandt invent while doing this work?

As you might guess, this viewing experience produced such dramatic results because the questions and answers encouraged

viewers to look beyond their own ideas and feelings about the work. The lesson of this story is that you need to view or listen to art actively—even if that means playing twenty questions with yourself. By taking an active role when you observe, you not only increase your enjoyment of the art but also draw out your feelings and ideas so you can tap them later in your own creative work. You never know where your observation can lead. Many great writers and artists got their inspiration from studying the masters of their fields. Creators in any business can find inspiration in observing art; one entrepreneur designed a line of umbrellas after viewing a special collection of Monet paintings.

MINI WORKSHOP

NINE ART OBSERVATION EXPERIENCES
Refresh your C.O.R.E. with a dose of art the next time you feel blocked or when you're seeking fresh insight into a problem.

1. **GO TO AN ART MUSEUM OR GALLERY.** Take a notebook with you. Spend some time looking at whatever type of art you feel drawn to on a gut level. Don't intellectualize about what you "should" see; simply head toward a room that speaks to your mood. Pick out a painting to study closely. Without thinking too deeply about your reactions, write down the following:

- What emotions the painting arouses
- What visual images come into your mind as you look at it
- Who or where it reminds you of
- Three ideas for stories you could tell based on the picture

2. **LISTEN MINDFULLY TO A PIECE OF MUSIC.** Select a cassette or CD from your own collection, or go to a music store and purchase something. Sit

down, relax, and listen to the music as attentively as you can, maybe with headphones to eliminate outside distractions. What feelings does the piece inspire in you? When was the last time you felt this way? Can you harness this feeling for a project you are working on?

3. LET ART CLARIFY YOUR VISION. If you are confused about a problem or you are trying to develop a vision for a project, spend a day viewing art or listening to music that helps you relax. You need to unclutter your mind and slow your body down so you can take in what you are seeing or hearing. Find art or music that helps you enter into a contemplative mode — moving quietly, reflecting on the paintings, photographs, ceramics, tapestries, or other art in front of you. By soothing you or filling you with pleasurable sensations, by altering your mood, art and music can put you into a frame of mind in which your natural creativity can flow more freely.

4. TRY TO APPRECIATE NEW ARTISTIC MODES. Visit a gallery that features art you instinctively feel you won't like. Ask the curator about the artwork; try to open your mind to learn why what you consider bad or disagreeable art is celebrated (and valued in monetary terms) by others. Be prepared to have your curiosity piqued and your beliefs challenged.

5. VISIT A CRAFTS STORE. Which craft attracts you most — pottery, quilting, woodwork, sewing, ceramics, stained glass, jewelry making? What does your intuitive connection to this craft tell you about yourself? Is there an item you see that inspires you?

6. STUDY A SPECIFIC STYLE OR SCHOOL OF THOUGHT IN MUSIC OR ART. Select a period in art or music history, such as Renaissance, Baroque, Romantic, Classical, or one of the modern isms. Read up on it to understand its basic concepts and philosophy. Then read up on the period immediately before or after that period, and try to understand what prompted the change in style. Was there a change in social beliefs? politics? aesthetics?

After your study, think about how the process of transition from one style to another might apply to your own work. Is your creative work suffering from a bias or belief that you ought to abandon? Should you make a transition to a new style? Can you look at your creative work in a different way than you have previously?

7. REFLECT ON HOW ART HAS SHAPED YOUR PERCEPTIONS. Have you ever seen a piece of art or heard a piece of music that completely changed the

way you think or feel? Many baby boomers feel that the lyrics of Paul Simon, Joni Mitchell, Bob Dylan, the Beatles, and the Grateful Dead changed their social and political views—and even their lives. Picasso's *Guernica* brought home the horror of the Spanish Civil War. When was the last time art changed your views?

8. **REGAIN YOUR PERSPECTIVE ON YOUR PROBLEMS BY VISITING AN EXHIBIT OF ANCIENT ART.** Remind yourself that your problems are taking place in a minuscule moment of time compared with the length of human existence. Take inspiration from seeing how humankind solved a problem thousands of years ago.

9. **EXAMINE ART THAT EMBODIES CULTURAL MYTHS.** Study Greek vases, Eskimo sculptures, American Indian pottery, or African masks. Learn about the myths it portrays and what they tell us about the resiliency and diversity of human nature. Is there a character in a myth with whom you identify? Can you make up a myth recounting your own creative struggle?

The inspiration and new perspectives you get from these experiences (and others like them that challenge your observational skills) can generate many ideas. You might return from one of these assignments with a plan to redesign your house, start a business, or write a poem to your lover. Tapping into your emotions or challenging your artistic prejudices might give you an insight into a problem you were hoping to solve. Use these activities over and over again. Do them once alone and then invite a friend to share reactions and ideas.

Own Your Own Museum

You might also collect art that especially pleases or satisfies you. Many people fill their offices and homes with beautiful or thought-provoking objets d'art—paintings, vases, wall hangings, or whatever. They find that art that is interesting, colorful, lively, funky, or culturally unique recharges their creative batteries. Even if you can't afford to collect pre-Columbian pottery or fine paintings, you *can* collect art. Every museum has a gift shop selling inexpensive posters and reproductions of art that you can place on your desktop.

Many art institutes hold exhibits of their students' work, which is often available for purchase, and many talented watercolorists, fiber artists, potters, and other artisans sell their work very reasonably at craft fairs and flea markets. Used bookstores often yield a treasure trove of books with fine engravings or plates that can be framed, and even postcards of subjects that intrigue, elate, amuse, or inspire you can be displayed as "art." If you would like to own an original artwork but cannot find a sculpture or painting you respond to in your price range, consider investing in photography, a still affordable but increasingly hot area for art collectors.

And of course music is readily available: Attend student recitals at local music colleges. Subscribe to a concert series. Invite a local musician to play at your next party. Tape live performances from radio (or simulcasts on PBS). Go to free open-air concerts. Go dancing at a country-and-western bar.

Observing and appreciating art is easy, whether your income approaches that of the likes of J. Paul Getty or that of a former postal worker and his wife who, over several decades, acquired a world-class collection of paintings, fiber arts, and sculpture that they donated to the National Gallery of Art in Washington, D.C.

Ars Gratias Artis

The famous movie opening for the film studio MGM has a roaring lion, beneath which is inscribed "Ars gratias artis"—art for art's sake. This endorsement applies to every creative endeavor. Think of it this way: art for art's sake means "make art your creative force." Whether you decide to become involved with dance, opera, photography, glassblowing, performance art, or any other type of artistic expression, art offers you the opportunity to move beyond your existing knowledge base and explore new feelings, images, and ideas. Any time spent in appreciation of art—whether as an observer or as a participant—will pay off by making you feel more alive, and ultimately creative.

Further Readings

The Artist's Way: A Spiritual Path to Higher Creativity by Julia Cameron (Los Angeles: Jeremy P. Tarcher, 1992).

The Customer Comes Second: And Other Secrets of Exceptional Service by Hal Rosenbluth and Diane McFerrin Peters (New York: William Morrow, 1992).

Drawing on the Right Side of the Brain: A Course in Enhancing Creativity and Artistic Confidence by Betty Edwards (Los Angeles: Jeremy P. Tarcher, 1979).

Free Play: Improvisation in Life and Art by Stephen Nachmanovitch (Los Angeles: Jeremy P. Tarcher, 1990).

Freeing the Creative Spirit: Drawing on the Power of Art to Tap the Magic and Wisdom Within by Adrianan Diaz (San Francisco: HarperSanFrancisco, 1992).

The Inner Game of Music by Barry Green (New York: Doubleday, Anchor Press, 1986).

On Not Being Able to Paint by Joanna Field (Los Angeles: Jeremy P. Tarcher, 1983).

Wild Heart Dancing: A Personal, One Day Quest to Liberate the Artist and Lover Within by Elliot Sobel (New York: Fireside Books, 1994).

Writing Down the Bones: Freeing the Writer Within by Natalie Goldberg (Boston: Shambhala, 1986).

Writing on Both Sides of the Brain: Breakthrough Techniques for People Who Write by Anne Henriette Klauser (San Francisco: HarperSanFrancisco, 1987).

Plug into Technology

Technology is another word for "tool." There was a time when nails were high-tech. — TOM CLANCY

There is an old story of a monk and a winepress that exemplifies how some people fail to recognize the constant technological improvements arriving into the world. An old Italian monk had a reputation for making wine using the time-honored practice of stomping on grapes with his feet. A wealthy man enjoyed the wine so much that he gave the monk one of the first winepresses available. But when the man visited the monk a few weeks later, he was surprised to observe the monk stomping grapes with his feet. "Why do you continue to stomp the grapes instead of using the new press?" asked the wealthy man. The monk replied that he enjoyed using the new winepress, but it added heavily to his workload. "Why do I need to use a press to crush the grapes after I've already done such a good job stomping them?" he asked with a dumbfounded look.

The message of this tale is simple: If you don't keep up with today's technological revolution, you may completely misunderstand the benefits it offers. So stop stomping grapes and learn to use technology as your newest creativity enhancer.

This chapter examines two ways technology serves your creativity.

• **Technology as a facilitator of the creative process in every field.** Thanks to the personal computer, the very shape of work is changing for many of us. From word processing and databases to idea-generation programs and on-line resources like the Internet, every aspect of creativity has been affected by computers and successive generations of powerful and sophisticated software.

• **Technology itself as a form of creative expression.** Many artists don't think of technology as a creativity tool for them because it

AMAZING BRAIN TOOLS

Idea-generation software is based on a variety of methods discovered by creativity researchers to stimulate new ideas. Here are a few of the best known:

➤ **IdeaFisher.** IdeaFisher was invented by Marsh Fisher, founder of Century 21 Real Estate and a man of many creative interests. This program is another example of how "fun and play" can be a creativity tool because it is an outgrowth of Fisher's passion for humor. He was fascinated by why some people write better jokes than others. The answer, he learned, lies in *associative thinking,* the ability to make word and situation associations from one context to another. IdeaFisher assists creativity by facilitating this kind of thinking, helping you form connections between ideas and execute mental leaps. It is used widely by creative types like writers and comedians, but can also be used to generate ideas appropriate to just about any business or personal situation.

➤ **Mindlink.** This program is like a playground for the mind, featuring a variety of ways to approach issues and be creative. The software encourages you to view problems from many perspectives. Its underlying assumption is that because you don't know in advance what you'll need to know to solve a problem, your goal is to generate as many fresh ideas as you can. To accomplish this, the software provides a variety of triggers to help you form associations among ideas and get into "divergent" thinking outside your comfort zone.

You might be asked, for example, to bring an interesting object back to your desk, where it triggers images, phrases, sounds, or feelings. Or you may be asked to pretend you are someone else, like a fighter pilot, while you write about what you see and hear. Such bizarre antics are aimed at loosening the kind of self-censorship that limits creative thinking. The program then "reconverges" your ideas onto the original problem. Mindlink is lots of fun to use, and it offers a specialized module called the Mind Gym that works to unfetter your thought processes in several ways.

➤ **Inspiration.** This software is a combined "idea collecting," mindmapping, and "electronic outliner" tool. It helps you develop and organize your ideas in several ways. Inspiration takes the basic concept of outlining and combines it with the technique known as mindmapping (explained in detail in the next chapter) to capture information quickly and display it visually through symbols. This is an excellent tool to facilitate group thinking.

doesn't have the reassuring feel of a paintbrush, a sculpting knife, or any of the other tools they typically associate with the creative arts. However, while a computer may not give you the same warm, fuzzy feeling as an easel or a loom, today's technology is creating whole new industries for creative people.

If you already own a computer and are fairly computer literate, you will immediately understand the ideas presented in this chapter. If you are not yet comfortable using a computer—and even if you don't know hardware from software—you can still benefit from reading this chapter and taking its suggestions to heart.

NOTE: The bulk of this chapter focuses on personal computers, software, and peripherals because these are the most prevalent technologies available to the average person in the home or workplace.

Technology as Facilitator: Touching Every Creative Process

Computers are revolutionary in the way they increase the speed of many tasks and the sophistication of the work you produce. (For a good picture of how far technology has advanced in less than fifty years, consider the fact that the novelty birthday cards offered today that allow you to record a humorous message and cost just a few dollars contain more computing power than existed on the entire planet before 1950.)

Think about the simple act of writing. If this book had been written a mere fifteen years ago, I would have had to handwrite my ideas and thoughts into a notebook, then pound out several drafts on an IBM Selectric, physically cutting and pasting sections together and making the revisions requested by my editor by retyping most of the manuscript. Needless to say, computer word processing has radically simplified this lengthy and tedious process.

But word processing is just the tip of the creativity-facilitating technology iceberg. Several types of software and on-line options enhance creativity regardless of your profession. The following sections discuss these subjects:

- **Idea-generation programs**
- **Information managers**

- **On-line resources**
- **Digital reference resources**
- **Groupware and Intranets**

FEED YOUR HEAD WITH IDEA GENERATORS

Purchase one of the idea-generation programs mentioned if you do not already have access to one. Then give yourself an assignment to invent a new product, write a poem, resolve a business dilemma for your company, or solve whatever problem has plagued you in the past. Use your software to try to bust out of the blocks you may have in thinking or writing. After a few tries, you will undoubtedly be surprised at how much you have learned about your thinking process as well as the possible ideas or solutions the software has helped you develop.

Information Managers

Information managers (IM's) are based on database programs. A database is essentially like the pigeonholed filing boxes used in offices years ago. Just as you sort items into different pigeonholes, databases store information in their electronic equivalent. The power of the software is that it can search through millions of these boxes and retrieve any data you want within seconds.

Information managers can help anyone who needs to collect—or who enjoys collecting—information. Prompted by the flood of data the average person in our society deals with and the fallibility of our memories, information managers represent a powerful innovation that facilitates many types of information-intensive work. Whether you are a writer, researcher, manager, or sales representative, if you use or have a need to store thousands of ideas, quotations, facts, statistics, or articles, you will find an information manager an extremely valuable tool.

Information managers have two amazing features: the ability to store data from many disparate sources and the ability to do many types of sophisticated and complex searches of that data. Most IM's can use Boolean logical terms like *and*, *or*, and *not*, which multiply your power enormously when you need to search

 and find many related items or to pick out one item from among thousands. For example, the information manager I use, InfoSelect, stores thousands of famous quotations and the text of articles that I collect on subjects of interest to me. I either type in the information or scan it in. Then, whenever I am consulting with a company or giving a seminar and need to locate a specific quotation or a fact to spruce up my presentation, I can type in one or more keywords for what I need. For example, if I am giving a speech on creativity, I can tell the software to search all the records I've entered containing the words *Einstein* or *Jung* and *imagination*. Within a second, the program produces a list of quotations, such as the following:

- **"Imagination is more important than knowledge." — Einstein**
- **"To raise new questions, new possibilities, to regard old problems from a new angle, requires creative imagination and marks real advance in science." — Einstein**
- **"The debt we owe to the play of imagination is incalculable." — Jung**

Using an information manager can substantially enhance many creative endeavors that benefit from having a storehouse of facts and data available, such as writing, public speaking, researching, and so on. Rather than letting the tidbits of knowledge you encounter over the years lie fallow, this type of software lets you build a powerful personal knowledge bank that you can access whenever you need it.

In the future, information managers along with high-speed scanners and advanced storage options such as "writeable" CD-ROM's (large-volume disks on which you can store data) will allow you to keep virtually any and all documents that pass through your hands. Imagine the power of being able to track and recall information from every "project" you've ever done—from your high school papers through your master's degree thesis to the memos you produce at work. The historical value of this type of archived information is significant. Consider what might have occurred if some of history's great creative thinkers had had access to this type of technology. What might we have been able to glean from the electronic notebooks of Einstein, Edison, or da Vinci?

Digital Reference Resources

Digital reference resources is a term I use for an assortment of sources that can have an enormous impact on your creativity because they give you access to huge amounts of data stored around the globe. They are relatively inexpensive to use, and with a PC, a telephone connection, and a simple software communications program, you can reach an amazing array of resources twenty-four hours a day. Digital reference resources can be subdivided into (1) commercial on-line services, the World Wide Web, and (2) CD-ROM multimedia. The following clarifies the difference between on-line services, and the World Wide Web.

• **Commercial on-line services.** These include companies like CompuServe, America Online, Prodigy, and a variety of privately owned bulletin boards that may be run by small organizations or even home-based individuals who have the computer equipment to let other people dial into their facilities.

• **World Wide Web.** The World Wide Web is a part of the Internet that is a vast collection of information pages called web pages. A  home page is like the table of contents page in a book; it shows a small amount of information and sometimes graphics describing the topics contained inside. When you want to turn to one of the subjects listed, you don't need to shuffle through pages to find a piece of information; hypertext links, which you activate by clicking on one of the underlined or colored words or pictures on the home page with a mouse, immediately transport you to another page or group of pages that contain more information.

If you belong to a commercial on-line service you can now access the Internet, through which you can communicate with anyone on any other on-line service. This effectively means all subscribers to any on-line service in the world are connected to one another.

These information resources allow you to research anything and everything in the world as well as hook you into communication with literally millions of other people with whom you can share your ideas or who you can ask for advice. You can send electronic mail as well as documents and files to millions of people with a single click of your mouse. These resources also give you access to thousands of databases from which you can download a summary or the full text of articles, along with pictures and sometimes audio and video clips. For example, you can tap into magazine databases containing thousands of magazines and journals that offer hundreds of thousands of articles in many professional fields.

You can also go to one of the commercial services and join any of hundreds of "forums," (CompuServe users should "GO CREATE") which are like clubs that maintain libraries of information for research and "chat rooms" where you can converse "live" with other people by typing messages to one another while on-line. There are forums for every interest, such as one for people who work from home or run a small business, another for people interested in flying, and one for people who love to travel, as well as forums for trading information and encouragement with others involved in a variety of creative pursuits, like crafting, writing, and so on.

As the Web grows, the role of on-line services is likely to change dramatically to allow you to navigate (or "surf") the Web. This is because no matter how many forums the on-line services offer, they will never be able to match the depth and breadth of information on the World Wide Web. The Web allows millions of companies and individuals to publish their own pages, displaying whatever information they want. What makes the Web so powerful is the characteristic called hypertext, by which a home page can link up to another party's home page anywhere in the world. Thus the number of connections you might make in a single sitting is enormous. This is what is meant when people talk about "surfing" the Net: They go from one home page to another, stopping at whatever information intrigues them and hooking into whatever hypertext links catch their eyes.

For example, let's say you wanted to learn about adventure travel. You might begin your search by looking up home pages sponsored by popular travel agencies. In addition to their home pages, though, many companies have sets of backup pages containing more information. In this case, you might find one travel company that has a group of pages about trips down the Amazon or mountain hikes through Asia. While reading one of those pages, it is also likely that you will click on a hypertext word that sends you off to another group of pages, such as the home page for a hotel in Thailand or one for a tourist agency that specializes in bicycling trips, or even one for a museum in Bangkok. In the end, your cyberspace journey may have taken you around the world, jumping from one home page to another in an instant. This is the creative power of the Internet.

Furthermore, what makes the Web extremely exciting is that it is digital, so updating is easy and ongoing. New pages are added each day, and the owners of these pages are continually adding new links. Even if you access a particular home page every day, you may find new hypertext links that will take you to locations you've never seen before.

Another significant feature of the Web is that anyone can build a home page. The Web is thus a place for everyone to exercise personal creativity. You simply need to learn how to design your page and have something of interest to offer other Web browsers. You also need to own or lease space on a special computer "server" that can handle the electronic communications aspect of having other people "hit" your home page with their requests to read it. But both these requirements are relatively trivial and easy to set up.

The Internet also includes a wide range of electronic bulletin boards called newsgroups, on which people leave messages and ideas for anyone to read. Like the forums on the on-line services, there are newsgroups for nearly every interest and hobby, from professional newsgroups for doctors and lawyers to personal newsgroups for those wanting to discuss the latest episode of must-see TV. Most newsgroups also have files called Frequently Asked Questions (usually abbreviated FAQs). You can browse through these questions and discover what other participants already know. You'll find that members of most newsgroups and forums are eager to answer questions or participate in discussions designed to help you be more creative. At this time there is at least one newsgroup that is dedicated to creativity, called *misc.creativity*. There are also many covering aspects of creativity—the arts, painting, music, travel, etc. However, like everything on the Internet, this could change, so check out the Aha! home page once you get on-line to receive updates on newsgroups.

At this time, the on-line universe is becoming the most exciting and creative frontier in computing. With access to the information contained in thousands of museums, companies, government centers, and academic institutions throughout the world, plus the ability to send E-mail and chat live with people at all four corners of the earth, being on-line is a creative adventure of tremendous power. Whether you are seeking the solution to your business problems, scoping out a location for your next novel, or researching wine making or pottery, you will find inspiration and answers by hooking into the on-line universe.

AN INVITATION TO THE INTERNET

If you have not yet tried an on-line service or the Internet, it's time to overcome your reluctance. You can log onto services like CompuServe and America Online for a trial period very easily. Both services have a variety of trial offers, including free hours of service to test out their forums and chat groups. Both also offer free Web browsers and access to the Internet. To get the free software that allows you to do this, contact CompuServe at 800-848-8199 and America Online at 800-827-3338.

Alternatively, you can get access directly to the Internet through an Internet service provider (ISP) in your area. You can find an ISP by looking in the free computer magazines often distributed through your local bookstores and software stores or in nationally published computer magazines. Most ISP's charge a low, flat fee per month for unlimited Internet time. You may need to purchase a Web browser software package, such as Netscape or Microsoft Explorer, but some providers give you a copy when you sign on with them.

However you can access the Internet, I invite you to make your first stop at the Web site I have established for this book. I set this site up specifically to help readers learn about creativity on the Web. You can reach the Aha! Web site by typing:

> http://www.create-it.com

You will immediately be transported to my home page, where I will provide specific directions for readers of this book. I also invite you to send me E-mail with your feedback regarding the strategies you're reading about or other ideas related to the topic of creativity.

Groupware and Intranets

Groupware is another example of technology that is radically altering the business world. Groupware allows computer users connected through a network to work together on projects and share ideas. LotusNotes, pioneered by Lotus Development, is probably the best-known of these packages. The concept allows a manager in Kansas City and an engineer in Boise to access the same information and communicate with each other. The manager can share the information developed by the engineer, and vice versa, giving them a common frame of reference.

If an organization's groupware is effective, there's no excuse for project participants to claim ignorance, absence, or exclusion from meetings and conversations. In fact, management experts believe that groupware will allow organizations to maximize their knowledge, increase productivity, and reduce conflicts. The premise behind groupware is that it encourages open communication and destroys personal fiefdoms built through secrecy and hidden agendas.

More and more companies are expected to find groupware an exciting option, and it will become easier and cheaper to use because of the development of intranets—internal versions of the World Wide Web on which companies can establish informational pages for employees to browse and use.

Software Reference Tools

This type of reference product comprises information resources stored on CD-ROM, such as Microsoft's Encarta and Compton's Interactive Encyclopedia, as well as a wide assortment of specialized databases in finance, business, and other areas. The amount of information stored on a single CD-ROM disk is enormous— every phone book in the United States can be stored on two disks. And many of the items are accompanied by photos, video clips, or audio clips, which increase the enjoyment and poignancy of your learning.

For example, let's say you wanted to explore Renaissance art; when you type in those two keywords, Microsoft's Encarta delivers nearly three hundred entries you can read, including complete entries on the period's most noted artists and photos of dozens of famous Renaissance paintings. Similarly, if you were eager to learn about jazz, typing in that keyword delivers more than 125 entries, including hundreds of short excerpts from a wide range of pieces that you can listen to on your computer. This technology gives free rein to your sense of wonder and curiosity while satisfying them immediately!

Technology and the Underground Revolution

In certain fields, such as publishing, music, and film and video, technology has had a significant impact on production processes, enlarging the creative potential for everyone involved. Most important, however, the advances of technology have opened up these professions in a truly unexpected way: by empowering anyone and everyone to participate in them. In other words, computers have effectively "democratized" these fields, so that anyone with a home computer and an idea can be an active producer, not just a consumer, of ideas and information.

Publishing

While the old days of publishing required an army to produce a document, today's technology makes it possible for one individual to publish single-handedly and influence millions of people. Anyone with something to say, a PC, and a printer can publish a document. Thousands of poets, writers, screenwriters, and many other word artists can now disseminate their own works, or even start their own publishing companies. With the World Wide Web, they can get their information to the desktops of millions of people.

Today's sophisticated desktop publishing software packages, like Aldus PageMaker and Quark, provide an amazing assortment of powerful features, including the following:

- **Ability to generate any kind of document, from one-page fliers to 500-page books or even color mail-order catalogs**
- **Access to thousands of typefaces so anyone can design a document as elegantly or smartly as any major publishing or design house**
- **Ability to bring in (import) illustrations from thousands of inexpensive and commercially available collections of artwork and photographs on disk and CD-ROM**
- **Ability to "separate" color photos and artwork into the four layers of film needed for color printing**
- **Ability to lay out text automatically in any number of columns and to make every page look different**

GET PUBLISHED

To learn something new and get your creative juices going, try designing and producing a simple newsletter using a desktop publishing program like Microsoft Publisher or Aldus PageMaker. If you do not have access to one of these programs, either buy an inexpensive version or rent time at a computer or copy shop like Kinko's or a library that leases computers by the hour. Some libraries also have computers for general use.

Your newsletter can cover any topic you wish: news about your family, your business, or a favorite hobby. Spend a few hours writing articles, selecting typefaces, and scanning in artwork appropriate to your newsletter if possible. By the end of this exercise, you will be amazed at how professional looking your product is, regardless of your background, thanks to the power of today's desktop publishing software.

New publishing hardware is also aiding the transformation of the profession. New printers allow you to print small quantities of material of a quality that is nearly indistinguishable from professional printing, even in color. Scanners let you add photos, artwork, newspaper clippings, or anything that can be copied to your documents.

The recent proliferation of privately published newsletters is an example of how the written word has spread. An estimated 1.5 million newsletters are now published in North America, according to the Newsletter Publishers Association. Many of these are produced by home-based individuals or small studios, and report news of interest to clubs, associations, and hobby groups.

Graphic Arts

The entire graphic arts field has also benefited from recent innovations that have expanded creative potential. The most significant advance is a generation of highly sophisticated software that allows anyone with an interest in art to use the computer screen as an electronic canvas or camera. Programs like CorelDRAW, Aldus FreeHand, Kai's Powertools, and PhotoShop are loaded with features that artists of yesteryear could never have even imagined. With a few simple clicks, even an untrained user can draw any shape he or she wants, merge in predrawn objects and artwork from others, adjust the colors and hues with precision, move objects, flip or rotate objects to any angle, enlarge proportions, create shadows or duped images, and employ dozens of other mind-boggling possibilities.

In fact, one program makes the point that today's software is the artistic tool of choice. Painter is packaged in a one-gallon paint can—as if to drive home the idea that the software is your paint and your paintbrush, while your computer is your canvas. Developed by musician Mark Zimmer, Painter has become one of the hottest artistic programs on the market, winning many awards. Zimmer's product provides a way to create works of art using *virtual* media on a *virtual* canvas rather than real media on a real canvas. With Painter, you simulate drawing with crayon or painting with oil right on your computer screen. You can even get realistic watercolor effects that change just like the real thing when you spritz your painting with *virtual* water. Painter also offers chalk, pastels, even Magic Markers to produce computer art so close to the real thing that only the artist knows for sure. You can also use Painter to alter existing images. For example, by scanning in a photograph and using the cloning technique, you can modify the photo so that it appears to have been painted in the style of a great master. Imagine your family portrait as done by Rubens, Renoir, or van Gogh for example. (Painter also has a little brother called Dabbler, which costs less and has fewer features.)

Whether you are a professional artist, a dabbler, or a businessperson who needs to use graphics in your work, it's time to take advantage of the incredible possibilities opened up by the tools of high-technology art. Whatever your training or background, you will be amazed at what you can accomplish after even a few hours with these innovative new programs.

Music

The field of music has also been revolutionized by computers and specialized high-technology recording equipment. As in publishing and graphic arts, the advances in music technology are neither minor nor optional; they have completely altered the landscape of how people create music, how it is recorded, and even how the rest of us listen to it.

It began a few decades ago with Moog synthesizers, machines that simulated the sounds of orchestral instruments using computer-controlled electric impulses. Today, those relatively simple synthesizers have given way to a vast assortment of artificial music machines that have the capability not only to imitate any and every instrument ever made but also to produce sounds never before heard. And what's more, the cost of such equipment has come down so far that even a child can own an electronic keyboard that synthesizes several dozen orchestral instruments while producing a few hundred background rhythms, from bossa nova to bebop, at any speed and pitch desired.

The fact is, technology is completely revamping how professionals and amateurs alike make music, expanding not only the ease of their work but also the range of creative expression available to them. If you have any doubt about how technology has changed the music business, consider these creative innovations:

- **Even if you do not have a music background, you can compose your own music and have it automatically transcribed using a computer and specialized scoring software.**
- **For less than $5,000, you can set up a professional recording studio in your home or garage with enough power to mix up to thirty-two tracks of sound and cut quality demos that might get you a professional recording contract.**
- **Many popular music groups, like Mannheim Steamroller, use nothing but electronic instruments that synthesize the sounds of their music.**

The creative implications of such advances are enormous. First, technology has created more opportunities for new musicians and composers than ever before. The proof of this is evident in any large music store; recordings are released every day by artists who, a few years ago, would never had had the opportunity to get their work before the public. Similarly, there are dozens of new recording studios, and some of them strike it rich with songs that hit the charts and garner the neophyte artist and producer a recording contract from a major studio.

Film and Video Production

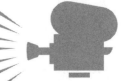

Technology is also completely modifying the film and video industries with an array of new creative techniques and equipment. In addition to new hardware like small digital video cameras, with greater sophistication and sensitive new sound recording equipment, the most important revolution comes from computers like the Macintosh and the Amiga "video toaster," along with specialized software that allows film or video images to be viewed and edited on a computer monitor.

Today's filmmakers can edit film or video footage entirely on computer. In the process, they can add millions of special effects. By freezing each frame on the monitor, the filmmaker can modify the image by adding or subtracting color, removing a character, adjusting a costume, or even superimposing one piece of footage on another. In fact, the 1994 Academy Award winner *Forrest Gump* was made using many of these tricks, and the 1995 hit *Toy Story* was created entirely by computer—in about half the time and at a third the cost of conventional animation techniques.

Naturally, the use of computers to create films and videos is not restricted to powerful celebrities and big studios in Hollywood. The recent explosion of so-called low-res films shows that anyone who has a video camcorder, a computer, and an idea can be a filmmaker. While Hollywood still takes months to shoot and edit a film that ultimately costs from $20 to $100 million, dozens of new filmmakers are breaking into the business because they can shoot and produce their films in a matter of weeks or even days and air them over the Internet or at local art galleries and film festivals. In fact, the production of low-res films became so popular in 1995 that a new low-res film festival began touring the country.

Many related businesses have also changed because of the technological advances in film and video production. Advertising agencies, management training companies, and industrial film companies all commonly write and produce films or videos for their clients. In these businesses, too, technology has expanded the limits of creativity, giving advertising executives and educational or training consultants many new tools with which to produce their products.

Business and Personal Affairs

The arts are not the only fields to have been touched by technology. Many of the basic processes of the business world and even our day-to-day personal lives have been revolutionized by new technology that has expanded the ways we think, create, and perform.

Personal digital assistants (PDAs) such as Apple Computer's Newton or Sharp's Wizard are other examples of technology altering our creative potential. Although PDA's have not yet reached the level of popularity that their originators had hoped for, it is conceivable that within a few years these portable electronic tablets will be the vanguard of the personal information revolution, allowing us to track our business schedules and personal affairs with tremendous ease, as well as to communicate with anyone else on the planet from wherever we are.

Apple's Newton is an early example of PDA technology. The Newton lets you use a penlike stylus to write on an electronic tablet. It then translates the handwriting into a file that can be edited and printed just like any word-processing file. As an experiment, I actually wrote this section of the book on a Newton, using its text recognition feature to convert my scrawls to text. Despite a few mismatches on the recognition side, the unit did the job, and it provided some great opportunities to capture my ideas on the run. With time, the technology of the Newton and other machines like it will improve, and in all likelihood PDA's will soon be able to recognize and respond to voice commands. As their costs come down and their sophistication rises, PDA's will enable the average consumer to write down ideas as spontaneously as they come, or even research a topic from anywhere in the world using satellite technology hooked into the Internet.

Combining PDA's with a new generation of what are called smart agents—software programs that can be *trained* based on your personal preferences and needs—will soon make technology an even more indispensable tool for the creative person.

- presort your electronic mail and organize it by priority based on the agent's knowledge of your current interests and information needs;

- **keep an eye on your investments and alert you to critical changes in your portfolio;**
- **search on-line for key information on a continuous basis and let you know when something of interest becomes available.**

PDA technology is still in its infancy, but smart agents will eventually improve the way we process and collect information in our work and personal lives and reduce or eliminate information pain. In the information age, finding the information you need is often a daunting task that interferes with your ability to be creative or access the information needed to achieve your goals.

Video conferencing is yet another example of new technology that has radically altered the ability to be creative in the workplace. Like the fax machine, video conferencing gives people the opportunity to communicate with others at remote locations, especially when it is important to share visual information. With advances in video technology and lowered costs, it is even possible to participate in videoconferencing right from your office or home using a personal computer equipped with a small optical lens.

Technology as a New Form of Creative Expression

So far in this chapter, we have seen how technology is a creative facilitator for many endeavors, and also how it has been a radical agent of change in many fields. But there is a third way that technology has played a role in expanding our creative potential. It has given rise to a new type of creative expression: multimedia.

As the name suggests, multimedia integrates the characteristics and talents of several media, including but not limited to writing, graphics, music, photography, film, video, animation, and painting. Just as the invention of the movie camera by the Lumière Brothers and Thomas Edison introduced an entirely new artistic genre that sparked the creative genius of such masters as Charlie Chaplin, Orson Welles, François Truffaut, and Steven Spielberg, today multimedia is spawning a generation of artists who are driven to break new ground in their creative work. Because of the nature of multimedia, artists may work in teams to take advantage of a variety of talents. The market for multimedia has mushroomed to the point where many of the most prestigious entertainment companies and film studios, such as Paramount, Disney, LucasArt, and DreamWorks, have spun off divisions devoted solely to developing multimedia projects.

Multimedia products commonly take the form of either a CD-ROM game, game cartridge, or edutainment disk, as well as a page on the World Wide Web. These programs are completely transforming the definition of entertainment. Coupling high-action stories with computer-generated 3-D graphics, music, old movie clips, still photos, and whatever else the developers can think of, these disks push creativity to new levels. Their most innovative feature is the ability to be interactive, that is, to let the user have a choice in how the game works, which characters appear, or even how the story ends.

Furthermore, multimedia is quickly evolving. Just in the past few years, additional developments in hardware and software have allowed producers and artists to begin creating a more advanced and creative form of edutainment that holds tremendous excitement and promise: virtual reality. Virtual reality technology aims to offer the most complete multimedia experience—making you feel as if you were really there. The applications of virtual reality will be enormous, such as teaching medical students to perform surgery, helping student drivers learn to drive safely, and giving thrill seekers the scare of their lives through lifelike interactive horror movies.

In terms of creativity, virtual reality will have several implications. First, the genre will be the preferred choice for many new forms of entertainment, education, and relaxation for people of all ages. Virtual reality machines will supersede the game machines now filling video arcades. More important, the development of both the hardware and the software from virtual reality will open up thousands of jobs for creative people. Many companies are already preparing to be leaders in what might be called techno-tainment (edutainment created by technology), by hiring writers, graphic artists, programmers, and hardware gurus of all kinds. In this sense, the role of technology in spurring creativity is quite clear: technological creativity = a job.

Technology — You Gotta Love It!

There is little doubt that technology plays a major role in most creative ventures today. Computers and software are already taking over the way people write, invent, decide, experiment, and learn. Artists of all kinds are also increasingly turning to technology to help them discover new ways to express their thoughts and to entertain and enlighten audiences.

The exciting part is, technology is never static. *The Wall Street Journal* has reported on microchips with the ability to "smell." While recent technology might sound far-fetched, consider its impact on such processes as making wine and mixing perfume. Your goal is to tune into technology and allow yourself to be turned on by its continually evolving magic and power.

Think of it this way: With major technological improvements in personal computer hardware occurring about every two years, and a constant stream of new software, if you don't incorporate technology into your creative work, you will find yourself living in a modern version of the "dark ages" before you know it!

Further Readings

Being Digital by Nicholas Negroponte (New York: Alfred A. Knopf, 1995).

Cyberarts—Exploring Art & Technology (San Francisco: Miller Freeman, 1992).

The Road Ahead by Bill Gates (New York: Viking Press, 1995).

Technotrends: How to Use Technology to Go Beyond Your Competition by Daniel Burrus (New York: HarperBusiness, 1993).

PowerThink Your Challenges

Many people would sooner die than think. In fact, they do. —BERTRAND RUSSELL

Few people think more than two or three times a year; I've made an international reputation for myself by thinking once or twice a week. —GEORGE BERNARD SHAW

If I gave you twenty-four hours to think up the concept for a new children's toy, or told you that you had just three days to figure out how to turn a 20 percent loss into a profit, could you do it? Can you be creative under pressure? Can you find a way to force your mind to generate ideas and manipulate information so you can complete an assignment with the clock ticking— and the world watching? Situations like these arise more often than most of us would like, requiring us to trigger our creativity under duress.

But even when there is no external pressure, at times we feel an internal pressure to be creative. Think of those moments when you *want* to tackle a problem or get over a creative hump in a definitive way. You wake up in the morning, rush into your office, and sit down at your desk, furiously scribbling notes or sketching out an idea. Or you are watching TV at night, and bang, you suddenly race over to the kitchen table and, jolting your mind into gear, begin racking your brain to pin down an idea you just had for restructuring your company.

Situations like these call for a different style of creative thinking, one that is highly focused and helps you find your target within minutes or even seconds. You need to telescope the traditional preparation and incubation stages of the four-step creative process, and you don't have time to use the tools of travel, reading, playing, or visiting a museum or gallery until the inspiration muse visits you or serendipity tumbles into your path. You are facing a creative emergency, and your mind (or your boss) is screaming out to you, "Let's get moving; we need that idea or solution *now.*"

At these times you need what I call *PowerThinking,* a collection of concentrated thinking strategies that can help take you from "no idea" to "new idea" in a short period of time. PowerThinking strategies are all highly focused, intentional, and conscious. Most of them rely on what is called divergent thinking, to generate lots of possible ideas. They are all generally geared toward increasing your idea "count," in other words, getting as many ideas out there as possible by tapping your brain's ability to make connections. Naturally, you must ultimately evaluate and analyze all the ideas you develop in order to select the best one, but what counts first (and most) in any PowerThinking technique is generating quantity, not quality. As Alex Osborn, one of the pioneers of brainstorming, said, "Quantity! and more quantity! is the order of the day."

PowerThinking can be an especially valuable tool in a business environment. As today's corporations seek ideas, new products, or ways to reduce costs and improve profitability, even the smallest new idea can go a long way. Many companies use management techniques that focus specifically on encouraging new ideas from all employees to achieve "continuous improvement" in every aspect of the business. One excellent program called I-Power, short for Ideas Power, has as its key concept that employees must supply two new ideas per week to benefit the company, ideas that they can personally make happen. Martin Edelston, author of the book *I-Power: The Secrets of Great Business in Bad Times,* has used I-Power in his own publishing company, Boardroom, Inc., to generate thousands of ideas, many of which helped the company save millions.

The rest of this chapter presents eight PowerThinking techniques in detail. Specifically, those techniques are

1. **Brainstorming**
2. **Transformative thinking**
3. **Forced connections**
4. **Think "As if"**
5. **GNP thinking**
6. **Mindmapping**
7. **PowerJournaling**
8. **Role playing**

These are just eight of the hundreds of thinking techniques and strategies available, but they are among the most fundamental and serve as the foundations on which many other techniques are built. In my consulting experience, I have also found that these strategies are among the easiest to learn and are often the most effective in generating new ideas.

Brainstorming

Brainstorming is one of the easiest strategies to use, but it is often misunderstood and misapplied. The term refers to the process of putting two or more people together to generate ideas or solve a problem simultaneously. Pioneered by Alex Osborn in his classic book *Applied Imagination: Principles and Procedures of Creative Problem-Solving,* this technique has become particularly popular in the corporate world as a way to facilitate and maximize creative thinking. Rather than assigning one person at a time the task of figuring out a new design or solving a problem, management puts a group of people in a room and asks them to pool their ideas for the good of all.

Brainstorming is not just for corporate situations, though; it can be used whenever an individual cannot resolve a problem and can locate a group of people to assist in tackling it. Brainstorming is a powerful strategy that taps into important characteristics of group dynamics:

• **Collective energy.** Brainstorming takes advantage of synergy, the fact that the total energy of a group is greater than the sum of its individual participants'. The group dynamic that occurs causes everyone's energy to skyrocket.

• **Collective confidence.** When faced with a difficult task, a funny thing happens to many people: they underestimate their power to solve the problem. In some cases, the magnitude or complexity of the task daunts them; in other cases, people think they don't have the skills or expertise necessary to think an issue through. In the seminars I give, I demonstrate such loss of confidence with a simple experiment. I ask who in the audience can name twenty birds in one minute. Few if any people volunteer. However, as soon as I put the people in groups, an amazing confidence develops, naming twenty birds becomes a trivial task, and all involved realize they could have done it on their own. So it is with many difficult creative situations; what one person thinks he or she cannot accomplish alone becomes child's play for a large group.

• **Divergent thinking.** Divergent thinking is developing as broad a range of ideas as possible on a given topic. Brainstorming maximizes divergent thinking because each individual in the group has his or her own perceptions and attitudes. In solving a problem, each participant in a brainstorming group is almost sure to see the situation differently and to come up with unique and distinctive ideas.

• **Collective associative thinking.** Each statement in a brainstorming session triggers the other participants to think of associated ideas. A chain reaction naturally occurs, as people take cues from one another and piggyback ideas. For example, picture a group of people brainstorming a new way to augment the computer education program in the local school district. One person might suggest approaching local businesses for equipment donations. This idea triggers another person to think about approaching those businesses that cannot afford to donate equipment to allow their employees to come to the schools a few hours per week to teach. That idea then triggers another person to think about sending the students to the local businesses once a week to get hands-on computer experience in business settings.

• **Delayed judgment.** A prerequisite of all brainstorming efforts is that criticism and judgment are not allowed when an idea is first introduced; in fact, wild ideas are invited. This principle helps the group's creativity in two ways: first, people tend to be able to produce more ideas when they know that quantity, not quality, counts. Second, when people are confident that no one will judge them, they become less inhibited and more willing to take risks, often resulting in more exciting, less predictable new concepts.

Brainstorming is more than just a group of people sitting around a table and haphazardly talking. To be most effective it should be a structured event that follows a specific four-step sequence.

Step 1. Orientation/Problem Statement

One person introduces the topic to be explored. It is best to present the topic using a clear and specific statement of the desired outcome, expressed in positive terms, such as "We are seeking new ways to increase customer satisfaction on phone orders" or "We are looking to develop a product that makes use of our new printing capability." Everyone and anyone may ask questions until they fully understand the situation.

Step 2. Idea Generation

This step is the key to the brainstorming process. The group as a whole tries to generate as many ideas as possible. Remember, quantity counts, not quality. No idea is too absurd, and no judgments or evaluations of the ideas are allowed. A "facilitator" or "recorder" writes all the ideas down quickly on a large easel or flip chart for everyone to see.

There are a variety of ways to elicit ideas during this stage, including the following three:

• **Freewheeling.** In the most common freewheeling approach, anyone can call out any idea at any time. Think of this as an idea "free-for-all" that benefits from fast thinking and momentum. In this approach, the facilitator or recorder needs to write quickly and not interrupt the synergy of the group.

• **Round-robin.** An alternative approach is the round-robin, in which participants are invited one by one either to propose an idea or to pass. The rounds continue until everyone passes. This technique is more thoughtful than the freewheeling approach, but its advantage is that there is likely to be more collective association since participants listen more closely to what other people suggest, thus triggering their own associations.

• **Closed eyes.** I find this extra feature adds power to many types of idea generating. With eyes closed, people tend to be less inhibited because they are not staring at their colleagues and feeling self-conscious. This can generate as much as 30 percent greater volume of ideas. In addition, I have noticed that groups tend to develop much more unusual ideas when people have their eyes closed. Sometimes this technique causes ideas to flow so quickly that a tape recorder is necessary to capture them.

Step 3. Discussion and Evaluation

During this stage, the group first discusses each idea written down to make sure they understand what it is and how it might help them. The team then evaluates the pros and cons of the ideas, without any reference to who contributed each one. There are usually some overlapping ideas and places where parts of several solutions might work when combined. The solution to a complex problem is often a synthesis of ideas and approaches, reflecting the group's synergy. In other cases, the solution comes in the form of a sudden insight that a single person received, thanks to another idea someone else contributed.

Step 4. Decision and Implementation

In the last phase, the group selects the best solution. Sometimes a unanimous decision occurs because everyone was involved in the process and witnessed the chain of thinking that took place to get to the answer. Other times, however, two or more ideas may seem equally valid, so the group may need further discussion to select one alternative over another.

Brainstorming is one of the most potent PowerThinking strategies to use when several people are involved in a project. But you can also use brainstorming in your personal creative work by inviting close friends or family members to help you think through a problem or generate ideas. Some families even use this technique to plan vacations or solve family issues.

Don't expect results from your very first brainstorming session. As in any team effort, it usually takes time and experience for a group of people to feel comfortable working together and to learn to listen to one another without judging or criticizing.

BRAINSTORMING FOR QUANTITY

Using the preceding four brainstorming steps, gather a group of between four and eight people in your workplace. Practice developing good brainstorming form with one of the topics below or one of your own devising. Brainstorm for ten to fifteen minutes. Make your goal to see how many different ideas you can accumulate; focus on quantity, not quality. Remember, a "silly" idea is often the trigger to the best solution.

POSSIBLE TOPICS TO BRAINSTORM

- Ways to improve communication within your organization
- Ways to improve employee morale
- New uses for E-mail in your company
- New directions your company might take
- How to reduce conflict in your department
- How to solve a problem in your community

Try each of the techniques on pages 205 and 206. Continue generating ideas until everyone has exhausted all thoughts. How many ideas did you generate? Once your group is comfortable with the principles of brainstorming, move on to a more pressing topic that relates specifically to your creative concerns.

Transformative Thinking

Transformative thinking is a form of mental aerobics that helps you consciously twist and turn the gist of one idea until you arrive at a fully developed new idea. It utilizes the human mind's ability to apply many thinking strategies to a problem and to visualize or verbalize the results in advance. This technique can be used alone or with a brainstorming group.

Transformative thinking encompasses many mental processes. The concept is derived from an idea-generation technique called SCAMPER, an acronym developed by Bob Eberle based on one of Alex Osborn's techniques. In SCAMPER, each letter stands for a mental process you could apply to a budding idea. The letters stand for substitute, combine, adapt, magnify/minimize/modify, put to other uses, eliminate and reverse/rearrange:

- **SUBSTITUTE** — What can I substitute in the material, process, approach, ingredient, appearance, etc.?
- **COMBINE** — What purposes, ideas, processes, ingredients, flavors, colors, etc., from another product or service can I blend with this?
- **ADAPT** — What else is like this? What can I copy?
- **MAGNIFY/MINIMIZE/MODIFY** — what can I add? Can I lengthen it? strengthen it? make it thicker? add more value? What can I subtract to make it smaller or shorter?
- **PUT TO OTHER USES** — What are new ways to use what I already have?
- **ELIMINATE** — What can I take away? get rid of?
- **REVERSE/REARRANGE** — What can I transpose? turn upside down? turn inside out? look at backward? reschedule? resequence?

By applying these processes to situations when you are seeking a new idea or when you are trying to improve an idea that is not as strong as you'd like, you can often come up with many new opportunities. For example:

- **SUBSTITUTING** — Sugar Pops became Corn Pops, a more attractive name for a cereal to appeal to nutrition-conscious parents;
- **COMBINING** — Lipton combined various fruits and flavors with their teas to develop a new line of iced tea products;
- **ADAPTING** — Sony adapted their original Walkman concept to develop the Watchman (small television) and Discman (small CD player);
- **MAGNIFY/MINIMIZE/MODIFYING** — McDonald's is minimizing their stores and putting them in gas stations and consumer retail stores like WalMart and Home Depot;
- **PUTTING TO OTHER USES** — Arm & Hammer transformed their baking soda product into toothpaste;
- **ELIMINATING** — Saturn eliminated the fear of salesmen for the car-buying process;
- **REVERSING** — Rheinhold Burger reversed the physics of a cold Thermos to invent the hot Thermos.

With my colleague Deanna Berg, I have developed a transformative thinking technique in which the word *transform* is an acronym for thirty-six possible transformations that can help you take the seed of an idea to a new stage. We plotted these possibilities on a grid as shown on pages 210–11.

Here's how the Transform grid might help you. Using the grid, look at the words in any order and apply them one at a time to your issue. If a word triggers an idea in your mind, write it down; if it doesn't, move on to another word. Keep going until you run out of ideas. For example, let's say you wanted to increase sales in your organization by 10 percent. You might use the grid to get ideas like the following: *Trim* the price to increase orders, *add* a premium, *offload* some old stock, *shift* your next quarter orders into this quarter, *simplify* your ordering process to encourage customers to buy more, *network* in your industry to increase the number of orders, and so on.

The Transform grid is effective because the mind often has a tendency to freeze up when you are under pressure to think. The thirty-six words help you trigger associations. Even the best of us get stuck in a rut from time to time. You have probably experienced such a time when you were trying to solve a problem, and every time you thought about it, you kept coming up with the same answers. Eventually though, you discovered a new answer or a different solution once you had twisted the problem around or thought about it from a different perspective.

The secret to Transformative thinking is forcing the mind to think differently. In the words of Roger von Oech, author of several books on creativity, people often need a "whack on the side of the head" to get their minds moving in a different direction and to "get out of their box."

MINI WORKSHOP

TRANSFORMATIVE THINKING

Pick one of your projects — business or a personal hobby — to which you can apply transformative thinking. Write down the problem and begin twisting and turning it using the mental strategies evoked in the **TRANSFORM** grid on pages 210 and 211. Spend a few hours evaluating the strategies and see what you can do to advance your thinking. Is there a process among the thirty-six listed that you seem to be more successful with? Can you think of other mental aerobics you might perform on your ideas?

T	Transfer	Transplant
R	Reduce	Remove
A	Add	Adapt
N	Narrow	Naturalize
S	Substitute	Shift
F	Force	Fence
O	Organize	Off-load
R	Reverse	Recycle
M	Magnify	Maximize

Trim	Thicken	**T**
Rearrange	Rotate	**R**
Accelerate	Adopt	**A**
Neglect	Network	**N**
Shrink	Simplify	**S**
Flush	Frame	**F**
Oscillate	Optimize	**O**
Reform	Relax	**R**
Minimize	Move	**M**

Forced Connections

As powerful as traditional brainstorming is, it has a drawback: All the participants have a common understanding, a collective mind frame that traps them equally in the same box or comfort zone. They all think about the problem in the common terms, and as a result, the normal process of associations eventually becomes unproductive.

This is when you need to switch to another PowerThinking technique: forced connections. There are many variations on this strategy, but they are all based on the brain's ability to link two disparate items—such as words, objects, feelings, and ideas—and then use the new language generated by the linkages to think through the problem. It is called *forced* connections because it relies on random external triggers that force people to make a connection between the problem at hand and the trigger. These triggers cause people to broaden their perspective.

For example, when I conduct a forced connections session for one of my clients, I prepare for the group's meeting by assembling several "idea bags" of toys and trinkets. I include a variety of amusing and provocative items, such as plastic animals, photos, cards—whatever I can find that is compact enough to fit in a small bag but evocative enough to trigger ideas in an audience. I then give the bags out to small brainstorming groups and ask the participants to select anything they want from the bag. The group then must generate ideas by forcing an association between whatever object they have pulled out of the bag and the problem or situation they are working on. In this way, the idea bag introduces a new universe of potential cues from which to associate, spawning ideas that were not on the table before.

In one company I worked with, several human resources executives were grappling with ways to cope with a reduced workforce, such as how to continue meeting their deadlines with fewer people; how to minimize the disadvantages of being in a separate building away from the rest of the organization; and how to help their various divisions improve their relationships with the human resources staff. I met with the executives and used the idea bag technique to help them generate new statements that described the issues in different terms. In this case, the items in the bags included a plastic monkey, which helped generate comments like "We need to take the monkey off our back and ask the departments to help with some people issues," and "There's too much monkeying around on trivial policy instead of focusing on key issues," and a measuring tape, which helped generate ideas like "How do we measure the amount of work each person now does?"

By reformulating their concerns, participants were able to clarify the various problems in much greater detail, and they brainstormed a variety of ideas that helped them manage the expected problems with less uncertainty than they had envisioned.

There are several variations on the forced connections exercise. For example, you can hold the meeting without preparing a bag of ideas in advance; instead, ask each participant in round-robin fashion randomly to name an object. Don't begin the connection process yet; simply write all objects down on an easel in front of the audience. Once everyone has named an object, repeat the round-robin, asking everyone to begin making associations between the objects and the problem. Record the connections on the easel for all to see. If you want, you can then ask for a second round of objects and repeat the process. This often adds a deeper level to the ideas generated.

These variations, will also increase the range of ideas on the problem-solving table:

- **Project a variety of pictures or photos on a screen or overhead projector.**
- **Ask each person to bring in an object.**
- **Open a dictionary to any page and pick out a word.**

Like brainstorming, forced connections are particularly useful when your group is blocked while trying to generate new ideas or to solve problems. In these circumstances, it is usually imperative to introduce external triggers to get people thinking in new ways.

IMPLEMENTING FORCED CONNECTIONS

1. **Begin collecting items for your own idea bag. Go exploring in thrift stores, discount outlets, 99¢ stores, drugstores, and toy stores. Mail-order catalogs are another source of fun items. Emphasize amusing or weird objects that will surprise people and take them out of their usual frame of reference.**

2. **Conduct a forced connection meeting with people in your department or field to test out the power of this strategy for you. Put an easel in the room and write at the top of a clean page**

Write down a phrase that identifies a creative opportunity or problem you face. Perhaps it is a new product or a process you would like to improve. Then randomly select objects from your idea bag or as provided by the participants, or use a dictionary to start the connection process. The more unrelated the objects are to the creative opportunity, the better.

As you examine each object, imagine how it connects to your creative opportunity. For instance, if you pulled a plastic lion out of the bag, think how a lion could help your project — literally or figuratively. Associate freely from what the lion symbolizes to each participant. Allow people to brainstorm without any judgment or criticism; you never know where an idea might lead. By the end of the session, you are likely to have a list of new ideas for your project.

Think "As If"

This imaginative strategy is a fun and effective way to move beyond your habitual narrow perspective when viewing problems. Begin by having your group phrase your problem or issue as a question. Then have the group generate a list of well-known people: celebrities, historical figures, philosophers, artists, politicians, cartoon characters, movie heroes, and so on. Then, one by one, imagine how each person would address your situation given what is generally known about that individual's viewpoint and opinions. First Lady Hillary Rodham Clinton used this technique and had imaginary conversations with Eleanor Roosevelt. The press had a field day with this, with one newspaper intimating that she was conducting seances. It would be unfortunate if the bad press turned people away from this type of technique since it is highly effective.

This "think as if" technique is successful because it helps you remember to think in many styles. Your list of people may generate solutions that range from the artistic to the philosophic, from the humorous to the exotic. The technique is outrageously funny, and the element of humor both enlivens the group and sparks creative drive.

Here is a humorous example that illustrates the principle of thinking in many styles. The example, culled from a widely circulated joke on the Internet, shows dozens of ways that the proverbial question "Why did the chicken cross the road?" might be answered. *Why did the chicken cross the road?*

ARISTOTLE: To actualize its potential.

PLATO: For the greater good.

BUDDHA: If you ask this question, you deny your own chicken-nature.

KARL MARX: It was a historical inevitability.

GOETHE: The eternal hen-principle made it do it.

B. F. SKINNER: Because the external influences that had pervaded its sensorium from birth had caused it to develop in such a fashion that it would tend to cross roads, even while believing these actions to be of its own free will.

CARL JUNG: The confluence of events in the cultural gestalt necessitated that individual chickens cross roads at this historical juncture; therefore synchronicity brought such occurrences into being.

JEAN-PAUL SARTRE: In order to act in good faith and be true to itself, the chicken found it necessary to cross the road.

DARWIN: It was the logical next step after coming down from the trees.

ALBERT EINSTEIN: Whether the chicken crossed the road or the road crossed the chicken depends upon your frame of reference.

SALVADOR DALÍ: The Fish.

TIMOTHY LEARY: Because that's the only kind of trip the Establishment would let it take.

HOWARD COSELL: It may very well have been one of the most astonishing events to grace the annals of history. An avian biped with the temerity to attempt such a herculean achievement, formerly relegated to *Homo sapien* pedestrians, is truly a remarkable occurrence.

EMILY DICKINSON: Because it could not stop for death.

RALPH WALDO EMERSON: It didn't cross the road; it transcended it.

ERNEST HEMINGWAY: To die. In the rain. Alone.

MARK TWAIN: The news of its crossing has been greatly exaggerated.

JACK NICHOLSON: 'Cause it (censored) wanted to. That's the (censored) reason.

FRANK PERDUE: I breed the finest chicken I know how, and it crosses the road as part of a vigorous fitness program to raise the leanest, plumpest birds anywhere.

As you can see from this example, the possibilities are endless once you start looking at problems from the perspective of others.

MINI WORKSHOP

THINK "AS IF"

Think of a situation or problem in your work or personal life now. How would the following people approach this problem. Spend a few minutes now writing down one-or-two sentence answers representing how each person would solve the problem. Have fun.

- your favorite author
- a teacher or coach from your past
- Ted Koppel
- Peter Pan
- Walt Disney
- your favorite movie star
- your least favorite politician
- Ann Landers
- The Cat in the Hat
- Susan B. Anthony

GNP Thinking

GNP stands for goal-not-problem thinking, which is a strategy that doesn't come naturally to a lot of people. The essence of GNP thinking is similar to reframing, viewing a situation in a different light. When you perform GNP thinking, you begin by redefining your creative challenge as a goal you want to reach rather than a problem you have to solve. For most people, the act of reframing opens up a multitude of options that they had overlooked because they had been thinking strictly within the parameters imposed by the problem. Liberating their minds this way helps them to put the impediment in a completely new context and to find what means are necessary to overcome it.

Consider the following problem: You are alone in a room, and two strings are suspended from the ceiling, far enough apart so that you cannot reach one string with your outstretched hand while holding the other. The room is empty; you only have what is in your pocket. How can you tie the two strings together? Many people would examine this problem and phrase it as "How can I get to the second string?" They would usually try to hold one string while reaching out for the other.

However, if you phrase the problem as "I want the strings and myself to get together," you give yourself a clue to devising a solution. Now you might realize that you have some keys or a coin that you can tie to one string so that you would be able to swing it and make it come to you while you grab the other string.

An exceptional real-life example of GNP thinking is the story of the space probe *Galileo,* which reached Jupiter in 1995 after nearly a dozen years on the drawing boards and five years traveling through space. After *Galileo* had been designed in the early 1980s, the engineers were asked to go back to the drawing boards and rethink its rocket booster, which their colleagues feared would endanger the space shuttle's delicate cargo bay when the probe was launched. The problem, the engineers believed, was that *Galileo* could not reach Jupiter without a large rocket to get it moving. However, the solution they devised exemplifies GNP thinking; by changing the focus of their inquiries from a problem ("The booster we need to launch the probe may damage the shuttle") to a goal ("We must find a way for the probe to build velocity with little rocket power"), the engineers realized that they could actually make use of the gravitational force of Venus, which would swing the space probe around and naturally launch it toward Jupiter.

You can apply GNP thinking to many types of creative challenges, such as new product development and design, conceptualization of verbal or written presentations, or conflict negotiation. The more you practice GNP thinking, the more you find it facilitates your creativity. By focusing on what you *want,* rather than on what you *don't,* you invariably open yourself up to new ideas rather than confining yourself to unproductive and discouraging territory. As in the *Galileo* case, GNP thinking can free your mind from the constraints and operational definitions that you think you must follow to solve a problem or produce a creative result. The reframing of the problem grants your mind permission to abandon old paradigms in favor of new strategies.

MINI WORKSHOP

GNP THINKING
Is there a creative challenge you now face that you can rephrase as a goal rather than a problem? Take a large or small roadblock that is impeding your progress and write it down on a sheet of paper. Now rephrase it as a goal. Does the reframing of the problem change your perceptions about it? Do you now feel you have more options or greater leeway in resolving the issue?

Mindmapping

Mindmapping is a visual writing and note-taking process that helps you break through creative dry spells. Developed by the creativity expert Tony Buzan, mindmapping is related to the traditional outlining we all learned in high school, but it is a much more powerful tool. Rather than jotting down your ideas in a neat, sequential fashion, as you do when making a classical outline (Roman numerals I, II, III, and so on), mindmapping encourages you to put your ideas and information into visual patterns reflecting the interrelationships among the topics.

Mindmapping derives its creative power from two features:

• **It appeals to your visual intelligence.** Many people have a strong preference for visual information. By seeing their ideas in written form while viewing the connections between them, they understand the ideas better, remember them better, and, most important, are able to develop them more creatively. In fact, the power of our visual intelligence has been shown in many experiments. In one study at the University of Rochester, for example, subjects were shown 2,500 slides over several days. After the last slide was viewed, they were shown 280 pairs of slides, in which only one of each pair was from the original set. The test subjects were able to identify which slides they had seen before in more than 90 percent of the cases.

• **It energizes your creative right brain rather than your logical left brain.** When you write a traditional outline, you spend your energy figuring out the logical and sequential connections between your ideas. Mindmapping, on the other hand, focuses your attention on only the broadest strokes of ideas. As ideas flow from your mind, you need make only loose associations between them. You work in a nonlinear fashion, without worrying about coherence, order, or correctness. Slowly, your right brain takes control from your left brain, which tends to enhance your creative thinking.

Here's how to make a mind map. Take a clean sheet of paper and, holding it horizontally (to give yourself more space), begin by writing your goal or problem statement smack in the middle and circling it. It helps to print, rather than write in script or scribble your notes quickly. Once you have your center point, let your mind flow, using your natural transformative and associative thinking processes. See the words on the page in front of you, and let new ideas pop into your head, without censoring any of them. Write every idea you get down on your mind map, with each one radiating like a spoke from either the center point or another point to which it is related. Don't worry about linking all ideas or discovering a sequence among them. Let the visual effect of the mind map energize your creativity and fuel your associative thinking.

My friend Joyce Wycoff, who is the author of *Mindmapping: Your Personal Guide to Exploring Creativity and Problem-*

Solving, offered me the following tips to help you improve the quality of mindmapping skills:

• **Lighten up.** Let go of the pressure to find a cure for cancer or write a million-dollar screenplay—or the best report your boss has ever read. Mindmapping is simply a brain-dumping process that helps stimulate new ideas and connections. Start with an open, playful attitude; you can get serious later.

• **Think fast.** Your brain works best in five- to seven-minute bursts, so capture that explosion of ideas as rapidly as possible. To save time while writing, use only key words, or even symbols and images to provide a mental shorthand so you can record as many of your ideas as quickly as possible.

• **Judge not.** Put everything down that comes to mind, even if it seems far-fetched. If you're brainstorming ideas for a presentation on the use of carrots in cooking but you suddenly remember you need to pick up your cleaning, put down "cleaning." Otherwise your mind will get stuck like a needle in that "cleaning" groove and you'll never generate great ideas (When you're done, don't forget to get your cleaning).

• **Break boundaries.** Break through the eight and a half by eleven mentality that says you have to write on white, letter-size paper with black ink, no doodling allowed. Use newsprint, ledger paper, or easel paper, or cover an entire wall with butcher paper. The bigger the paper, the more ideas you'll have. Use wild colors—fat, colored markers, crayons, or calligraphy pens. (You haven't lived until you've mindmapped a business report with hot pink and Day-Glo orange crayons!) Feel free to draw with images or cartoons and to circle and highlight groups of words.

• **Center first.** Our linear, left-brain educational system has taught us to start in the upper-left-hand corner of a page. However, the mind naturally focuses on the center, so mindmapping begins with a word or image that symbolizes what you want to think about placed in the middle of the page.

• **Associate freely.** As ideas emerge, print one- or two-word descriptions of the ideas on lines branching from the central focus. Allow the ideas to expand outward into branches and sub-branches. Put down all ideas without judgment or evaluation.

• **Keep your hand moving.** If your ideas slow down, draw empty

MINDMAPPING

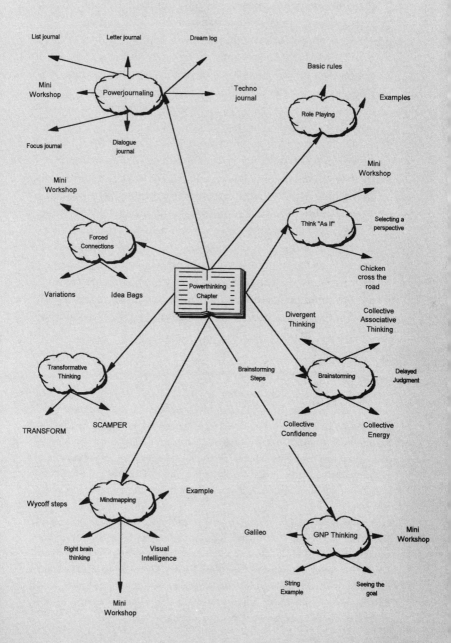

List journal

Letter journal

Dream log

Mini Workshop

Powerjournaling

Techno journal

Basic rules

Role Playing

Examples

Focus journal

Dialogue journal

Mini Workshop

Forced Connections

Mini Workshop

Think "As If"

Selecting a perspective

Variations

Idea Bags

Powerthinking Chapter

Chicken cross the road

Transformative Thinking

Brainstorming Steps

Divergent Thinking

Collective Associative Thinking

Brainstorming

Delayed Judgment

TRANSFORM

SCAMPER

Collective Confidence

Collective Energy

Mindmapping

Example

Wycoff steps

Galileo

GNP Thinking

Mini Workshop

Right brain thinking

Visual Intelligence

String Example

Seeing the goal

Mini Workshop

lines and watch your brain automatically find ideas to put on them. Or change colors to reenergize your mind. Stand up and mindmap on an easel pad to generate even more energy.

• **Allow organization only when you can.** Sometimes you see relationships and connections immediately and you can add sub-branches to a main idea. But sometimes you don't, so just connect the ideas to the central focus. Logical organization can always come later; the first requirement is to get the ideas out of your head and onto the paper.

You can use mindmapping as an idea generator for many types of work: organizing information and ideas for reports and memos; planning out your next novel, poem, or screenplay; masterminding a marketing strategy; reorganizing departmental responsibilities for your company; coordinating a charity benefit; mobilizing a community task force; and so on. Another value of mind maps is that they can easily be shared with others if you are working as part of a team or if you are asking others to comment on your ideas. As you will find, other people will enjoy looking at your mind map and will likely understand your ideas more readily than if you had asked them to read a traditional outline.

MAKE YOUR OWN MIND MAPS

1. To test the power of mindmapping, try this exercise. If you are like most people, you probably have at least one book idea in you. Why not mindmap a concept for the novel you have always wanted to write? Don't be afraid to try this. Take an hour and sit down with a large sheet of paper and some colored pencils or markers. Begin with either your central character or plot line in the middle of the paper. Then let your imagination soar and see what characters and subplots you can invent in sixty minutes.

2. Pick a project or problem related to your professional or personal creative work that you would like to shed light on. Spend an hour mindmapping the issues of that topic. Give yourself permission to think more in depth about this topic than you've ever done before. Use a large sheet of paper, colored markers, doodles, pictures, whatever note taking you need to develop your mindmap as fully as possible. Show your mindmap to your colleagues or friends, and get their feedback.

PowerJournaling

In Part I, I suggested that you keep a daily journal to record your thoughts and ideas as you read this book. If you haven't already started keeping this kind of journal, you might consider journaling now as a PowerThinking technique to generate ideas or get unstuck when you encounter a difficult situation.

Unlike a daily journal, used as a method of introspection or psychological discovery, a PowerThinking journal is intended specifically to help you capture your thinking processes or develop new ideas over a finite period of time.

PowerJournaling is effective in several types of situations, such as when you are handling a tremendous amount of information or options and need to categorize the data, or when you feel your mind is evolving an idea and you would benefit by writing down each stage of its development.

There are many techniques of PowerJournaling from which you may choose:

Dialogue Journal. In this technique, you record imagined conversations with other people so you can develop an exchange of ideas. For instance, you might pretend you are talking to a favorite musician who helps you think through preliminary ideas for your first song. You might imagine yourself speaking with an expert in your field and getting advice about how he or she would handle a problem you have been assigned. Or you might write up the dialogue you guess would occur if you approached your boss and presented some innovative ideas for the company. This imaginary dialogue would be a kind of dress rehearsal, in which you imagine how she would respond to your suggestions, allowing you to be better prepared with answers when the real occasion arises. If you have already generated solutions, you might have an imaginary dialogue in which the other person supports your idea or plays devil's advocate.

Focus Journal. In this technique, you write *everything* you can on a specific issue or theme. Your journal is a complete brain dump, showing you everything you know—or think you know.

(Mindmapping some of the information is useful too.) For example, if you were developing a new product, you might write *all* your thoughts about the product's attributes, benefits, and how people would use it. Or if you were doing a presentation to your management team, you might write about every aspect of the topic so you could eventually narrow down your thoughts to the most appropriate information.

List Journal. This technique is both fun and easy. Make a list journal in which you record as many ideas as you can on any subject you think about. For example, list the ten things you'd like to do by the time you're sixty-five, the three skills you'd like to develop in the next year, the five best low- or no-cost activities in your area, or ten things you want to teach your children. Such lists often trigger other thoughts and ideas, which you can then pursue as creative projects in their own right.

Dream Log. Keeping a dream journal has long helped people to understand the events transpiring in their unconscious. We will discuss dreaming in greater detail in the next chapter, but for the moment, it is useful to note that a dream journal can be an excellent tool when your dreams are particularly rich with the images and people that populate your current situation. Often a single powerful dream can unlock the secret to overcoming a problem. By writing the dream down in detail the moment you awaken, you can often remember and understand it better than if you had let it lie dormant in your mind for hours or days.

Letter Journal. Similar to a dialogue journal, your letter journal can be composed of real or imaginary letters you write to people about your ideas. You might write a memo to a real person in your life, to a celebrity, or to a historical character. As in dialoguing, you can also write your own response to the letter. Writing a letter to a person, living or dead, who's had an impact on your life can be a useful way to bring memories to the surface and track major influences on your ideas.

Techno-journal. If you find carrying a journal or a laptop computer everywhere you go impractical, try keeping a small pocket recorder in your purse or pocket. Some of today's personal recorders incorporate digital chip technology that makes storing and retrieving your notes and ideas very easy. A product called the Voice Organizer even allows you to keep track of your schedule and be reminded of meetings at specific times with a beep. A pocket recorder is especially useful if you drive or travel extensively (and, as we've seen, travel often inspires ideas). Bright ideas can come from anywhere; perhaps you pass by the new Moroccan restaurant in town and the aroma translates into a musical phrase or graphic design motif. Whatever the prompt, why wait until you reach your home or office to record these brainstorms? You can also use your techno-journal when you are cruising a bookstore or newsstand to record quotations, names of books and authors, or the insights that occur to you as you peruse the shelves.

Obviously you can't employ all these techniques simultaneously, or you'd have no time to implement your creative breakthroughs! Choose the one that feels most comfortable and corresponds to your most productive times. You can also combine several of these PowerJournaling techniques. For example, if you are in the midst of developing a new project at work, try spending one week consistently using your pocket recorder to maintain a list or a focus journal, *and* maintain a dream journal to catch the ideas that are stirring in your subconscious through the five nights. By the end of the week, you may be pleasantly surprised at how such diligent record keeping can help your brain PowerThink through the creative challenge. The careful scrutiny given to your thoughts coupled with precise tracking and recording of an idea's development keep your mind focused and organized.

Journalizing is an extremely effective technique to pull together your ideas and improve your creativity. The late Earl Nightingale, cofounder of the successful publishing company Nightingale-Conant Corporation, and one of the great proponents of Positive Thinking, believed strongly that people can benefit from writing down their ideas. He observed that most people "seldom indulge in serious, concentrated thinking between problems." Nightingale believed that we should all have what he called a "systematic daily plan of creative thinking." He proposed that each day, you spend one hour proactively thinking about the issues of your life. His technique for doing this was to write a problem statement at the top of a sheet of paper, and then jot down all the ideas that come to mind as you think about the problem. Through this exercise in journalizing, Nightingale believed that everyone could develop a sharper focus on all their problems and a clearer picture of their future goals.

MINI WORKSHOP

THINKING ABOUT POWERJOURNALING
1. **Recall the last time you did a special project for either your professional work or your personal creative pursuits. How long did it take you to come up with the seed of the idea you eventually pursued? Do you think you might have shortened the time if you had used a PowerJournaling technique? Is there another project you are developing now which might benefit by your keeping a short-term journal?**
2. **Do you own a pocket tape recorder? How frequently do you use it? What prevents you from using it every day to record all your ideas?**
3. **Write a letter to or dialogue with an author, actor, director, or executive you admire in which you discuss your ideas for a book, film, business program, or whatever. Explain your concepts as completely as you can. Play the other person's part as well in the correspondence or dialogue. Have you gained additional insights into your own ideas?**
4. **Over the next week or month, try spending a few minutes per day in proactive journalizing, as Earl Nightingale suggested. By investing this time in forward, goal-oriented thinking, you'll be able to draw from your well of personal, spiritual beliefs, and use your intelligence and energy to make changes and to develop new ideas for your business or your personal projects. If your experiment into GNP thinking doesn't produce immediate results, don't give up. As pioneer and business entrepreneur Henry Ford once said: "Thinking is the hardest work there is, which is probably the reason so few engage in it."**

Role Playing

Role playing is a creative mental exercise in which you pretend to be someone or something else. The value of role playing is that it gets you out of your own way of thinking, out of your comfort zone. When we take on different personae, we tend to release our inhibitions and let our imaginations soar.

A famous example of creative success in role playing is a group of executives who were brainstorming at the Gillette Company in 1980. The goal of the session was to develop a new shampoo product. The executives were asked to pretend that they were shafts of hair. While in this state of mind, they brainstormed about what qualities a hair shaft would most want. Some role-playing hair shafts wanted a powerful cleanser that would seek out dirt from the scalp; others wanted a gentle formula that would not cause split ends. By the end of the exercise, the executives had realized that what they needed was a shampoo that would adjust to every type of hair. The product they invented, Silkience, went on to become one of the most popular shampoos on the market.

I have used role playing in my consulting work with many companies. In one case, a group of engineers from NASA were trying to figure out new public-sector applications for a highly sophisticated acoustic baffle they had invented. On their own, the engineers decided to imagine themselves as sound waves moving through space and encountering a baffle. They were able to come up with new applications, such as a barrier to keep noise on freeways away from bordering neighborhoods.

Role playing can be done alone or with a group. Here are some important role-playing guidelines:

1. *The basic rule is that anything goes.* Just as in brainstorming, the moment a negative comment is made about a participant's ability or choice of character, all participants will become much less effective. Avoid critical comments, snide or mocking remarks, and even innocuous questions (such as, What are you supposed to be?) because they usually cause people to "break character" and become extremely conscious of their bodies, their voices, and their movements.

2. *Just as with exercising, before role playing do some warm-ups.* Have all participants do a few stretching exercises so their bodies are limber, they have released stress from their necks and shoulders, and they feel more free to use their bodies as they role-play.

3. *Don't limit yourself to "people" roles.* Remember, in the Gillette experiment the executives pretended to be hair, not chemists working on a shampoo formula. Give yourself the freedom to pretend to be animals, types of food, chemicals, metals, or any other animate or inanimate object.

4. *Role playing can occur in either a directed or a nondirected format.* In a directed role play, a group leader sets up a specific scene from which participants are to work. For example, the leader of a group of travel agents seeking to come up with a new idea for vacation packages might say that the agents have just landed in a country for a previously planned tour but their bus has broken down. They are then asked to pretend that they can do whatever they want as long as they return in three days.

In the nondirected format, each participant can do whatever he or she pleases, just as actors do in an improvisation. There are no predefined ideas, limits, or characters. The course and result of the role play depend entirely on what characters people choose to be, how they interact, and where they take the role play while they are doing it. For example, in the case of the travel agents, they would only know that they were trying to come up with ideas for new vacation packages. They would be allowed to play any role they wanted—a grain of sand on a beach, a bird flying over the Alps, or a monk in a Tibetan Buddhist temple.

5. *Don't push for results.* Some role plays work, others don't. Most role-playing games require ten to twenty minutes for people to warm up and develop their characters. In many cases, a theme or pattern slowly takes shape among the participants, and the best images or ideas are developed toward the end of the role play.

Role playing can be a tremendously powerful idea-generation strategy for a small group of people who are comfortable with one another, such as members of a department or division of a company or longtime friends working on a community or professional project. The strategy fosters teamwork and cooperation as well as encourages people to have fun.

Don't Underestimate Your Mind Power

It is difficult for most people to recognize their own thinking processes when they are blocked, stressed, or under pressure. We all get into a rut sometimes and lose our perspective in the process. We fail to see when our mental acuity has slowed down, or that we have begun to spin our wheels, trying the same approach over and over and over again.

This is why the eight PowerThinking strategies presented in this chapter are so effective. They all remind you to get out of your rut, to think in new ways. They all largely focus on helping you become more aware of your thinking processes, consciously test and experiment with new ways to perceive a problem, or create new words and images to express your nascent ideas.

These PowerThinking strategies are all reminders that your mind has enormous potential. So whenever you get stuck or blocked, don't underestimate your mental powers by giving up or slowing down—instead, turbocharge your thinking! Try the PowerThinking strategies either on your own or as part of a group thinking session, and you will very likely discover more answers than you ever thought possible.

If you are interested in more PowerThinking strategies, read several of the books listed under "Further Readings." All these books emphasize specific mental techniques to generate creative solutions.

Further Readings

Applied Imagination by Alex Osborn (Buffalo: Creative Education Foundation Press, 1993).

Idea Power: Techniques and Resources to Unleash the Creativity in Your Organization by Arthur B. VanGundy (New York: AMA-COM, 1992).

"I"-Power: The Secrets of Great Business in Bad Times by Martin Edelston and Marion Buhagiar (Greenwich, Conn.: Boardroom Books, 1992).

Mapping Inner Space—Learning and Teaching Mind Mapping by Nancy Margulies (Tuscon: Zephyr Press, 1991).

Mindmapping: Your Personal Guide to Exploring Creativity and Problem-Solving by Joyce Wycoff (New York: Berkley Books, 1991).

101 Creative Problem Solving Techniques: The Handbook of New Ideas for Business by James M. Higgins (Winter Park, Fla.: New Management, 1994).

The Pursuit of Wow—Every Person's Guide to Topsy-Turvy Times by Tom Peters (New York: Vintage Books, 1994).

Thinkertoys: A Handbook of Business Creativity for the '90s by Michael Michalko (Berkeley, Cal.: Ten Speed Press, 1991).

Thinking for a Change—Discovering the Power to Create, Communicate, and Lead by Michael J. Gelb (New York: Harmony Books, 1995).

Thunderbolt Thinking—Transform Your Insights & Options into Powerful Business Results by Grace McGartland (Austin, Tex.: Bard Productions, 1994).

Transformation Thinking by Joyce Wycoff and Tim Richardson (New York: Berkley, 1995).

A Whack on the Side of the Head: How You Can Be More Creative by Roger Von Oech (New York: Warner Books, 1990).

What a Great Idea! The Key Steps Creative People Take by Charles "Chick" Thompson (New York: HarperPerennial, 1992).

Release Your Alterconscious

Science has taken us far, yet we know so little about the brain and its mysterious powers beneath our state of waking consciousness. For the sake of simplicity, I call these powers the *alterconscious,* by which I refer generally to the *unconscious,* the layer of impressions and information under the surface of our minds, but also to the Freudian *subconscious,* the repository of repressed feelings that Freud hypothesized influence our thoughts and behaviors. In my view, the alterconscious should be thought of as that "nowhere" territory from which our ideas seem to arise.

Each year top neuroscientists uncover more information about the complex functions of the human mind, but we remain many steps away from full understanding of its deep inner workings. We know the brain is a peerless calculator, capable of processing billions of instructions per second. A recent article in *Psychology Today* estimated that the brain can process about 10^{15} billion instructions per second (BIPS), while the most advanced supercomputer is capable of only 10^9 BIPS. (To put this in an even more amazing perspective, today's cutting-edge personal computer is still measured in *millions* of instructions per second, or MIPS.) In short, the brain is an incredibly powerful thinking tool.

It is often said that we do not use much of our true brainpower. A few years ago, it was speculated that we use only about 10 percent, but more recent studies suggest that in fact less than one tenth of 1 percent of our mind's power is harnessed. Whatever the statistics indicate about how much of our brain is utilized, clearly there is wondrous capacity below the surface for us to tap into when we need it.

That is why this chapter explores a group of phenomena that are generally accepted as the visible manifestations of the alterconscious: intuition, daydreams, visualization, meditation, and dreams. These processes occur naturally in the brain, but in the background. They are worth examining because they appear to be linked strongly to how we create and invent new ideas, yet at the same time they are difficult to interpret because they are vague, sketchy, and hard to pinpoint. Unlike the strategies of transformative thinking or forced connections that you invoke consciously, you cannot force your alterconscious to come up with a new idea. Instead, you must train yourself to pay attention to the pearls of wisdom your mind produces on its own and perfect a method for capturing this information.

States of Mind Are Real

Recent research offers amazing insight into the alterconscious. This research focuses on the electrical activity in the brain, as measured with a machine known as an electroencephalograph (EEG). Through the use of EEG's, scientists have found that we have four different brain states. They have also found that each type of electrical wave is closely correlated with specific functions. The brain wave states are described as follows:

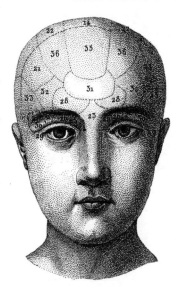

➤ **Beta.** Beta waves are associated with our awakened state of mind, when we are alert and thinking logically and coherently about concrete problem solving. The beta state also occurs when we are excited and over-stimulated by the environment.

➤ **Alpha.** Alpha waves are associated with those times when we are relaxed and have detached awareness; this is the state of mind that prevails when we daydream, imagine, or visualize. It is thought that this state of mind is the doorway to meditation. Without alpha, you do not remember your dreams when awakened.

➤ **Theta.** Theta waves are associated with the unconscious mind and are active during dreaming sleep and deep meditation. Theta waves are also thought to be the repository of our repressed emotions and suppressed creativity.

➤ **Delta.** Delta waves can be described as a kind of radar; they occur at the deepest levels of the unconscious mind, reflecting strong inner knowledge. Delta waves also occur in the deepest stages of sleep.

Greater knowledge of these brain wave states has been a boon to many fields. For example, educational experts have found that we learn better and retain information longer in an alpha state of mind rather than in beta, especially if the information is rehearsed and repeated many times; because we are more relaxed we are able to absorb the information more deeply into our unconscious. In response to this finding, the field of accelerated learning has adopted techniques such as relaxation exercises, controlled breathing, and repetition to help people learn subjects like foreign languages, and many actors apply the same techniques to learning their lines. Scientists interested in stress reduction have also widely accepted that slowing the mind down to attain an alpha state can help people feel calmer and more blissful, thus providing support for the centuries-old practice of meditation.

As it turns out, researchers today believe that the alpha, theta, and delta brain wave states are particularly relevant to creativity, helping us to focus inward and prepare our creative endeavors. Anna Wise has applied brain-wave research to the three important areas listed in the subtitle of her book, *The High-Performance Mind: Mastering Brainwaves for Insight, Healing, and Creativity.* Her work has shown that when we reach a peak of creativity, it can be detected on an EEG. By watching a subject's brain waves, Wise says she is able to determine the point at which an aha! or peak creative experience occurs.

With this enlightening news as our starting point, let's examine how intuition, daydreams, visualization, meditation, and dreams can be tools for your creativity.

Intuition: Know Thyself!

Perhaps you don't consider yourself particularly intuitive, or you may feel that logic exerts more force on your decisions than "gut feelings." Yet we all experience intuitive thoughts at times. Recall flashes of sudden insight that you have experienced:

- **The nagging urge to go somewhere or to take an alternative route**
- **That feeling that something has been left undone or that you need to recheck your work**
- **The hunch that you should try a certain idea or process to fix a problem**
- **The feeling that you will meet someone you know at a certain location**

More often than not these amorphous messages lead you to the right answer, an important discovery, or a generally creative experience.

I first saw the true power of intuition through my wife, Jan. Her sense of intuition is well developed, but I didn't realize how valuable it could be until it affected us dramatically. In 1987, we were contemplating buying a new home; we had been saving our money and investing in blue-chip stocks for some time. Our nest egg had grown, and we were house hunting, having saved enough to comfortably put money down on a new home. In our family structure, my wife handles the cash flow (payment of bills and so on), and I handle the investing. In the fall of that year, Jan said that she thought we needed to sell all our stock. However, given the hours invested in securing my business degree, I felt more qualified to make those decisions. She was so insistent, though, that, against my better judgment, I sold all of our common stock, keeping the balance (our down payment) in lower-yielding cash funds. The next day the stock market crashed. Had we not sold the stock, much of our investment would have been lost, and we would not have been able to afford our dream home, which we ultimately purchased, for a long time. From that point forward I decided to try to use intuition to guide us whenever it was present.

Until recently, it was difficult in Western culture to admit that intuition exists. Many people regarded it as mumbo jumbo, relegated to fortune-tellers and carnival sideshows. Those who admitted to following their intuition were quickly ridiculed and dismissed, even called mad.

However, intuition is now widely recognized as a true and distinct activity of the brain, not simply "fast reasoning" or "inference" as some people have claimed. All such flashes are likely the result of your intuition coming alive, a message from the deepest reaches of your alterconscious. Intuition plays a role in many endeavors, from the spark that helps us discover a new product, create a painting, write a novel, or compose a song to the little voice that tells us which questions to pursue when we are stumped, how to set up a science experiment, or where to look for supporting facts when we are researching something. In fact, in an excellent book on the subject, *The Intuitive Edge,* Philip Goldberg distinguishes six types of intuition, which can be summarized this way:

➤ **Discovery:** when the mind suddenly recognizes a new principle, such as the famous example of Archimedes understanding water displacement while taking a bath and yelling, "Eureka!" (I have found it!)

➤ **Creativity:** when the mind suddenly flashes with words or music or an image that gives rise to a new poem, song, painting, or invention

➤ **Evaluation:** when the mind suddenly makes a choice about one option over another, such as when Ray Kroc persevered in his efforts to buy McDonald's against the advice of his lawyers, or when Conrad Hilton changed his mind at the last minute and upped his bid for a Chicago hotel from $165,000 to $180,000, only to discover that the second highest bidder had bid $179,800. (As a footnote, Hilton made $2 million on the sale of the hotel a few years later!)

➤ **Operation:** when the mind suddenly knows what direction to go in, such as the breakthrough that led Alexander Fleming to pursue a line of investigation that resulted in the discovery of penicillin

➤ **Prediction:** when the mind suddenly senses in advance how an event will turn out, such as when people decide not to attend an event or board an airplane, only to find out later that they narrowly avoided being involved in an accident

➤ **Illumination:** when the mind suddenly feels at one with a higher power, such as a religious or spiritual experience.

Many of these are interrelated, distinguishable only by how much you might know in advance, or what type of decision your mind is making. Ultimately, though, like many researchers, Goldberg affirms that intuition is central to many creative works and discoveries. It appears to be the fundamental event occurring in the mind during the incubation stage of the creative process, when our brains mull over the information we have taken in during preparation, until the answer suddenly appears. But, as Goldberg points out, intuition does not always require a period of incubation to do its work; it can also happen spontaneously, even when we are in the middle of a sentence or a step, with no discernible preparatory stage having preceded it. In either case, intuition is responsible for delivering the answers to a problem or the image of a new product or the dialogue that will be exchanged between the main characters in a novel.

How does the mind "intuit," suddenly divining the answer, solution, or image that eventually guides us to creative success? Scientists are still baffled about that question. Some early theorists placed the seat of intuition, along with our other nonlogical mental skills, in the right hemisphere of the brain, believing that intuition was a reflection of nonlinear thinking. Other researchers have disagreed, suggesting that intuition coalesces information from the entire brain in a much more complex and holistic process. Some researchers led by the Stanford neurophysiologist Karl Pribram have even postulated that intuition reflects the fact that our brains are "holographic," meaning that all parts of the brain replicate the data stored in any one part so that information meshes as a whole without a logical set of steps. The fact that intuition seems to come out of nowhere and has no identifiable single location in the brain lends credence to this theory.

Obviously, much more must be discovered about intuition and its physical and electrical workings. However, given that intuition cannot be pinpointed like other thinking processes to a specific location in the brain, there does seem to be unanimity that it arises—at least metaphorically—from deep in the mind, precisely from what we call the unconscious or the alterconscious. The great psychiatrist Carl Jung long ago linked the unconscious and intuition when he wrote that the unconscious is "no mere repository of the past, but is also full of future psychic situations and ideas."

What makes the unconscious and its intuitive abilities so powerful is that, according to Jung, it is divided into two layers: the personal and the collective. The personal layer contains all the experiences and impressions that lie beneath the threshold of individual consciousness, while the collective unconscious holds what he called archetypes—universal images that allow us to process our thoughts and feelings instinctually. Jung clarified this by saying that archetypes are not literal memories or images we get from our ancestors but predispositions for experiencing the world that come from "the inherited powers of human imagination as it was from time immemorial." In other words, deep in our minds, along with our personal experiences, we all carry an innate sense of the "universal truths." In this Jungian view, our intuition and the creativity born from it thus express a sort of primordial instinctual knowledge. In a rather circular logic, we intuitively know that something is right or beautiful because our intuition tells us so. The intuition arises from so deep within us that we accept it as instinct.

It is now widely accepted that we are all intuitive—at least to some degree and in different areas. Your level of intuition, or more precisely your ability to be creative when being intuitive, reflects many factors. There are circumstantial or situational factors, such as people who are intuitive in business but not in their relationships or love lives. Many people believe that there are also cultural and gender factors; Easterners and women are thought to be more intuitive than Westerners and men. However, the vast majority of researchers now recognize that such stereotypes are based on ingrained biases and learned behaviors. In other words, in Western culture in general, and among men in particular, there is little belief in the power of intuition, so members of these groups learn to disregard intuition when it occurs.

How then can you use your powerful intuition for creativity? How can you tap into your unconscious mind with its precious insights and creative answers to your problems? This is the ultimate dilemma, because the first rule of intuition is that you cannot force it. Intuition works on its own pace and in its own way.

As Goldberg writes, "You can no more force intuition than you can force someone to fall in love with you."

The trick is therefore learning to prepare yourself for those moments when your intuition sends you a message. There are several issues to review in this regard. First, you must learn to become more accepting and respectful of your intuitive powers. Here are some suggestions that can help you provide a welcoming if not inviting environment for your intuition:

• **Believe in your mind's intuitive process.** You need to deprogram your mind from thinking you are not intuitive and eliminate internal dialogue that negates your ability to listen to your inner voice.

• **Trust your feelings and thoughts.** Low self-esteem can cause you to mistrust your feelings and turn away from intuitive messages.

• **Be confident and independent.** These qualities allow you to be open to unpredictability and surprise, two major elements of intuition.

• **Be flexible and playful.** The intuitive mind needs room to maneuver, and time to play while it tests and experiments with ideas.

• **Don't oversimplify problems; be prepared for complexity.** Intuition is uncanny in that it works best when you allow it to tackle the true problem. When you simplify something, you tend to develop simple answers that don't require the kind of creativity that arises from your unconscious mind.

Second, to become more intuitive, you need to learn how to shake intuitions loose. While your intuition cannot be forced, you can often jar it into action. The surest way to do this is to follow the four-step model of creativity. If you are blocked on a project or problem, it can be well worth your effort to begin with an intentional preparation step, by researching, collecting data, interviewing people, writing down your goals, traveling, reading —in other words, using all the strategies in this book. Then take a break from stress and pressure; go somewhere and put the issue completely out of your mind. It is almost axiomatic that during this downtime your intuition will pull together the data you have collected and reveal the answer. During incubation, your brain reaches into the alterconscious to access additional data and perhaps, as Jung believed, to consult the archetypes embedded in the collective unconscious. Whatever is transpiring behind the scenes, there is no doubt that the period of incubation calls directly on your intuitive abilities for the answers.

Another way to jar your intuition is to seek out opportunities for serendipity and synchronicity. As I've said often throughout this book, inspiration sometimes occurs spontaneously, such as when you meet a new person who turns out to be just who you were seeking or when you stumble on a newspaper article that contains exactly the information you need for an upcoming presentation. In these cases, you weren't in the midst of doing preparation; your intuition simply jumped out of nowhere and was right on target. This is why activities like travel, reading, and the arts create excellent conditions for your intuition to appear—they expose you to opportunities for serendipity and synchronicity.

Finally, and most important, you need to learn when your intuition is "speaking" to you. As the great thinker Buckminster Fuller said, intuition is like cosmic fishing: "Once you feel a nibble, you've got to hook the fish." This means that you must learn to recognize the signs of intuition, which might include the following:

• **Sudden thoughts.** These are the most common signs of intuition—flashes of ideas that usually arrive in your mind instantaneously, moving so fast you almost feel you can't capture them. Although you have no way of comprehending their origin, you feel confident that these thoughts are correct. Sudden thoughts can occur at any time: in the middle of walking up a staircase, in the shower, while you are listening to someone else speak, or when you are playing basketball.

• **Repeated thoughts.** Sometimes it is not the suddenness of a thought but rather the repetition of the same thought that tells you to listen to your intuition. Most people can recall having a "nagging" feeling at some point in their lives.

• **Sudden visions.** These are images and pictures that, like sudden thoughts, pop into your mind with no obvious origin. The visions might be fully fleshed out, in color or even in three dimensions, but they may also be sketches or blurs of something in the distance that you can only barely make out.

• **Gut feelings.** These are recognizable as distinctive, uncomfortable physical sensations, usually located in the stomach or chest, that direct you to do something, go somewhere, get up, or sit down. If you don't do what your gut feelings tell you to do, you don't feel right and you often fail to function well. Gut feelings usually hit quickly, and, especially when you're trying to be creative, are relaying a message you should listen to immediately.

• **Instinctive emotions.** These are often associated with what some people call women's intuition, although men experience them too. They are strong flashes of emotion relating to a situation, issue, or person you've just met. They may be positive feelings that draw you to someone or something or negative impulses that warn you to stay away. Instinctive emotions are somewhat related to gut feelings, except that instead of a strong physical component they begin as a more generalized frame of mind that filters through your body.

• **Sudden "spiritual" feelings.** Anne Durham Robinson, a leading expert on intuition, defines this intuitive sign as a message from within that often deals with extremely deep personal growth issues and reveals itself as an epiphany.

As you can see, many of these signs demand that you learn to feel what is happening inside your body—from free-floating emotions to the teeniest twitches in your stomach or skin.

However intuition manifests itself, remember that intuitive insights usually occur when you are distracted, relaxed, or generally not thinking about your creative challenges. This is precisely the alpha brain wave state, when the brain moves out of its normal waking state and tunes in to the alterconscious. This suggests that there is a strong correlation between creativity and the alterconscious. It seems to be both a source of data that you can use in generating creative ideas and the home of the mysterious function we call intuition.

If you find yourself resisting your intuition, defeat this censoring mechanism by focusing on why you may be blocking this valuable method of getting new ideas. If the answer is rooted in your personal belief system, begin to work on changing it. Think of your intuition as a sixth sense; if you don't use it, you are wasting that part of your perception. By wasting it, you are letting great creative opportunities slip through your hands.

GET TO KNOW YOUR INTUITIVE STYLE

1. What is your attitude toward your intuition? Can you name some events or decisions you have made that demonstrate your intuitive ability in any of the six areas perviously outlined: discovery, creativity, evaluation, operation, prediction, illumination?

2. Are you backwards intuitive, in other words, do you have a tendency to think intuitively but deny your verdict until you have proven your thesis with hard data? I have worked with managers who seemed to make the best decisions based on their "gut feel" but did not implement them until they had secured plenty of marketing reports, financial analysis, and white papers. Margaret Wheatley, a scientist and author of *Leadership and the New Science*, highlights the fact that many people make decisions on an intuitive level, then go off in search of data to back the decisions up.

   If this is you, try this test: the next time you have an intuitive response to a decision, write it down concretely and clearly, then put it away. Get the backup data you need to make your decision, but review your original intuitive answer. After you do this several times, you will begin to trust your intuitive judgment. You will slowly gain confidence in relying on your intuition for increasingly complex decisions.

3. How do you experience intuition? Go through some recent scenarios in which you were particularly creative. Close your eyes and ask the following questions as they relate to the time immediately before your creative inspiration took place:

   a. Was there a strong feeling in your gut pushing you in a certain direction?
   b. Did any thoughts or visions inexplicably pop into your mind?
   c. Did you have repeating thoughts?
   d. Did your emotions cry out for you to take action?
   e. Did you experience any stomach pain, goose bumps, or other physical manifestations?

Your answers to these questions can guide you the next time you need to be creative and want to tap into your intuitive voice. Assessing your symptoms can help you recognize intuition when it occurs. Anne Durham Robinson noticed that if she hears something repeated three times in her mind, it is a good indication that she is experiencing intuition and should heed the message. She suggests that if you really want to connect to your intuition, keep a log of your intuitive experiences.

DAYDREAMING TIME

Our culture tends to dismiss daydreams and reveries. In fact, we often chide those who take refuge in daydreams as slackers. But daydreaming is another avenue into your alterconscious that allows you to tap its vast reserves of images, ideas, and experiences that lead to new connections, that is, creativity. Through daydreaming, you invite the intuitive muse to visit. A well-known story about Henry Ford illustrates this point perfectly. Ford once hired an efficiency expert who examined his organization and recommended that a certain employee be fired. The expert explained that each time the efficiency team walked by the man's office, he had his feet up on his desk and seemed to be daydreaming. Ford acknowledged that although this worker didn't appear to be working as hard as other employees, his last idea had dramatically increased sales. "Let him daydream," Ford admonished the consultant.

What exactly is daydreaming? In the context of the alterconscious, daydreaming is a hypnogogic state of mind, in which the brain is between beta and alpha waves but has not yet fallen asleep. In this state, the mind is less focused and tends either to roam freely from one topic to another or to loosely toss about a single topic without a specific agenda. Daydreaming is characterized by willingness to ponder in a playful way, without concern for realistic scenarios, true motivations, or a specific outcome. Daydreaming can lead you to weird thoughts, crazy outcomes, and even erotic images. It produces just the right frame of mind in which to incubate previously collected information or to stumble upon an answer offered by your intuition.

Visualization

Related to daydreaming is the technique of visualization, a powerful tool for tapping into the alterconscious. Visualization is a form of mental rehearsal or making a "movie in your mind." It differs from daydreaming in that you intentionally prompt your mind to visualize, whereas daydreaming happens more on its own accord when your mind needs a break. Visualization works because the brain has a strong visual inclination that allows us to experience events as if they were truly happening. Visualization allows you to run a scenario in your mind, showing how an event might take place, how a problem can be solved, how a new product idea should be implemented, or what an artistic composition will look or sound like.

Visualization produces three powerful benefits. The first lies in the fact that, during the process neuromuscular templates—patterns of mind-body reflexes that prepare you for what you are going to do—are created. Researchers have shown through electromyographic studies (measurements of minute electrical activity in the muscles) that when you visualize an activity, your muscles undergo electrical impulses corresponding exactly to the physical actions you are imagining. Your muscles effectively "learn" what you want them to do through your visualized mental workout.

Visualized rehearsal and learning help many types of creative work that involve physical activity, such as acting, playing an instrument, speaking in public, or putting something together, as in designing a new product. There is a well-known story about the Chinese pianist Liu Chi Kung, who was imprisoned for seven years during the Cultural Revolution. Although he could not play the piano while in prison, when he was released he had not lost his mastery, and many said he played better than ever. Asked how this was possible, he responded, "I did practice, every day. I rehearsed every piece I had ever played, note by note, in my mind."

Surgeons also are known to visualize their procedures. Dr. Charles Mayo (for whom the famed Mayo Clinic is named) rehearsed in his mind the night before an operation. Many athletes also use visualization to practice how they will perform at an upcoming event. Several books have reported, for example, how the former Soviet Union athletes all received extensive training in visualization, to which they attributed their impressive record of success in the Olympic Games. Muhammad Ali cited the visualization of his fights as a key to his championships, and many world-class skiers and gymnasts visualize their entire routines before a competition. Visualization has been proven so effective that it is now being used in physical rehabilitation and to combat serious illnesses like cancer, for which patients imagine a white light or other healing energy attacking their diseased cells.

The second benefit of visualization is that the technique allows you to get out of your comfort zone. As you conjure up the images of a forthcoming event or a scene in your mind, you become disassociated from the actions, as though your were a bird watching the event from above.

Noted medical doctor and health writer Dean Ornish uses the following analogy to explain how visualization can help you examine a problem or situation from a new perspective. Assume you are standing next to a train track. The train coming by is like your creative challenge; you see each car as it passes. This is similar to how your linear mind views a problem. By contrast, if you can visualize yourself up in a balloon, looking down at the same setting, you can see the train, the track, the village, and many of the surrounding towns. Your new vantage point allows you to take in a much larger picture. This is what happens when you use visualization to solve a problem. With the change of perspective, you become aware of the overall context of your situation—and the numerous places a resolution could be found.

Finally, the most salient creative benefit of visualization arises when you call on your intuition to assist you. When you visualize deeply, you relax your brain into the alpha state, inviting input from your alterconscious. When you imagine a scene or event that you do not fully understand or haven't worked out before, your mind somehow reaches back into its resources and begins to throw out imagery, symbols, and seeds of ideas that your conscious thinking had not proposed.

As in a dream, these images can sometimes be confusing, but they often point you in the direction you need to go. Your intuition may tell you to proceed on a certain course, or to move the part you put on the right over to the left, or it may warn you to avoid talking with a certain person. Sometimes these messages reflect your inner wishes or fears about a situation that are not realistic, rather than intuitive thoughts from your alterconscious. Practice will enable you to distinguish between the two, so that you can rebuff unwarranted fears and control unrealistic wishes while paying attention to meaningful intuitive messages from your alterconscious. Your intuition during visualization can also reveal how you feel about other people.

When you visualize a scene or a conversation, you can get in touch with deep emotions and feelings that you may be neglecting. In this way, your alterconscious helps you imagine the dialogue that may occur or the actions someone else might take. By hearing or seeing the scene in advance, you may get an inkling of someone's strategies, secrets, and inner motivations that your mind has intuitively absorbed but your conscious mind has overlooked or neglected. Your new perception of the situation can then help you select the best strategy to use when you next meet that person.

An excellent example of the use of visualization is the story of the great inventor Nikola Tesla, discoverer of alternating current and developer of many fundamental concepts that laid the groundwork for satellites, microwaves, robots, and computers. Tesla visualized all of his designs in advance. He wrote, "Before I put a sketch on paper, the whole idea is worked out mentally. In my mind, I change the construction, make improvements, and even operate the device. Without ever having drawn the sketch, I can give measurements of all parts to workmen, and when completed all these parts will fit, just as certainly as though I had made the actual drawings."

Here are five general rules to follow in learning how to use creative visualization in your work:

1. Always begin with some relaxation exercises, such as breathing deeply and slowly for five minutes, or by sitting quietly in a comfortable chair and clearing your mind. A relaxed state of mind is essential to release your conscious attention from its agenda so you can enter into your alterconscious.

2. Set your visualization scene slowly. You can either imagine going on a journey to a special location where you rehearse or visualize the problem or issue you want to see or set your scene in its natural location (your office, home, or wherever it would normally occur). Many experts recommend that you choose an exotic location, such as a mountaintop, a cabin in the forest, an island beach, or your own distant "planet," so that you feel as if

 you are going on a journey to a special location known only to you. In this location, you find wisdom and truth, because it metaphorically represents your alterconscious.

3. Only when you get to this location and have relaxed there for a few minutes should you begin asking the question to which you need an answer, or playing out the event you want to rehearse. In setting up the scene, figure out any way that makes sense for you to learn what you seek. If it's a business problem, you might imagine yourself talking with your colleagues or your boss in the office. If you are looking for information, imagine yourself in a library, laboratory, or bookstore. If it's a personal decision, picture yourself standing at a crossroads, wondering which direction to take. You can play out your scene in many ways and even try several options in multiple visualization sessions spread out over a week or so.

4. Don't force anything or impose your conscious voice. Wait for a few moments and see what images, ideas, or characters appear in your visualization. Whatever is evoked from your alterconscious, accept it without judgment or analysis. Become a spectator, as if you were watching the action in a movie theater.

5. Emerge slowly from your visualization. Jot down notes about what you saw or learned.

This procedure can be used for any purpose, whether it is a business question, a conflict negotiation, or the search for a new idea.

VISUALIZING YOUR CREATIVE CHALLENGES

Start by setting up your personal visualization space. You may choose to envision a quiet room, or a unique location — but it must be a place where you can feel total peace and calm.

First, relax and do deep breathing for about five minutes. As you exhale, release any tension that you may be holding in your body. Then start exploring your space; make it an ideal spot where you feel totally at harmony with yourself. See the location in vivid detail, and use all your senses to smell, hear, feel, and even taste the surroundings. Construct your place in your mind using any furnishings or details you want.

Go there now in your mind, but don't take a problem to solve or an event you want to rehearse. Make this first instance a brief visit just to get comfortable in your space. Consider this retreat your special place, to which you can return at any time you want peace, serenity, and a location to work on your ideas, opportunities, or problems. Know also that you can change the location in any way you feel appropriate, by adding or taking away furniture or details as you choose. The key is that this should always be the most welcoming place you can visit, a place where you have no fear or stress.

Once you have designed your special location and visited it a few times in your mind, try a full visualization in which you rehearse an event, ask a question about an issue you are working on, or make a decision about a problem. Follow the five general instructions at left.

What happened in your visualization? What discoveries did you make? Did you sense your intuition alerting you to a solution or a path to follow? Even if you get no concrete results, did you enjoy the experience? Continue visualizing over the next month, perhaps once a week or even once a day, to perfect your technique and get in closer contact with your alterconscious. You may be surprised to find that within a few sessions you feel a change in your ability to find answers to your creative blocks.

For those people who have difficulty visualizing, creativity consultant Win Wenger proposes what he calls Image Streaming. This technique uses all your senses to generate images that might trigger your creativity. In his book *The Einstein Factor,* Wenger proposes that you learn to use Image Streaming in three steps:

Step 1. Learning How to Generate Images Based on Real Objects

➤ Sit in a comfortable chair, close your eyes, and turn on a tape recorder to record what you will say.

➤ Begin describing *out loud* in rich and vivid terms the room where you are sitting or a scene outside your window. Use all your senses to drive your narration; describe how objects feel, look, smell, and taste. Keep talking without editing your narration or worrying about your grammar. Full sentences are not necessary. However, be sure you speak loudly rather than whisper or think your narration (the tape recorder helps reinforce speaking out loud).

➤ Repeat this process for several days in a row, always speaking into the tape recorder. Wenger points out that this type of practice assists you in learning how to narrate your thoughts and describe things in your mind.

Step 2. Learning to Generate Images Based on Imagination

Once you develop the skill of describing, begin describing scenes and pictures that are not there—that is, those from your imagination. Follow the same technique as before in describing these mental images. Close your eyes and imagine any setting, person, or object. Still using the tape recorder, describe whatever your mind sees in as great detail as you can.

Step 3. Learning to Generate Spontaneous Images

You are now on your way to using actively Wenger's Image Streaming. The first two steps were simply a prelude to *spontaneous* imagery, in which you don't imagine or picture anything in particular but wait for images to pop into your mind of their own accord. These images are messages or triggers from your unconscious mind, which, like visualizations, can help you solve a problem, find an answer, or generate a new idea. To invite spontaneous imagery, stay alert. Don't force anything, but, as Wenger says, "the moment an image appears in your mind, describe the dickens out of it!" Don't worry if the image fades; continue describing it as you first saw it. Don't be concerned with accuracy in your descriptions either; just keep saying out loud to your tape recorder whatever comes to mind. Use all five senses in your descriptions to make your narration more vivid. Just keep describing whatever images appear in your head for ten or fifteen minutes.

According to Wenger, the spontaneous imagery technique helps the mind tap the wellspring of thoughts and images it has stored within. As the boundaries between the senses break down, we begin describing colors in terms of taste or smell, and smells in terms of images. This merging of the senses is called *synesthesia,* and the process aids in strengthening the power of images as well as the associations we make from one image to another. Little by little, Image Streaming becomes self-reinforcing; as you describe each image that pops into your mind, your description makes you think of another image, and soon you have strung together a chain of images. One of these may be the spark your creativity needs.

In evaluating these images for answers to your creative challenge, Wenger suggests that you review the tape recordings you made and try to determine why your mind chose certain types of images, why they were sequenced the way they were, and whether some of the images contain particularly poignant emotions that might tip you off to the answers you seek.

Meditation: A Path to Pure Alterconscious

Meditation is perhaps the truest path to your inner self and hence an enormously effective way to contact your alterconscious and invite your creativity. Most people think of meditation as emptying the mind, blanking out, or becoming exceptionally still, which are all valid descriptions but somewhat simplistic. At its best, meditation is a technique for cleansing the mind. In this sense, it is said that the real value of meditation is not what occurs during it but what happens to your thinking *after* you have meditated. Thanks to the clarity of mind you experience following a meditation session, you have a greater chance of freeing your creative spirit and being able to think through your creative challenges.

How does meditation work? There are actually dozens of meditation techniques, so the question cannot be answered briefly.

However, many meditative traditions are aimed at teaching you to achieve a state of illumination, in which you transcend your consciousness by becoming at one with it. This is difficult to understand, but it is analogous to the flow state of mind, in which you function perfectly but effortlessly. In the illumination state, you are able to clear your mind of all consciousness by *becoming* consciousness itself. In *The Transcendental Meditation TM Book,* Dennis Denniston writes, "The Transcendental Meditation technique is a simple, natural, effortless process that allows the mind to experience subtler and subtler levels of the thinking process until thinking is transcended and the mind comes into direct contact with the source of thought."

Some meditation techniques have you concentrate on a single object or idea to clear your mind of all extraneous thought; other techniques have you think about something such as God or Oneness; and still others suggest you blank your mind until you are "aware without thought." Whichever practice is used, the general goal is to release all tensions from your mind and induce a state of blissful relaxation. While other kinds of relaxation such as daydreaming and visualization also create the conditions for creativity, meditation is reputed to be one of the most powerful. People who meditate regularly say that they come out of a meditative experience with restfully alert minds and find afterward that they often have more frequent and perceptive insights that come from deeper within. Some academic research has also shown that long-term meditators scored significantly higher on certain types of creativity tests.

Meditation must be done regularly and consistently to truly benefit from it. Although instructional tapes and books are available, many meditators suggest that it is best to learn the technique from a master, who can evaluate your personal situation and make sure you learn correctly.

A SIMPLE MEDITATIVE RELAXATION TECHNIQUE

Here is a simple but effective breathing technique from the ancient Chinese healing art of chi kung (also spelled gi gong). The technique, if practiced regularly and properly, will help you release tension and, with enough practice, move you easily into a hypnogogic or meditative state. Read the directions, then try the exercise. It can be practiced anywhere at any time, with or without the eyes closed.

Close your eyes and get in a relaxed sitting position. Place your hands comfortably on your lap. Allow your body to release its inner tensions with a couple of deep, cleansing breaths. Now imagine that in your stomach is a large bowl. Inhale through your nose, in a slow and measured manner so that no sound is made as the air passes through your nostrils. Imagine the air flowing into your body and slowly filling the bowl in your stomach. When the bowl is full, imagine that a weight has been put on top of the air in the bowl, and slowly, again without being able to hear the rush of air through your nostrils, let it leave your body. Repeat this sequence for approximately five minutes (or until you choose to stop). Concentrate only on the breathing. Relax and emerge slowly from your position.

If you are interested in meditation, consult your yellow pages under Meditation Instruction to find schools and courses to teach you. Many community colleges and even hospitals also offer courses in meditation.

Dreams: Secret Gateway to Your Alterconscious

Dreaming is one step further along the way to the alterconscious, beyond the alpha brain wave state to the delta and theta states of sleep. It has long been accepted that dreams are signals of intuitive messages or advice from the alterconscious. Perhaps more than any other creativity tool, dreaming figures in a plethora of stories testifying to the famous decisions, inventions, and artistic pieces that were delivered to their makers while they slept:

- **Mozart heard his music in his dreams.**
- **Robert Louis Stevenson dreamed the plot of _Dr. Jekyll and Mr. Hyde._**

- **Stephen King claims that all his ideas come out of his dreams.**
- **William Styron's dream of a woman he had known in his earlier years led to his novel *Sophie's Choice*.**
- **Bette Nesmith Graham invented Liquid Paper (correction fluid) after a dream gave her the idea. Her invention had delivered her $50 million by the time she died in 1980.**
- **Elias Howe was able to complete his invention of the sewing machine after a vivid dream that told him to add an opening to the needle at its base.**

For all the dreams that have occurred in the history of the world, we are still far from understanding where dreams come from and what they may be telling us. For most of history, dreams were little understood, though most philosophers considered them obvious doors to the inner mind. Aristotle thought dreams were early warning signs of illness. Many kings and queens had dream interpreters to help them determine their courses of action. In the seventeenth century, Thomas Hobbes promoted the theory that dreams were nothing more than "distempers" of the internal organs. Since that time, sleep researchers have learned that we dream all night but that the most vivid and longest dreams occur during four or five periods of time called REM (rapid eye movement) sleep, which alternates with deeper sleep stages. We usually begin our first REM period about 90 minutes into sleep and have four or five more REM periods during an eight-hour night, for a total of about 90 to 120 minutes of vivid dreaming. Oddly enough, beta waves are associated with REM dreaming, indicating brain activity that suddenly interrupts the deeper stages of sleep, in which your brain is usually producing delta waves.

Freud and Jung were both quite interested in dreams. Freud called dreams "the royal road to the unconscious mind." One of Jung's major works was entitled *Individual Dream Symbolism in Relation to Alchemy,* a book in which he analyzed more than 1,000 of a patient's dreams and developed his theories on the universal symbolic nature of dream imagery. However, even Jung began to understand that the images and symbols that come to us in our dreams are truly not open to formulaic interpretations and instead reflect much about our individuality. Jung is known to have encouraged his students to learn as much as they could about dream symbols but then to forget it all when they were analyzing a dream.

Nevertheless, dreams can be your personal source of information, delivering messages from your alterconscious to guide your creativity. Dreams can reveal a path to take in your life, a decision, or a full-blown image of the artistic creation you are working on. The power of dreams to inspire you is best stated by the fact that nearly everyone automatically looks to dreams for advice. It is almost impossible to wake up and, remembering a dream, not want to know what it was telling you. You have an intuitive sense that your dream is a metaphor or symbol for something your mind is suggesting—and that is probably because your dream truly reflects your alterconscious telling you something.

The number of dreams you remember and understand appears to be related to how interested you are in working with them. People who have no curiosity about what their dreams tell them tend to remember very few. But people who believe that their dreams offer insights or intuitive messages tend to remember many more dreams than the average person and to listen to them more closely. If you are interested in using your dreams to boost your creativity or as a door to your alterconscious, experts recommend the following specific techniques:

- *Dream capture:* remembering and recording dreams
- *Dream control:* determining what you want to dream
- *Interpretation:* gaining understanding or meaning from dreams
- *Action:* deciding what to do as a result of the dream experience

Dream capture is actually an ancient practice that figures in the mythology of many cultures. Native Americans created beautiful dream catchers, circles of leather woven around nets of thread that trap your good dreams while letting the evil ones pass through the holes in the net. A technique based on Australian Aboriginal folklore is to put a glass of water by your bedside, drink half before you go to sleep and drink the other half immediately upon awakening. (This worked for me.) Today most dream experts suggest that you approach dream capture systematically by recording your dreams as soon as you awaken either in a written dream log or in some other form that you can refer back to from time to time. I use my laptop computer, but others use notebooks or sheets of paper on which they mindmap the dream or even narrate their dreams into pocket tape recorders. The key is to record as many details as possible right away so that you can come back to the dream later for analysis.

Dream control refers to the fact that you can learn to "program" or "seed" your dreaming. Psychologists maintain that this can be accomplished by quietly suggesting to yourself—before you go to sleep—the topic on which you want to dream and that you want to remember it. Alternatively, as you prepare for sleep, review your day or the creative challenge before you and then consciously pose yourself a question that you want your dream to answer. Think about the problem as you lie in bed and let yourself fall asleep. Not everyone can achieve this level of control, but trying to do so may at least make you more aware of your dream process.

Understanding and interpreting the messages of your dreams is the most challenging aspect of using dreams for creativity. Some dreams are self-evident. You dream about being berated by your boss, and you finally realize that he is too critical. You dream about seeing your clarinet in a dusty cabinet, and you realize that you haven't practiced in a few days. However, many dreams require a much deeper analysis to understand their symbolism— and you are as likely to misinterpret them as not. As one dream writer put it, dreams are catch-22's—they are a door to your intuition, but you need to be pretty intuitive to understand them.

As I have indicated, dream interpretation and the decision to take action based on your dreams are quite personal. It can take years of practice to get good at fully understanding the meaning of your dreams. If you intend to approach dreams for more than occasional amusement, it is useful to read several books on dream interpretation or even to work with a trained dream therapist. Many people benefit greatly by incorporating dream analysis into their creative process as a complement to the many other techniques for reaching the alterconscious.

DREAM ON

If you would like to see how your dreams reflect your creative challenges, here are five techniques used by many analysts to get to the meaning of dreams. These techniques are just a starting point; see "Further Readings" for more help in dream analysis.

1. If the dream has no ending, sit down and write an ending to it.
2. Make a work of art based on the dream. What characters or types of people did you create? What were the key characteristics evident in the drawing or other type of artwork?
3. Is there a character in the dream that seems to have some specific reason for being there? Write an imaginary dialogue with that character, asking about his or her purpose in the dream, and what idea or thought this character may have to reveal to you.
4. Make the dream concrete. Re-create the central action of the dream. If it is about painting, paint; if it is about dancing, dance. Pay particular attention to the feelings accompanying the dream.
5. Ponder the presence of any creatures or animals in your dream. Why are they there? Use active imagination to interpret their significance.

Honoring Your Alterconscious

All the techniques of this chapter—intuition, daydreams, visualization, meditation, and dreams—are actually servants of your alterconscious. By honoring these servants—calling upon them, listening to them, and letting them come to you as they please—you can significantly enrich your creative spirit. Like the ancient Chinese symbol of yin and yang, your creativity results from a combination of your rational mind and your inner mind. As the intuition expert Daniel Cappon, M.D., stated in a 1994 issue of *Omni* magazine, intuition and deductive reasoning "ideally work in balance, yin and yang. If logical reasoning and analysis have brought knowledge to the crown of human intelligence, then intuition—and its inseparable twin, creativity—form the jewel in the crown."

Further Readings

Creative Breakthroughs: Tap the Power of Your Unconscious Mind by Jill Morris (New York: Warner Books, 1992).

Creative Dreaming—Plan and Control Your Dreams to Develop Creativity, Overcome Fears, Solve Problems and Create a Better Self by Patricia Garfield (New York: Simon & Schuster, 1995).

Creative Visualization by Shakti Gawain (New York: MFJ Books, 1978).

Developing Intuition (audiotapes) by Shakti Gawain (Novato, Cal.: Nataraj Publishing, August 1989).

The Einstein Factor: A Proven Method For Increasing Your Intelligence by Win Wenger and Richard Poe (Rocklin, Cal.: Prima Publishing, 1996).

F-States: The Power of Fantasy in Human Creativity by Steven Starker (Van Nuys, Cal.: Newcastle, 1985).

Intuition Workout—A Practical Guide to Discovering and Developing Your Inner Knowing by Nancy Rosanoff (Santa Rosa, Cal.: Aslan Publishing, 1991).

The Intuitive Edge—Understanding Intuition and Applying It in Everyday Life by Philip Goldberg (Los Angeles: Jeremy P. Tarcher, 1983).

The Intuitive Manager by Roy Rowan (Boston: Little, Brown, 1986).

A Little Course in Dreams: A Basic Handbook of Jungian Dreamwork by Robert Bosnak (Boston: Shambhala, 1988).

The Mind Workout Book by Vernon Coleman (London: Viscount Books, 1989).

Sixth Sense: The Whole-Brain Book of Intuition, Hunches, Gut Feelings, and Their Place in Your Everyday Life by Laurie Nadel (New York: Prentice Hall Press, 1990).

The Theft of Spirit by Carl Hammerschlag (New York: Fireside Books, 1992).

Tools for Exploration (catalog) 800/456-9887.

Working on Yourself Alone by Arnold Mindell (New York: Arkana, 1990).

Connect with Your Creative Soul

Of all the strategies we have so far explored to inspire your creativity or contribute to the successful production of ideas, this last one is by far the most difficult to describe. Connecting with your inner self requires that you be open to the idea that within each of us are the seeds of great ideas. Some of us don't have the ability to hear our own ideas, or lack the willingness to listen to our creative souls. There are many different paths to hearing our inner self clearly. Some people find that clarity comes from following a spiritual path. Some follow a road that offers new ways to reflect on the inner self. And still others will find that alternative, what some may call New Age, approaches work best for them. Regardless of the method, like most of the creative strategies discussed in this book, any road that "works for you" can lead to untapped creativity.

There are many ways to explore and discover your spiritual side so that you can introduce or incorporate it into your creative work. The methods we will explore in this chapter include prayer, affirmations, rituals, meditation, movement, retreats, pilgrimages, and oracles. This chapter examines these methods not in the context of any specific doctrine, but rather as practices that cross many traditions.

Spirituality

Before explaining the relationship between spirituality and creativity, let's differentiate between the terms *spirituality* and *religion*. *Spirituality* can be defined as a feeling of connection with something beyond our ability to comprehend but not beyond our awareness. Although it is outside our sight, we know it is there.

Spirituality provides us with comfort and a sense of peace. It is intuitive but inexplicable. The term *religion* does not necessarily point to spirituality. Many people are religious in the sense that they embrace a specific set of beliefs. Not all of them are spiritual, though. Religion itself does not create spiritual awareness, because that must come from inside. Think, for example, of the many native peoples who embraced religions brought to them by missionaries from far away but who continued to live according to their old spiritual beliefs. A Chinese friend who was brought up in the Philippines related to me that when he was a child, many people in his community were converted to Catholicism, yet they continued to bring traditional Chinese spiritual beliefs into the daily rituals of their new religion.

So how does spirituality fit into the creative process? For some people, the connection is quite direct. They believe in a God or higher power from which they feel their creative blessings flow. For these people, the higher power is a voice that continually guides them on their creative path. For others spiritual feelings connect them to their inner souls, from which their creativity blooms. For still others, spirituality is a connection not to a higher power in the traditional religious sense but to the inexplicable harmony between the individual and the universe.

In all three instances, spirituality is the inexplicable element that contributes to inspiration. It is interesting, in fact, to look at the word *inspired,* which derives from the Latin meaning "to breathe into"; when we look at one of our creative works and say that it is inspired, we are acknowledging that the life of the idea comes from beyond ourselves. Many people also say that the idea for a beautiful piece of art, an elegant building, or an invention came to them "out of thin air." In a sense, this thin air is our spirituality; it is the air we have breathed to become inspired.

Other than offering this simple explanation of inspiration as an aspect of spirituality, it is difficult for me to explain ways that spirituality can help boost *your* creativity or add to *your* ability to generate profitable ideas. This is because my sense of spirituality cannot be transferred to you; it must be experienced directly by you. The pioneer of American psychology William James wrote, "Spirituality defies expression, . . . no adequate report of its content can be given in words. It follows from this that its quality must be directly experienced, it cannot be imparted or transferred to others." In other words, the extent to which your creativity may be changed, influenced, or enhanced by your spiritual feelings relates directly to how *you* experience spirituality. This is the perennial conundrum of defining spirituality.

Nevertheless, whatever your religious beliefs, an exploration of your spirituality can benefit your creativity in many ways. First, most spiritual teachings encourage you to slow down, concentrate, and focus on your feelings to achieve harmony and inner peace. If you are stuck on a problem or unable to grasp an idea bubbling inside, being quiet and gaining internal equilibrium can often break the block and reveal the path you need to follow. Slowing down also allows you to listen more attentively to the stirrings of your thoughts—which reflect the process of incubation that may be occurring in your mind. In our high-pressured society, we frequently lose our creative way because we are simply moving too fast from one event or idea to another. We leave our work only partially done, or we don't give a budding idea the time and space to grow fully.

Spirituality can also provide a source of energy you didn't know you had. Throughout the ages, many artists, scientists, explorers, writers, and poets have acknowledged the sustenance that spirituality has provided them in the face of adversity. Some people pray for this energy; others get it through the practices of contemplation and meditation.

It is probably true that, for most of us, creativity arises from our desire to do good, to make the world a better place, and to leave something of ourselves behind for future generations. Such a desire to achieve world peace, harmony, and prosperity for everyone provides basic elements of nearly every spiritual tradition. In this sense, feeling at one with the world—and at peace with one's soul—imparts a healthy focus to our creative urges. I am sure you, like most people I know, feel more creative when you are working on a project that benefits others than when you are involved in something that destroys or depletes our limited resources. Depending on your intent, charity can actually be a creative act that carries back into your other creative work. As the ancient biblical expression metaphorically reminds us, "As ye sow, so shall ye reap."

Your spirituality can also bolster your self-confidence and self-esteem, necessary ingredients for many creative endeavors. This is not to say that you cannot be confident if you are not spiritual, but exploring your deeper spiritual nature almost always leads to self-knowledge and self-assurance. When you don't believe in your own ideas, they seldom see the light of day. Without self-confidence, self-censorship takes over, killing your imagination and creative thoughts.

Finally, thousands of years of spiritual and religious history have created a body of work in many arts that can trigger creativity. Whatever your beliefs, it is impossible not to recognize the extraordinary human effort behind the ceiling of the Sistine Chapel, or the intelligence embedded in a 2,000-year-old holy scroll, or the absolute presence of the Great Buddha at Kamakura. Many writers, poets, artists, and composers have drawn on previous works of art and spiritual teachings to create great works enjoyed by modern audiences. Consider, for example, the success of such theatrical pieces as *Jesus Christ Superstar* and *Joseph and the Amazing Technicolor Dreamcoat* and films like *It's a Wonderful Life* and *Little Buddha*.

Prayer

Prayer is a ritualized and active form of meditation and contemplation—directed outward to communicate with God. Prayer can be highly formalized or extemporaneous; its goal can include praise, thanksgiving, a petition for oneself or others, confession, or a request for forgiveness.

From a creative perspective, prayer can function either as a request for inspiration, guidance, or assistance, or as an offering of thanks for the successful completion of a goal. Some artists and businesspeople use prayer in a very direct way to boost their creativity; they simply ask God to deliver an idea or solution to a problem. Other people use prayer to rebuild their spirits or get in touch with their creative souls.

Prayer is extremely personal, and must be discovered and

understood on your own terms. There is a poignant folk tale that wonderfully highlights the highly personal nature of prayer. The story recounts that there was once a rich and powerful emperor. One day, the emperor found out about a man whose reputation was quickly spreading as the most holy man in the kingdom. It was said that this man prayed constantly. The emperor decided he must visit this man. He set out on the journey to a faraway island, where the man lived. Much to his surprise, when he arrived, the emperor found a poor and simple fisherman praying on the shore. He asked of the man if he might watch him pray; the fisherman agreed and began praying.

The emperor watched the man closely for an hour. The fisherman closed his eyes, held his head skyward, and moved his lips as if in prayer, but he did nothing else. Finally, the emperor stood up and asked the fisherman to stop praying. He then began scolding the fisherman, telling him that his method of prayer was completely incorrect. He insisted that the fisherman learn to pray according to the methods used throughout the palace. The fisherman listened patiently as the emperor gave him lessons, repeating the words and the phrasing just as the emperor told him to. When the lesson was over, he humbly thanked the emperor, bowed, and left the shore to return to his home.

The emperor boarded his boat to return to his palace, proud of the good deed he had done in instructing the poor fisherman how to pray correctly. Suddenly though, as the boat was approaching a quarter-mile out to sea, one of the servants on the boat came running to the emperor, frantically pointing back toward the shore. The emperor gazed into the distance, and lo, he saw the fisherman running after them—on top of the water. Within a minute, the old fisherman was literally standing next to the boat, his feet gently washed with waves, as he bowed with reverence to the emperor. "Excuse me, your Highness," the fisherman called out from the side of the boat, "but I have forgotten the words you taught me. Would you please instruct me again?" The emperor waved his hands to the fisherman, gesturing him to go back to shore. "No, no," he apologized to the old man. "Forget what I have taught you. Just continue praying as you did before my visit."

So, whatever your creative venture, I can only recommend that you use prayer in whatever way you have always used it, or in whatever way that you discover works for you.

Quieting the Mind
Through Meditation and Movement

In the last chapter, I spoke about meditation as a gateway to your alterconscious. Techniques like Transcendental Meditation are aimed at clearing the mind and body to allow your creative energy to flow. However, meditation can also be a path to higher spirituality and enlightenment, as in the Zen school of Buddhism. Zen teaches that people can grasp the oneness of the universe not through logic, rational thought, or verbal doctrine but through meditation and contemplation. Zen masters spend years learning how to concentrate on what the West often calls "nothingness." They also use the tea ceremony, calligraphy, music, and Zen gardening (which employs stones and sand raked into patterns) to clear their minds.

Many cultures have developed a form of slow, quiet movement that, like meditation, helps integrate body and mind. Just as an hour of aerobics or even a walk around the block makes you feel reinvigorated, these types of physical movement free the mind from conflict and put you in touch with your inner energy. A refreshed and balanced body releases your inner wisdom and permits your inspiration to flow.

One of the most widely used spiritually oriented body movement techniques is yoga, a system of breathing and postures that has been practiced for more than six thousand years. Yoga, which means "union," teaches you to be at one with your body and mind. The greatest yogis (those who practice yoga) are revered because of their ability to unite spiritually with what they call the life force, the energy that flows through all forms of life. Yoga teaches you to be highly attuned to your body. Through its practice, you learn to be sensitive to your nerve fibers and muscles, and to develop natural ways to manipulate and direct the energy channels in your body. There are many types of yoga, which differ in the postures they use and in their spiritual orientation. One of the most popular in the West is hatha yoga, which uses postures and breathing to relax and stretch the body.

The recent resurgence of interest in the martial arts also reflects not simply an interest in self-defense but a growing recognition of the spiritual connection between body and mind. Martial arts such as aikido, tai chi chuan (also spelled kuan), and chi kung are all fundamentally based on learning how to control the flow of the life force *chi* (Chinese, also spelled *qi,* which is *ki* in Japanese) through body movement. I studied chi kung under a Chinese master and found that, when practiced, it significantly improved my health and, more important, profoundly increased my awareness of the world and my ability to feel creative. In the traditions from which each of these martial arts arises, the spiritual connection is a critical component in mastering them.

Many cultures—including the Native American, African tribal, Australian Aboriginal, and Islamic—have body movement techniques, some more spiritual than others, that facilitate a reconnection to your inner force, clearing away obstacles to your creativity and nourishing your spirit. Even in some Christian traditions, there is a meditative walk called the labyrinth, which is a spiral maze that appears on the floor of some medieval churches. The most famous one is at Chartres Cathedral in France.

Most cities have centers where you can learn yoga, tai chi, or other movement traditions. If you are interested in studying any of these, many sports centers and even community colleges offer courses. You might also look in your yellow pages under Martial Arts, Yoga, or Tai Chi Instruction.

Affirmations

Affirmations are short statements made to yourself that help you refocus your spirit and pay attention to yourself. While some argue affirmations are little more than quick fixes to inspire self-confidence and positive thinking, they can be powerful reinforcing thoughts that inspire you to be mindful and caring of your soul. This is the aspect of affirmations that makes them part of a spiritual path.

You can recite affirmations to yourself in the morning upon awakening, at night before sleep, or any time you feel anxious and unbalanced. Some people write their affirmations on large slips of paper and hang them on their walls or even on their refrigerators so they can be constantly in view.

Writing affirmations to assist your creativity should be done with care. Write in the present tense, using positive words so that you actually see yourself performing the way you would like to. Affirmations program your alterconscious in the same way that a mental rehearsal does. For example, a songwriter might create an affirmation like "I effortlessly compose music with pleasant harmonies." A busy manager might write, "I take the time to think each problem through."

I recommend that you write affirmations for each element of your creative C.O.R.E. so you can constantly remind yourself of your creative spirit. For instance, a general affirmation to inspire curiosity is, "Today I seek the awe and wonder that is my life. I am willing to explore each new idea and opportunity that comes my way."

Celebrations and Rituals

Rituals demarcate many universal experiences, such as birth, death, coming of age (confirmation and bar mitzvah), and marriage. We usually celebrate these rituals by getting together with friends and family, eating a fine meal, perhaps sharing a glass of wine. The value of rituals is that they help us mark the milestones of life, celebrating the progress we've made or mourning something we've lost so that we can continue with the rest of our life.

The power of rituals can be applied to creative work, too. Just  as in other aspects of life, you can devise many types of "creative rituals" to boost your spirit and take stock of your progress. For example, many artists make it a point to celebrate the start of each new project with a festive party or gathering, announcing to themselves and the world that they are entering a new phase in their life. Such a kickoff party can literally stir up enough creative energy and excitement to propel you forward—at least during the initial days when an extra boost is often useful.

A creative ritual does not have to be complex, lengthy, or expensive (although, technically speaking, it should be repetitive to be a ritual). You can devise a simple creative ritual to use any time you need to renew your spirit or give yourself support. In developing your ritual, the goal is simply to design something that allows you to reconnect with your creative C.O.R.E. and makes you mindful of your deepest feelings and thoughts. Rituals that involve "grounding" elements (earth, wind, water, and fire) are particularly useful for this. For example, you might decide to make it a ritual to do some gardening or to go for a walk in the woods or at the beach whenever you get stuck on a problem and need to refocus your concentration. For some people, an excellent creative ritual is to brew an afternoon pot of tea and sip it while reflecting in a favorite chair by a fireplace before sitting down to work.

MINI WORKSHOP

DEVISING YOUR OWN RITUALS

Do you use any rituals to inspire your creativity? If not, develop some ideas for rituals that could help you, such as in the following circumstances:

- **Starting your creative work each day**
- **Kicking off your next big project**
- **Overcoming impasses or blocks**
- **Celebrating a success**
- **Mourning a creative failure and moving on to a new project**

Be creative and feel free to invent any type of ritual you would like. For example, when I was writing this book, I had a ritual to begin writing sessions: I put on drumming music and sat for a few moments with my eyes closed while my body and mind prepared for the work. Through this ritual, I found that I became more focused and energetic, and I can recall many sessions when the ritual literally put me into a flow state of mind that allowed me to write freely and easily.

Remember, your rituals do not need to be overtly spiritual or religious in nature; even going to an amusement park can be a bona fide ritual if it actually helps you to reconnect with your artistic C.O.R.E. Give yourself free reign to devise whatever type of creative rituals you are drawn to design.

Even companies can devise rituals to boost creativity when employees are about to begin a new project or to celebrate closure when a successful job ends. These rituals can serve as important touchstones to focus everyone on a common vision. Although they are performed in the neutral business environment, they are as spiritual as any celebration because they transform the ordinary into the special and show respect and honor for employees. Here are some ideas for rituals you can implement in your company:

- Kick off projects with a celebration for those involved.
- Hand out awards in a public forum so everyone can share the sense of accomplishment.
- Acknowledge failures by wrapping them up and burying them so everyone can feel good about having tried.

Take some time now to develop three rituals that might be helpful in making your company a more creative place to work.

Retreats: Getting Back in Touch with Yourself

Nearly all cultures and religions recognize that focusing on yourself and connecting with the soul often requires you to "leave" the world for a time to seek peace. This leaving, which many refer to as a retreat, allows you to honor yourself and pay attention to your creative spirit. Even corporations are using retreats to help their executives or staff discover themselves, create new ideas, or develop a shared vision.

A personal retreat can be as simple as setting aside a weekend to be in your own home, doing nothing but contemplation and rest to refresh your creativity. Another type of retreat can be a house you rent in the mountains, surrounded by streams and forests that remind you of the marvels of nature, or in the desert, where you can see enormous vistas of stars that remind you of the infinity of the universe. You can also take a retreat dedicated to cleansing and purifying your body and mind through activities such as sweating and fasting. The physical component of sweating out toxins from your body and completely eliminating waste from food is actually an impetus for the body to undertake renewal and rebalancing. Many cultures have sweat-inducing retreats like saunas or sweat lodges. A sweat lodge is similar to a

Scandinavian sauna, except that its orientation is personal and spiritual. It is usually a tent where a group of people sit in a circle around a bed of hot rocks. In Native American cultures, this practice is said to prepare you for a spiritual journey.

Yet another type of retreat focuses on pampering yourself and become totally relaxed. Going to a spa for a massage and a mineral or mud bath, or spending a weekend at a hotel filled with alternating periods of exercise and relaxation can make you feel like a new person. Although such a retreat may feel more like an indulgence than a spiritual experience, it serves the same purpose of refreshing your mind, rebalancing your body, and putting you back in touch with your creative spirit.

CREATING YOUR OWN RETREAT

Organize your own formal or informal retreat. You can either do this yourself or invite a spiritual guide to help you reconnect with your soul through specific assignments. You might do your retreat in your own home or find a formal retreat, sanctuary, or religious center nearby. Some monasteries and temples permit visitors of any denomination to stay on their grounds.

If you choose to make a retreat in your own home or at a house in the mountains or desert, find a simple space. Clear out any distractions and turn off your phone. This is a time to shut out the outer world and tune in to your inner world. Fast (check with your doctor first) or eat simple foods like homemade breads, soup, and fresh fruit. You want your body to be tuned in to its whole self, not preoccupied with digestion. Have books, paper, pens, and perhaps art supplies to inspire your creative spirit. During your retreat, become attuned to your surroundings and your inner thoughts. Notice the noise in your head, the way the light shines through the window, the smell of the air, the way the floor feels under your bare feet, aches and pains in your body, and memories that float to the surface. Practice being mindful and noticing your being.

Pilgrimages

To rediscover your creative soul, it is sometimes useful to take a journey or pilgrimage to a distant place that you consider sacred or venerable. When we think of pilgrimages and sacred sites, we may imagine a long walking trek among the great cathedrals of Europe or an extended trip to faraway holy sites such as Bethlehem, Mecca, the Sinai, or the Ganges River. However there are many other places in the world that can constitute creative and spiritual pilgrimage destinations; the mind knows when it is filled with awe and reverence. Many locations—such as the Carlsbad Caverns, Haleakala on Maui, the Acropolis, the pyramids of Egypt, and the monoliths of Stonehenge—inspire an appreciation for the harmony we have with nature or the power of the human mind.

A pilgrimage can have any number of purposes related to your creative needs: wonder and awe, meditation and mindfulness, silence and reflection, a vision quest, contemplation and self-realization, or healing. Perhaps the greatest value of a pilgrimage is what you get not from seeing the site itself but from the feelings and emotions it stirs in your creative soul. In *Sacred Sites: A Guidebook to Sacred Centers and Mysterious Places in the United States,* travel writer Frank Joseph points out, "A sense of wonder is essential to a full-bodied appreciation of any sacred center. But our higher purpose should be to communicate with it, if not in words, then in emotion."

PILGRIMAGE SPACES

Make a list of five places that create awe and wonder in your mind when you think about them. Select the one that attracts you most and develop a plan to visit it within the next year. Then detail a plan to honor and experience the spiritual power you feel about the site. This plan should be spiritual in your own personal way, not necessarily something you gleaned from your religious background. It may be a natural site such as Yosemite National Park or Sedona, Arizona, or a traditional sacred shrine, such as the Wailing Wall in Jerusalem. Use this experience to create something, like a collage, a drawing or visual art project, or a musical composition, to be a continual reminder of spiritual feelings that exist within you.

Oracles

Oracles are believed by some to be voices from a higher power that address questions posed by seekers of illumination. In ancient Greece, people turned to oracles to hear the gods' predictions of the future. At the famous Oracle of Delphi, a priestess called Pythia ate the leaves of the sacred laurel tree and breathed intoxicating vapors to put her into a trancelike state. Priests recorded her strange sounds and reported them as revelations from the god Apollo. Honored with gifts of pure gold and silver, the oracle exerted a powerful influence over Greek history. The ancient Greek people consulted oracles before wars and other major events with the same zeal some twentieth-century people consult astrologers or psychics.

Most other cultures have looked to oracles to help predict the future. Native Americans have used special methods of divination, and African tribal cultures have relied on oracles ranging from South African bone divination to the sacred system of worship used by Ifa priests in southwestern Nigeria. The Germanic peoples who occupied what is now Greenland and Scandinavia millennia ago used small stones called runes to gain insight into themselves and the future.

One well-known system of oracles, which is becoming increasingly popular, is the Chinese *I Ching*, the "Book of Changes." The *I Ching* celebrates the balance between the feminine force, yin, and the masculine force, yang. Consulting the *I Ching* is simple. You pose a question, then toss three coins three times to produce one of sixty-four hexagrams (previously defined combinations of the coins). By consulting the *I Ching*, you determine the hexagram's meaning and relevance to your question.

How do oracles work? One theory is that they draw on the same quality of knowledge as intuition. The answers they provide actually reflect the inner wisdom of the asker, and the answers' effectiveness depends on the asker's belief and how he or she interprets the results. In this sense, oracles are closely related to the wise ancient advice "Know thyself," which according to Plutarch was inscribed on the Oracle at Delphi.

Today, as in ancient times, some people use oracles as guides to self-understanding and creativity. The oracle doesn't foretell your specific future as much as it directs your mind to follow a certain path or allows you to look at a problem or issue from a fresh perspective. Oracles can thus be used to stimulate ideas or restructure your thoughts.

EXPLORING ORACLES FOR YOUR CREATIVITY
Many bookstores have popular guides to a variety of oracles, such as the Norse runes, the *I Ching,* tarot cards, Native American medicine cards, and so on. If you are not familiar with these ancient methods of divination, it can be fun as well as revealing to try one of them as you develop a creative project. Even if you are not inclined to feel a spiritual connection to the oracles, the chances for serendipity and synchronicity still exist. You never know!

Tuning in to Your Spirituality

All the techniques in this chapter, at their core, help you center yourself, reconnect with your emotions, and reinvigorate your creative spirit. The extent to which you link these techniques with a religion or a belief in the existence of a higher power does not interfere with their effectiveness in balancing your body, mind, and soul. Respecting your powers through affirmations, taking time for yourself on retreats, or inspiring your awe for the inexplicable through a pilgrimage all open you to establishing a way to listen to your own creative spirit.

I have defined a spiritual path for myself that has guided me through many creative endeavors, including the writing of this book. I invite you to glean what works for you from this chapter and use it in any fashion that nourishes your C.O.R.E.

Further Readings

Doorway to the Soul: How to Have a Profound Spiritual Experience by Ron Scolastico (New York: Scribner, 1995).

The Heart Aroused: Poetry and the Presentation of the Soul in Corporate America by David Whyte (New York: Doubleday, Currency, 1994).

Nourishing the Soul—Discovering the Sacred in Everyday Life edited by Anne Simpkinson, Charles Simpkinson, and Rose Solari (San Francisco: HarperCollins, 1995).

The Present Moment: A Retreat on the Practice of Mindfulness (audiotapes) by Thich Naht Hanh (Boulder, Colo.: Sounds True Audio, 1993) 800/333-9185.

Sacred Sites: A Guidebook to Sacred Centers and Mysterious Places in the United States edited by Frank Joseph (St. Paul, Minn.: Llewellyn, 1992).

The Theft of Spirit by Carl Hammerschlag (New York: Fireside Books, 1992).

The World Atlas of Divination: The Systems, Where They Originate, How They Work edited by John Matthews (Boston: Little, Brown, 1992).

epilogue:
Ideas into Action

Everyone is creative, and people are working on creative ideas all the time. The problem is putting the ideas into some form. That's where it all falls apart. —BETTY EDWARDS, AUTHOR OF *DRAWING ON THE RIGHT SIDE OF THE BRAIN*

If you actively use the strategies in this book—the one or two that most appeal to you or all ten—you will assuredly begin to have more and more ideas about everything in your life: how to decorate your home more beautifully, how to raise your children more joyfully, and how to solve creative challenges in your professional work or personal life more effectively. Each tool assists you in its own way, but try to remember that all of them are at your disposal. They are a holistic system: the more you use any one of them, the more you will be tempted to use others, because they are closely interconnected.

The next time you are seeking a new idea, need to get unblocked, or want to develop a business or personal project, use the chart that follows to remind yourself of the broad spectrum of techniques and strategies available to help your creativity thrive and flourish. You might even photocopy this chart and hang it on the wall, in your office, in your studio, and in your home—wherever you most need to gain access to the creativity within.

Making Your Ideas Happen

To complete your transformation into a more creative person, you need to keep in mind one additional point. Creative people fall into two camps: those who are great at coming up with ideas, and those who are great at coming up with ideas and making them happen. The first group of people are often labeled

Techniques and Strategies

People	Pay attention to synchronicity and serendipity in all your meetings and encounters.	Join a creative community or start your own.
Environment	Enhance your environment by redesigning your lighting, furnishings, and comfort.	Use aromatherapy to spark memories and experiences that can fuel your creative output.
Travel	Use travel to find inspiration for new ideas and to refresh your creative soul.	Take a creative emergency trip anywhere in your local area when you become blocked and need to refresh your mind.
Play/Humor	Put fun back in your life by engaging in amusing and enjoyable activities and humorous games.	Develop a playful environment at work; encourage employees to have fun in meetings to generate ideas.
Reading	Start a "creative reading" plan that teaches you to read across a wide spectrum of sources.	Go to a newsstand and pick out the top-left-hand corner magazine or any magazine that you would otherwise never read.
Art/Music	Actively participate in doing some type of art to connect with your deepest, natural creative feelings.	Reevaluate your negative judgments about not being able to do art "correctly"; engage in art for yourself only.

Find a mentor to support and guide you.

Network to expand your contacts and idea connections.

Observe your own pet peeves and needs, and those of others, to come up with new entrepreneurial ideas.

Surround yourself with environmental art to spur your thinking.

Eliminate detractors and "crazy makers" from your creative work, or change jobs.

Find your "creativity trigger," a cue that automatically reminds you of your peak creative performance.

Seek out synchronicity and serendipity as you travel; be open to new people, ideas, and lifestyles.

Go on a "themed" travel expedition to explore or learn about something that can help your creative work by giving you new information.

Turn all your trips into entepreneurial excursions to seek out new products and ideas to import, or new markets to which you can export your business products.

Go on fun field trips or bring a bag of toys for people to use to get inspiration.

Invite humor into your work environment to encourage people to explore their most wacky, wildest, and weirdest ideas.

Engage in play with your family and children to inspire your own creativity.

Use deep reading to approach a topic from many points of view.

Cruise bookstores looking for serendipity or synchronicity by randomly selecting titles to browse.

Go to a library to tap "library angels," who seem to help you find the information you need.

Learn to play a simple musical instrument and express your natural sense of rhythm, melody, and harmony.

Seek out fun and challenging art observation experiences at museums, galleries, and other venues where you can see what others have done and inspire yourself.

Go to unconventional art exhibits and concerts where you can see how artists are constantly challenging the status quo and the traditional way of thinking.

Techniques and Strategies

Technology	Start using an information manager to keep track of ideas and data that you collect to help all your creative projects.	Purchase and learn to use "idea-generation" software that can inspire new ideas and help you burst through creative blocks.
Power-Thinking	Implement brainstorming as a primary strategy to generate new ideas in your work.	Use the TRANSFORM grid (page 210) as a reminder of the many mental techniques available to you to develop new ideas or modify old ones.
Alterconscious	Learn to respect your intuition and its messages. Become more aware of when and how your intuition appears to you: what are its symptoms and cues?	Use daydreaming to encourage the free flow of your mind. Let yourself daydream in a relaxed state to invite your intuition.
Creative Soul	Practice spirituality in any way that is meaningful to you and that supports your creative spirit.	Write your own affirmations to build your self-confidence and commitment to creative success.

idealists. You have probably met many of them in your life. They are the ones who, when they see a good idea, remark, "I thought of that six months ago. I just never could get the funding [didn't have the time, wasn't sure which step to take first, et cetera]." But those who put their ideas into action are the ones our society admires the most, even though they are frequently derided as simply lucky people who happened to be in the right place at the right time, or who were born to good fortune.

There is no need to belabor the point: The ultimate joy of cre-

Get on-line on the Internet or a commercial service to begin taking advantage of the resources available to you. Visit the Web site for this book at http://www.create-it.com.

Learn to use one of the newest software products in desktop publishing, music, or video/filmmaking that let you become your own producer.

Take part in the newest creative field, multimedia, as a form of expression. Produce your own multimedia games, educational products, and more.

Experiment with strategies like forced connections and role playing to get people to think in new ways.

Learn to mindmap your ideas to introduce a powerful visual tool into all your creative thinking.

Use one or more journaling techniques as a powerful tool to track your ideas and help them develop more fully.

Begin practicing a meditation technique to learn how to empty your mind completely to release a refreshed creative spirit.

Practice visualization regularly to mentally rehearse an event you will do, and to seek in advance answers to your creative challenges by tapping into your intuition and unconscious mind.

Learn to seed and/or remember your dreams to benefit from the creative messages they may be bringing you.

Use ritual to celebrate your successes and to pay attention to your self.

Go on a quiet retreat to refresh your mind and reconnect with your creative spirit.

Take a pilgrimage journey to a "sacred" site of your choice that provokes a sense of wonder and awe in your creative spirit.

ativity is moving your ideas from the *dream* stage into the *steam* stage. Make them happen, if only just for you! The world is filled with disheartened and disenfranchised people who, for lack of follow-through, left their good ideas sitting on the roadside of life, only to be run over or swept up by some other person ready to drive them to success.

When I was in business school studying marketing, a concept that many professors called the "Four P's" was repeatedly pounded into our heads. Marketing success was said to consist of product, place, promotion, and price. There was a time when I felt that if I could master those four simple concepts, the world of advertising and marketing would welcome me. Today I am indeed convinced that the Four P's are critical to success—but we were concentrating on the *wrong* Four P's in college. The future does not belong to corporate clones who can sell products using a formula. The future, corporate and at large, belongs to idea people—those with creative vision, willing to be curious and open, able to take the risk to make new things happen, and possessing the energy to move them forward.

The creative individual needs to use a new set of "Four P's": plan, persistence, patience, and passion.

Plan

No idea just happens. Yes, occasional fads take off with wings of their own, but, much like the wax wings of Icarus, they soon fail. (Have you seen many pet rocks for sale recently?) After using the strategies outlined in this book, the idea person must become a pragmatist and assemble a concrete plan to move the idea to the next stage—off the drawing board, so to speak, onto the shop floor.

Persistence

According to research by Dr. Mihaly Csikszentmihalyi, persistence or perseverance is among the major factors of creative success for people who have made significant contributions in their fields. As he told me in an interview, "you cannot falter when it comes to implementing your ideas." In taking a risk, idea people have to learn never to take no for an answer, to come back swinging and swinging until they hit a home run.

Patience

When you have an idea, you can't always control the timetable. You never know how long it might take for all the pieces to fall into place, or you may need to step back and be willing to change some part of it. If you lack patience, your idea may flame out before the world is ready for it.

Passion

No great discovery or invention happens without the passion of the person who owns the idea. You can move an idea forward, but unless you are passionate about making it a reality, you will never get others to join in your quest. Men and women of great passion can rally others to their cause, and often it take others to breathe life into your ideas. If you are committed heart and soul to making your idea happen, your passion will bring it to life.

The Steps to Turning Your Ideas into Creative Opportunities

It can be interesting to look back over time, say the last six months, and reflect on your experience in developing ideas. If you are like most people, you may discover most of the ideas you had in the last six months stopped at the idea phase. Few made it to the "creative opportunity" stage, at which point you take some action to move an idea forward. The action can be as simple as writing the idea down, but the moment an action occurs, the idea acquires substance. Unfortunately, ideas fade into oblivion every second of every day because people don't know how to translate them into action steps.

So, how can you push your ideas into the creative opportunity stage? Here is a seven-part regimen:

Step 1. Translating the Idea into a Goal

Once you have firmly established that an idea is worth pursuing, begin by setting goals for bringing it to the real world. It is impossible to act on a dream, difficult to act on an idea, but relatively easy to set a personal goal moving toward a desired result. The key is to turn ideas into goals, no matter how nebulous those goals may seem.

Step 2. Thinking "As If"

Now that you have established the desired end result, and expressed it as a goal, write it as if it already exists. Although this process may seem peculiar, it works to establish the goal in your mind as a reality and will be extremely beneficial when you start to sell your idea to others. Do whatever you can to make your creative goal as concrete as possible.

In my own life, to solidify the end result of this book in my mind, I went to the sections of bookstores where this book would ultimately be shelved. I then visualized the book on the shelves. I would do this every time I went into a bookstore, and I would replay it over and over in my mind. The creative goal was getting the book done. I didn't know how I was going to make it happen; I only knew that I could see what it looked like on the shelves. I even asked some bookstore community-relations people to send me letters inviting me to conduct book signings in their stores when the book was finished (and I hung these letters on my office wall). I did everything I could do to bring the experience to life. Through this envisioning process, I came up with the methods needed to do the research, find an agent and a publisher, and get the book written. This was a process that I knew nothing about before I started. What you now hold in your hands is a tangible example of this powerful concept.

Step 3. Selling Your Ideas

Bringing your ideas to fruition often involves selling to others. When I use the term *selling* I mean both the literal sense of exchanging it for money, and the metaphorical sense of convincing or persuading someone of its validity, such as in a negotiation. Either way you need to get other people to accept your creative suggestion.

Unfortunately, many people feel uncomfortable with selling. If you are one of these, you have to change your attitude, because the first rule of selling is that it starts with your own deep conviction. You need to be 101 percent behind your idea. If you fail in this measure, you are doomed at the start. The world is filled with salespeople who do not believe in what they are selling, and the results are almost always the same—poor sales. This holds true even more for the sale of ideas, because in most cases, at least in the early stages, you are selling an intangible. Without something solid to grasp, the only thing people can buy from you is your enthusiasm.

Step 4. Making Your Pitch

The next important step in the selling process is the sales presentation. You must develop what salespeople refer to as a pitch. It does not matter if you are outlining the idea for a person on a napkin in a bar or using multimedia presentation techniques in the boardroom of a Fortune 500 company—the process follows a similar pattern. You need to communicate the basic idea you have, along with its key benefits that are important to the customer (or the person you are pitching the idea to). If the benefits don't hit the customer's "hot button," you won't go far.

We have all experienced salespeople trying to sell us something we don't want. Often they just rattle off the features, paying no attention to the fact that none of these features offers *us* a benefit. Your idea must address a need or deliver some benefit to the prospect, or it just isn't going to sell.

Step 5. Handling Objections

Assuming that you have delivered a successful pitch, the person will likely respond with a variety of objections, which you need to be ready to address. If the person doesn't come back with some objections, either you have lost him or her or you need to start asking some revealing questions to get at the customer's true feelings. An objection is really a customer's way of saying, "I am interested in what you are telling me, but here are some holes that I see." You can prepare for this phase by using several idea-generation techniques, like brainstorming, to determine every possible objection. You need to know all your idea's shortcomings as well as its strengths so that you can reduce its chances of rejection. Answer all objections one at a time, and answer them convincingly.

Step 6. Getting Commitment

Once you have done that, it is time to get the buyer to commit to your idea. You should know exactly what you are asking for when you start out. I have found that it usually helps to write some sort of commitment for the close. You can state it as your objective for having the meeting, something to the effect of "By the end of this meeting, I will have convinced Ms. Smith to use the process I am suggesting" or "Before leaving Mr. Buffet's office, I will have convinced him to become my partner in the new project and have secured his commitment to provide me with the $10,000 needed to make it happen." When you get to the close, if you have successfully done all your homework up to this point, you will have a customer who is ready to buy. However, if you don't know what you want the prospect to commit to, you will have nothing to sell.

Persistence counts, regardless of what you are selling or pitching. If you get to the close and you don't secure the commitment that you came looking for, circle back and try again with additional support to your idea, further enhancements to your initial offer, or new ways of meeting needs you know the potential client has. There is an old saying in the sales profession: "Close quickly and close often." In our culture, if a customer fails to buy, he or she will probably give you some reason or objection. Use this as a way to start the process again. As Winston Churchill said, "Never ever ever give up."

Step 7. Overcoming Discouragement and Becoming an Innovator

Don't be discouraged or dissuaded if your idea fails to sell quickly. Many ideas must suffer a great deal of doubt before they get a single yes. Sometimes selling an idea requires finding a visionary out there who also sees its beauty. Keeping the idea going is sometimes the hardest part of the selling process. Having dwelt in the halls of corporate America for many years, I know that some ideas will never sell, and that some may take years to sell. When you are in an organization, part of being a creative person requires that you don't become fixated on one idea, and get so hung up on selling it that you get fired in the process. Continue to generate ideas even if your first one or two or three aren't implemented.

In the corporate environment, it can be very beneficial to be seen as a person who brings continuous creativity and innovation to the organization. You will become an extremely valuable asset, and others will seek you out when new projects are initiated. Few corporations delegate the job of developing new ideas to one individual—developing ideas can and should be a part of everyone's job. For the most part, however, it won't be spelled out in your job description. *You* have to take the initiative and make it happen.

In corporate environments discouragement often is the result of corporate politics. If you are in an organization where politics seem to inhibit ideas, you need to step back and decide if you are playing the political game properly. Very few people are able to survive and sell their ideas in a corporate setting if they are completely ignorant of (or intentionally disregard) their organizational culture. This is one of the few situations in which it is necessary to follow the rules to a certain extent. What you need to sell an idea in a politically charged climate is an understanding of and sensitivity to the politics. With political savvy you can create innovative ways of working through the system. In most organizations, ideas are most readily sold by the individuals who learn to use the same creative power they employ to generate their ideas to wind their way through the politics.

Once you are recognized in your organization as an innovator, tolerance for your political infractions will increase, and you will be given more latitude in the way you work. However, the best rule of thumb whenever you sell is, always try to work within the system. If this fails, try to work within the system *creatively*. If this fails, break the rules, but do so with the knowledge that you are stepping outside the bounds. Then if the idea fails to sell, or you are reprimanded for your action, you won't feel stung because you realized the risk involved at the outset.

Take up the Strategies for Action

The strategies I have presented here are available for you to use as much as you want and whenever you want. The question is whether you choose to use them. As you close the pages of this book, open new pages in your life. Take these strategies and create wonderful, new life experiences that combine with the other elements of your creativity—problem-solving techniques, serendipity, synchronicity, and chaos—so that you can help create a better world along with many others of us out there. The strategies are in your hands: *you* must take the action.

index

Jordan Ayan is a frequent keynote speaker on creativity technology and innovation. His company conducts a variety of seminars and workshops where participants learn to increase creativity and develop new ideas. For further information on Jordan's speaking programs, seminars, and consulting work or to share how the strategies in this book have worked for you, write him at:

Create-It Inc.
P.O. Box 3003
Naperville, IL 60566

You can also visit the Create-It! Inc. Web page at

http://www.create-it.com

or E-mail Aha@create-it.com. The Web page contains updated information on the strategies covered in this book, as well as links to other Internet resources related to creativity.